Anna May Wong's Lucky Shoes
1939 Australia Through the Eyes of an Art Deco Diva

by

Derham Groves

with a foreword by **Elaine Mae Woo**
and photographs by **Lee McRae**

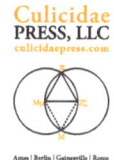

Culicidae
PRESS, LLC
culicidaepress.com

Ames | Berlin | Gainesville | Rome

Culicidae Press, LLC
918 5th Street
Ames, IA 50010
USA
www.culicidaepress.com

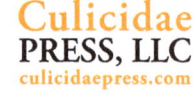

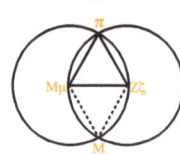

Ames | Berlin | Gainesville | Rome

ANNA MAY WONG'S LUCKY SHOES:
1939 AUSTRALIA THROUGH THE EYES OF AN ART DECO DIVA
Copyright © 2011 by Derham Groves and Lee McRae.

For more information address Culicidae Press, LLC
918 5th Street, Ames, IA 50010, USA
or send an email to: editor@culicidaepress.com

ISBN-13: 978-0615860688

ISBN-10: 0615860680

Cover design by Huey Groves
Interior layout by polytekton.com
Photography and digital imaging by Lee McRae, University of Melbourne, Melbourne, Australia

For
Khoo Ping Tiang

Table of Contents

Foreword

The Chinese American actress, Anna May Wong (1905-1961), was—and still is to this day—one of the most glamorous and memorable female movie stars of color to ever grace the silver screen. She was the first Asian-American actress to achieve international stardom.

Anna's career in Hollywood began as a lamp-bearing extra in the silent film, *The Red Lantern* (1919), starring Alla Nazimova. She went on to star herself in *The Toll of the Sea* (1922), Technicolor's ground-breaking two-color film, and *The Thief of Bagdad* (1924) with Douglas Fairbanks Sr., while *Shanghai Express* (1932), the talking film directed by Josef von Sternberg in which she co-starred with Marlene Dietrich, is still a classic.

Anna was involved in over sixty films. She was a versatile actress who constantly wanted to prove herself not only in motion pictures, but also as a performer on radio, stage, television, and—surprisingly—in vaudeville throughout the world.

In many ways, *Anna May Wong's Lucky Shoes: 1939 Australia Through the Eyes of an Art Deco Diva* by Dr. Derham Groves reflects the desire of many people to bring back to the spotlight this puzzling Chinese American woman who was nearly forgotten, but has resurfaced in the last few years and is finding her proper place in our cinema history. It will help people around the world and in the future to know a little more about this marvelous pioneering actress, who at a particular time in history persevered when there was much discrimination towards people of Chinese origin and only limited opportunities for them in Western society.

Intriguingly, Derham's detailed research on Anna's visit to Australia in 1939 is illustrated with pairs of shoes designed and made for the actress by architecture students from his Popular Architecture and Design course at the University of Melbourne.

Elaine Mae Woo wrote, directed and produced the documentary, Anna May Wong—Frosted Yellow Willows: Her Life, Times and Legend *(2007).*

Anna May Wong in Australia
"Oh, How the Ghost of You Clings"[1]

Derham Groves

Anna May Wong's Lucky Shoes: 1939 Australia Through the Eyes of an Art Deco Diva showcases the amazing shoes created by the architecture students who did my Popular Architecture and Design course in 2010 at the University of Melbourne (Australia), where I teach, for the remarkable Chinese-American actress, Anna May Wong (a.k.a. Wong Liu Tsong), who was born on Tuesday the 3rd of January 1905 and died suddenly on Thursday the 2nd of February 1961. But before viewing the wonderful photographs of the shoes taken by the Melbourne University photographer, Lee McRae, let me say something firstly about Wong, and secondly about the shoe project.

Acting Career

Ever since I first saw Anna May Wong in the otherwise somewhat dreary Sherlock Holmes movie, *A Study in Scarlet* (1933), I have been smitten

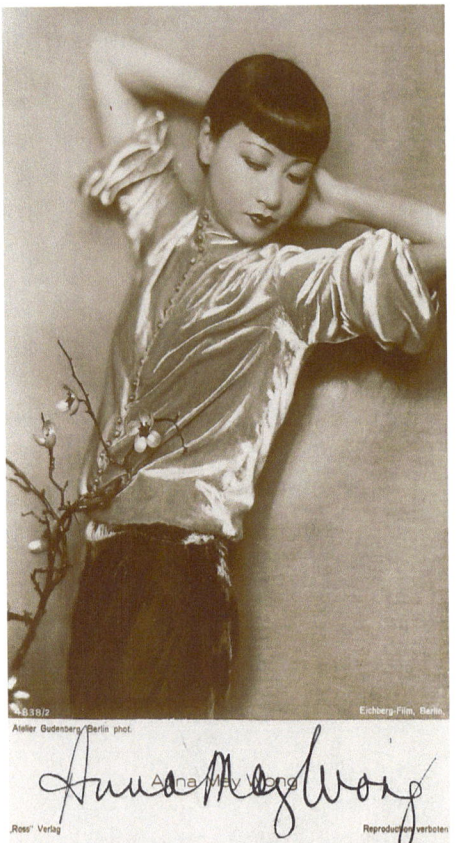

Fig. 1: Anna May Wong. (Derham Groves' collection.)

by her drop-dead good looks and Steve McQueen coolness (Fig. 1). Reading Graham Russell Gao Hodges' biography of the actress, *Anna May Wong: From Laundryman's Daughter to Hollywood Legend* (2004), I learned that she had come to Australia in 1939 to star in a variety show called *Highlights From Hollywood* (1939) at the Tivoli Theater in Melbourne. However, Hodges does not say very much about her trip, and nor do Wong's other biographers.[2] My curiosity piqued, because I live in Melbourne I felt that I was well placed to fill in some of the gaps. Therefore, I have tried to give a thorough, chronological account of Wong's stay in Australia, based on local newspaper reports, and using her own words whenever possible. As it turns out, the 107 days that she spent in Australia provides a snapshot of the actress at a crossroads in her career and the country unwittingly on the verge of war.

Anna May Wong's acting career more or less spanned the years between World War One and World War Two (1918-1939). On the eve of her arrival in Australia, the Melbourne (Victoria) newspaper, *The Age,* published the following summary of her film and stage credits (which I have edited and corrected where necessary): "Anna May Wong […] made her [American] stage debut in New York as Minn Lee in […the] play, *On the Spot* [(1930), by the prolific English writer, Edgar Wallace (1875-1932)…] She first appeared in films at the age of […14 in *The Red Lantern* (1919)…] As an extra [in *The First Born* (1921)] she carried a tray to Sessue Hayakawa [(1889-1973), a Japanese actor who is probably best known in the West for playing Colonel Saito in *The Bridge on the River Kwai* (1957),] with whom she was later featured in *Daughter of the Dragon* [(1931)]; she played roles with Lon Chaney [(1883-1930), an

American actor who was nicknamed "The Man of a Thousand Faces," in *Outside the Law* (1921) and *Bits of Life* (1921)]; and [she] became an established actress in such films as *The Alaskan* [(1924)], *The Thief of Bagdad* [(1924)], *The Chinese Parrot* [(1927)], *The Devil Dancer* [(1927)], *Mr. Wu* [(1927)], *The Toll of the Sea* [(1922)]—the first full length film in Technicolor—*Daughter of the Dragon, Shanghai Express* [(1932)], and *Limehouse Nights* [a.k.a. *Limehouse Blues* (1934)…In] 1928 […] Wong left Hollywood on a contract to appear in German films […] In Berlin, her first picture, *Song* [(1928),] was an immediate success, and she was requested to go to London where she was starred with Gilda Gray [(1901-1959), a Polish-born American actress,] in *Piccadilly* [(1929)]. Returning to Berlin, she made *The Pavement Butterfly* [(1929)…] Basil Dean [(1887-1978), an English director and producer…] purchased the Chi-

nese play, *The Circle of Chalk* [(1929),] especially for her […which had] a long run at the New Theater in London […] Wong starred in *The Flame of Love* [a.k.a. *The Road to Dishonor* (1930),] her first tri-lingual picture […] speaking her part in English, German and French. Since 1933, the film star has been making stage and nightclub appearances in England, Europe and America. Four years ago [i.e. 1936,] she toured China […] Her most recent films for Paramount have been *Daughter of Shanghai* [(1938)], *Dangerous to Know* [(1938)] and *North of Singapore* [a.k.a. *Island of Lost Men* (1939)], which was completed in April,"[3] wrote *The Age.* Indeed, Wong made the latter film only shortly before she came to Australia, as the Canberra (Australian Capital Territory) newspaper, *The Canberra Times,* reported: "Anna May Wong will leave for a personal appearance tour in Australia after she finishes work on her current picture, *North of Singapore.*[4]

7

For most of Anna May Wong's career, Chinese actresses were not allowed to kiss Caucasian actors in movies. In 1930, the Darwin (Northern Territory) newspaper, *The Northern Territory Times,* justly ridiculed this absurd and racist ban: "The British Board of Film Censors has issued a mandate forbidding John Longden [(1900-1971), an English actor,] to kiss Anna May Wong in the new talkie, *The Road to Dishonor.*[5] He may sit at her feet; sing her a love song; kiss her hand; clasp her in his arms; but on no account must he kiss her lips. In the story, Longden plays the part of a Russian officer who is madly in love with a Chinese girl played by Anna May Wong. But love kissing is forbidden, because Miss Wong is Chinese and the censors have put a ban on 'parti-colored kissing.' If the part was played by a white girl dressed as a Chinese it would be allowed, and the decision of the censors is farcical in the extreme."[6]

Banning interracial kissing on the screen in effect ruled out Wong from playing the female romantic lead in films. As a result, she was often cast as a villain. Prior to departing for Australia, Wong told Lon Jones, the Hollywood reporter from the Sydney (New South Wales) newspaper, *The Sydney Morning Herald:* "I can't for the life of me understand why a white man couldn't fall in love with me on the screen [...] without breaking some terrible censorship law. What is the difference between a white girl playing an Oriental and a real Oriental, like myself, playing them? The only difference I can see is that in most cases I would at least look the part, where the white girls definitely do not. If it were possible to overcome this terrible censorship barrier, a new field would open for me, giving me endless chances to act in good parts. I don't want to play white girls, but I do think I should have the chance to play the roles that are mine by rights. Is the moral any different because a white man makes love to a white girl who is playing an Oriental? I think not."[7] A photograph showed Jones and Wong stiffly sitting side-by-side on a tiger skin-covered sofa. When Wong arrived in Australia, *The Age* asked her whether she enjoyed playing threatening roles. "No," she replied, "except when I am really effective in them. Actually, I have been doing sinister roles for so long that I have got mental indigestion."[8]

Although Anna May Wong had virtually no choice but to play villains, she was nevertheless criticized for presenting Chinese women in a bad light on the screen, especially by Mainland Chinese, as she told F.K.M., a journalist from the Australian magazine, *Table Talk:* "All these sinister parts I'd been playing hadn't been making me at all popular with my own people. They felt very strongly that in my portraying unpleasant types of women so consistently, I was bringing discredit upon the Chinese race—despite the fact that I pointed out to them that right always triumphed in the end, and I was really pointing a moral in showing girls what *not* to be. But this explanation didn't satisfy my people to any extent at all."[9]

On the other hand, the British author, W.J. Passingham, believed that Wong was a positive role model for Chinese girls. In his essay, "Influences of Screen on Lives of Women" (1936), which was published in *The Sydney Morning Herald* on Tuesday the 7th of July 1936, Passingham wrote: "Pictures of modern life in the most progressive and prosperous nations have penetrated to the earth's most secluded corners, sweeping away age-old customs and ideas, breaking down barriers that have held women in slavery for centuries. In Asiatic countries, for example, where until recent years women were classed with cattle, the influence of films has wrought changes of tremendous significance [...] What Josephine Baker [(1906-1975), a sexy, American-born Afro-French dancer,] did for Negro girls, Anna May Wong has done for the Chinese."[10]

Going to Australia

Frank Neil (1886-1940) was the general manager of the theatrical company, the Tivoli Circuit, from 1934 until his death in a suspicious car accident—possibly a homophobic motivated murder—on New Year's Day in 1940.[11] He regularly traveled overseas to book artists for the circuit's two theaters in Melbourne and Sydney,[12] and on one such trip to England in 1934 he announced: "Negotiations are almost complete for Anna May Wong, the Chinese cinema actress, to appear in Melbourne in January [1935]."[13] Wong was working in London at the time, rather than in Hollywood. However, in August 1934, *The Sydney Morning Herald* ended the speculation over her proposed forthcoming visit: "Recent reports that Anna May Wong would come to Australia during the Centenary [of European settlement] celebrations have been scotched by the cabled announcement that she is proceeding to Hollywood, there to appear in American pictures."[14] Wong's ensuing work commitments prevented her from making the long voyage to Australia and touring the country until 1939. "Mr Frank Neil has been trying to persuade me to come out here for a couple of years now, but this is the first time that my contracts have permitted me to do so," she told F.K.M. "Fortunately, my contract with Paramount has always been a happily elastic one."[15] (Ironically, the elastic "snapped" while Wong was in Australia, but more about this later.)

Before heading to Australia, an excited Anna May Wong told Lon Jones: "I want to see those big countries 'Down Under,' because I've met so many people who rave about Australia and New Zealand."[16] However, the most important reason for her going to Australia was her almost desperate desire for time and space away from Hollywood in order to reassess her own acting career, as Wong—suddenly in a pensive mood and feeling vulnerable—went on to explain to Jones: "You see […] I'm a unique personality in motion pictures. I'm the only Oriental star in the world, and for that very reason I'm hampered.[17] People insist upon looking at me as a freak—something akin to a five-legged dog or a two-headed calf. I want to be an actress, not a freak. I want to feel that people go to see my pictures because I perform well, not just because I am an Oriental. That's the main reason I want to get away from Hollywood. I want to examine myself closely and find out if I have anything really to offer the public or whether I must just go on being regarded as a freak. I'm hoping that I'll find out that it is not the latter."[18] A shorter version of Wong's remarks was also published in the Melbourne newspaper, *The Herald*.[19]

Anthony B. Chan, the author of *Perpetually Cool: The Many Lives of Anna May Wong (1905-1961)* (2003), the first full-length biography of the actress, in my view wrongly claimed that Wong went to Australia primarily to raise money for China, which was at war with Japan at the time. "After 1936 she was no longer restless," wrote Chan. "Although she toured Australia with a vaudeville troupe in 1938 [sic], this travel was a manifestation of her China War Relief efforts to raise money for her grandparents' homeland, not a longing to seek out the unusual or to acquire yet another foreign experience."[20] Likewise, in his biography, *Anna May Wong: From Laundryman's Daughter to Hollywood Legend*, Graham Russell Gao Hodges also rather overstated the political and fundraising aspects of the film star's trip to Australia. "Her intention was to lecture and host subscription campaigns for China aid,"[21] said Hodges. While Wong did highlight the plight of the occupied Chinese in her vaudeville act, even if this was merely by accident, as I will explain later; and she did raise money for war-torn China, even if the amount was fairly insignificant—the proceeds from the "Anna May Wong Ball" in Sydney;[22] these things were not her main reasons for going to Australia. As Wong told Lon Jones from *The Sydney Morning Herald*, she visited the country to escape Hollywood in order to consider her future in the movie business.

Anna May Wong's forlorn assessment of her own acting career was largely a result of being seen as neither completely Chinese nor wholly American by moviegoers—and sometimes even by herself. Most confusingly for the actress, in the United States she was looked upon as Chinese, while in China she was regarded as American.

Indeed, Wong talked about feeling betwixt and between to *The Sydney Morning Herald:* "I told one of my friends how I felt [...] She told me I was in 'mental conflict,' because I had inherited the Chinese attitude to life, but had had an American upbringing. The Chinese are an ancient people, they have foreseen the end of personal ambition, they relax and 'ride along.' On the other hand, America is a young, bustling country."[23] It seems to me (and also to others) that Wong never satisfactorily resolved this dilemma, either on the screen or in her own mind. [24]

On Thursday the 4th of May 1939, Anna May Wong left San Francisco for Honolulu,[25] most likely onboard the *S.S. Lurline,* a luxury steam ship operated by the Matson Line, which sailed express between the two cities.[26] Newspaper photographs showed her wearing one of her signature fur coats in anticipation of spending winter in Australia.[27] After several busy days in Honolulu, Wong boarded the *R.M.S. Aorangi,* a well-appointed Royal Mail steam ship operated by the Canada-Australasian Line Ltd., which traveled between Vancouver and Sydney via Honolulu, Suva and Auckland (Fig, 2).

Initially, Anna May Wong wanted to bring to Australia her brother, Richard Wong Kim Ying (born in 1922), as her pianist, and her sister, Mary Wong Lew Huang (1910-1940), as her secretary, but for some reason they did not go along with her.[28] Nevertheless, the actress did not travel to Australia alone, because the other American artists in *Highlights From Hollywood* were also onboard the ship. They were Merrill La Fontaine (1897-1976), Wong's pianist; "America's Young Comedy Star," Jack (Vinton) Lane (1916-2009); "Famous Dance Stars of the Screen," Betty (a.k.a. Elizabeth) Burgess (1917-2002) and Sonny Lamont (1909-1961); "Cuban Dancers," Alfredo (born in 1903) and Delores (Garcia); "the Radio Racketeer," Bugs (Howard Alan) Wilson (born in 1909); "the Mexican Troubadour," Joaquin (Aguilar) Garay (1911-1990); "South America's Foremost Instrumentalists," Frank (a.k.a. Francesco, 1906-1969) and Lawrence (a.k.a. Lorenzo, 1908-1974) Andrini (which was sometimes also spelled "Andreini"), who were known as the Andrini Brothers; and "Dance Creations on the Wire," (William Frank) Evers (born in 1903) and Dolores.[29]

But there was no doubt about who was the star of *Highlights From Hollywood*—Wong traveled first class on the *Aorangi,* while her fellow performers went cabin or second class.[30] Not that there was anything wrong with cabin class! For lunch on Sunday the 14th of May 1939, for example, the cabin class passengers were served their choice of grilled Canadian salmon steaks; fried chicken legs; curried sheep's tongues; or a cold collation, which included roast suckling pig, roast leg of mutton and roast beef.[31] While some of the tasty-sounding dishes on the cabin class dinner menu for that evening included

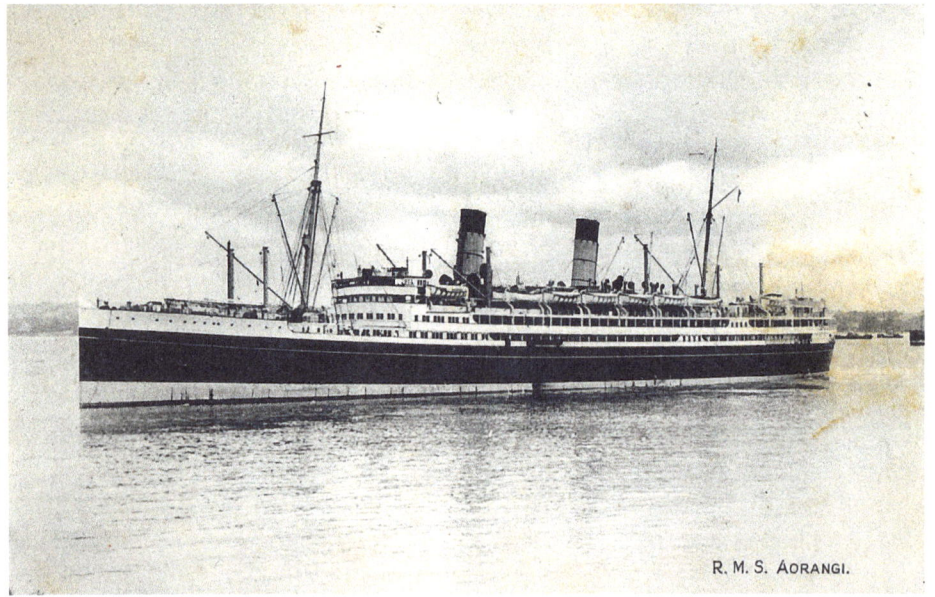

R. M. S. AORANGI.

Fig. 2: The *R.M.S. Aorangi.* (Derham Groves' collection.)

black game croquettes with perigord sauce and spaghetti a la president; roast Californian tom turkey with raisin stuffing and cranberry sauce; steamed black cod with sauce ecrivisses; and Florida pudding with sabayon sauce, for dessert.[32]

Anna May Wong also made friends with some of the other passengers onboard the *Aorangi,* especially Charles Lloyd Jones (1878-1958) and his wife, Hannah (died in 1982), who were traveling home to Sydney with their two young sons, David (1931-1961) and Charles (1932-2010), after spending nine months in England, Europe and the United States.[33] Lloyd Jones was the chairman of directors of his family's firm, David Jones Ltd., a large retail clothing company, as well as being a generous patron of the arts. Despite being extremely wealthy, he was very humble and down to earth, often describing himself as "a simple draper." Indeed, when Lloyd Jones' butler insisted that tradesmen could not use the front door of "Rosemont," the businessman's mansion in the posh Sydney suburb of Woollahra, he jokingly protested: "Well, I had better start using the back door then."[34] When *Highlights From Hollywood* was playing in Sydney, the Lloyd Joneses introduced Wong to their high society friends at several parties (more about these later).

Bringing Anna May Wong and the other American artists to Australia was expensive, so Frank Neil, who "liked to do things on the cheap,"[35] naturally wanted to earn as much money as he could from his headline act. While the *Aorangi* was still at sea, Neil's secretary, Charles Brandreth, wrote to Charles Moses (1900-1988), the general manager of the Australian Broadcasting Commission (A.B.C.), to offer Wong's "services for one [radio] broadcast weekly during her Australian season of 10 weeks [sic], from the stage of the theater only, at a fee of £75 per broadcast".[36] Moses asked his managers at the A.B.C. for their advice.[37] Ewart Chapple, the acting federal controller of music, responded as follows: "This artist is only known to me through her appearance in the film, *Shanghai Express*.[38] Before we negotiate with Mr. Neil, I think we should have some idea of how he is going to present her on the stage. It is difficult to know just how he will do this, and it is quite possible that she may not be a success on the stage, as was the case with Nina Mae McKinney [(1913-1967), a black American film actress who Neil had brought to Australia in 1937[39]]. As £75 a broadcast is a high fee, I would recommend that Miss Wong's act be viewed in Melbourne before any arrangements are made with Mr. Neil."[40] Accordingly, Moses told Brandreth: "Arrangements will be made […] for our manager for Victoria to see Miss Wong's performance as soon as possible after her opening in Melbourne, and we may then decide to discuss the matter with you further."[41]

Nothing happened, but things might have been different had Neil known that Wong was friends with Charles Lloyd Jones—the first chairman of the A.B.C. (1932-1934)!

On the other hand, Frank Neil had better luck with the instrumentalists, the Andrini Brothers, who performed live on A.B.C. radio while *Highlights From Hollywood* was playing in Melbourne. On Wednesday the 12th of July 1939, they were heard from 8.10 p.m. to 8.20 p.m. on 5AN in Adelaide and also 5CK in Port Pirie,[42] which are both in South Australia, and then from 8.40 p.m. to 9.00 p.m. on 7NT in Launceston in Tasmania.[43] Given that *Highlights From Hollywood* started at 8.00 p.m., and the Andrini Brothers was act number 15 on the program,[44] there was plenty of time for them to perform at the A.B.C. studios, which were located in a laneway off Russell Street, Melbourne, near Little Collins Street, and then get to the Tivoli Theater in Bourke Street well before they were due on stage.

Arrives in Sydney

The *Aorangi* arrived in Sydney on Sunday the 4th of June 1939. Its voyage had been mostly uneventful, although four children and one adult had been hospitalized onboard with chickenpox,[45] and bad weather between Suva and Auckland had delayed the ship by one day.[46] A crew from Cinesound, a local film company,[47] and reporters from the A.B.C.[48] and several Australian newspapers, met the ship before the passengers disembarked. Naturally, they all asked Wong about Hollywood.

The Brisbane (Queensland) newspaper, *The Courier-Mail,* reported: "Anna May Wong, the United States-born Chinese film actress, who reached Sydney today in the *Aorangi,* said that actors in Hollywood were today more sane and real than they had been. Producers in Hollywood were following Samuel Goldwyn's idea, that a film should be pictorial first, with talk subordinated to action. With a more intelligent approach today, the motion picture had become a more direct projection of the player's personality than was possible on the stage, where skilled technique was more apparent than real emotion. On the screen it was possible to give something of oneself to a role, to make acting more spontaneous. 'The film player is much more on his or her own today,' she said. 'In the days of silent films, people were directed more. Now the films demand a far higher standard of acting. Many players from the stage have come to Hollywood, too.'"[49] Two days later, *The Courier-Mail* published a photograph of Wong, tomboyishly sitting on the railing of the ship.[50]

The Sydney Morning Herald also quizzed Anna May Wong about her life away from acting. "There is one role in which I am a complete failure," she sheepishly admitted. "That is the task of playing the part of an actress off the stage […] I am afraid I do so much acting that when I am 'off duty' I forget all about it and become a completely practical person with ordinary interests."[51] Wong explained that she particularly enjoyed gardening and cooking: "When I am not at [326 San Vicente Boulevard in] Santa Monica, where I have a house, I live with my father and brothers at [241 North Figueroa Street in] Los Angeles, and there I have my own patch of garden. I am very fond of simple flowers, such as geraniums, stocks, ginger, and Chinese forget-me-nots. I have been learning Chinese cooking since I visited China, and it is absorbingly interesting, much more of an art than a science. You do not measure by teaspoons, but have to be able to guess when the proportions are right."[52]

Anna May Wong may not have played "an actress off the stage" in private, but she certainly played one in public, as indicated by the following colorful (literally) description of her onboard the *Aorangi,* which was published in *The Sydney Morning Herald* the day after she arrived in Australia: "Miss Wong, who has a quiet, serene manner, and a low-pitched speaking voice, was an impressive figure in a slim black frock, ankle-length and slit to the knees, to display long white trousers of embroidered sheer. She added a smooth black turban, with a gold ornament, and a silver fox cape. Her finger and toe nails were lacquered with a new colored polish, crushed strawberry, which is a deep red with an opalescent sheen."[53] *The Sydney Morning Herald* also published a photograph of Wong dressed-to-the-nines, as described, and clutching a huge bouquet of flowers—the first of many that she received in Australia.[54]

There were a number of other celebrities onboard the *Aorangi* besides the cast of *Highlights From Hollywood,* including George Zaharias (1908-1984), a colorful Greek-American wrestler, who was known as "the crying Greek from Cripple Creek;"[55] Zaharias' wife, Babe Didrikson (1911-1956), a dual gold medallist in track-and-field at the 1932 Olympics and also a champion golfer;[56] and 20 members of the Viennese Mozart Boys' Choir, who had joined the ship at Auckland on Monday the 29th of May 1939.[57] *The Sydney Morning Herald* wrote: "The 20 rosy-cheeked small boys who form the Viennese Mozart Boys' Choir would have delighted any mother's heart when they arrived in Sydney in the *Aorangi* yesterday morning […] Their most popular hobby at the moment is preparing scrapbooks, and whatever one does, all the rest imitate […] They were all very excited to see Miss Anna May Wong on board, and yesterday I discovered 12 of them knocking at her door to ask for her autograph! She has given them all a photograph of herself for their books."[58] Within a week of the overseas celebrities arriving in Australia, a Cinesound newsreel featuring Wong, Zaharias, Didrikson, and the Viennese Mozart Boys' Choir was being shown in cinemas around the country.[59]

The day before Wong's ship moored at Cockatoo Dock in Sydney, a notice in *The Sydney Morning Herald* announced, "Anna May Wong arrives *Aorangi* tomorrow, Sunday morning at 8," and also invited her fans to "Be there to welcome this illustrious daughter of China."[60] Indeed, Dr. Chun-Jien Pao, the Consul-General for China, and his American wife, Edith, were among those present who warmly welcomed the actress to Australia.[61] Because the *Aorangi* had arrived a day late, a formal reception for Wong arranged by the Paos on Saturday the 3rd of June 1939 had to be cancelled.[62] However, when *Highlights From Hollywood* was playing in Sydney, the Paos introduced Wong to their circle of friends in the local diplomatic core at several functions they attended (more about these later).

Doris Chen, a representative of the Chinese government who had been in Australia for about eight months raising money for Chinese war refugees, was another who greeted Wong at the dock. She had delayed her departure from Sydney so as "to meet Anna May Wong, an intimate friend, with whom she had been associated with in Hollywood," reported the Cairns (Queensland) newspaper, *The Cairns Post*. "Miss Chen met the celebrated Chinese actress on her arrival from America and spent several days with her [in Melbourne?] before sailing for home. Two years ago, Miss Chen was assigned to the technical staff of Metro-Goldwyn-Mayer during the production of the memorable picture, *The Good Earth* [(1937), which was based on the novel of the same name by Pearl S. Buck (1892-1973), a Nobel Prize-winning American author]."[63] Wong was bitterly disappointed when she missed out on playing O-lan, the leading female role in the film, which went to Luise Rainer (born in 1910), a German actress.

Arrives in Melbourne

At night on Sunday the 4th of June 1939, Anna May Wong and the other American performers in *Highlights From Hollywood* left Sydney onboard the *Spirit of Progress,* an elegant, Art Deco-style, inter-capital-city express steam train, which arrived at Spencer Street Station in Melbourne on Monday morning at 11.30 a.m.[64] *The Age* published a photograph of Wong at the station, wearing the same outfit that she had on the day before, holding a big bouquet of flowers, and smiling broadly.[65] Two days earlier, *The Age* had announced: "Meet Anna May Wong. The exotic star will arrive by car in front of the Tivoli Theater, Bourke Street—12.30, midday, Monday next, June 5."[66] Hundreds of people turned up at the theater to greet Wong.[67] The event was broadcast live by the Melbourne radio station, 3KZ,[68] and also covered widely in the Melbourne press: *The Argus* published a candid photograph of Wong being led through the large crowd at the Tivoli by two young Chinese girls wearing national dress,[69] while a photograph in *The Sun News-Pictorial* showed the film star striking a pose like a mannequin, which highlighted her very slim waist.[70]

Te Pana (a.k.a. Nelson Burns), the film critic from *The Argus,* was clearly taken with the Chinese-American actress: "Anna May Wong, American-born Chinese film star, who arrived in Melbourne yesterday to begin a season at the Tivoli Theater, is a young woman with a sense of humor, and something of the philosophy of her ancestors," he wrote. "She has a pretty turn of wit, but is not to be drawn on the subject of Hollywood. 'It is a comfortable town,' she told me, 'where the traffic lights are out at 10 o'clock. A sensible, reasonable place, all in all.' Unlike most of Hollywood's stars, Miss Wong enjoys a uniform popularity throughout America, England, the Continent, and far into the East. She is untrammeled by screen artifices, taller than she appears in pictures, unmarried, intelligent, but by no means profound either on the subject of her work or its meaning to the public. 'Playing in films and on the stage is my means of livelihood,' she said, 'and I take my work seriously. It has given me an opportunity to travel, has broadened my education and, above all, has brought me into contact with many very interesting people. I might have been just another girl in Hollywood. Thus I am grateful to the films and the fans.' Brown-eyed, with a dark fringe of hair, and a warm, friendly smile, Miss Wong is as attractive in person as in the shadow shows. Filmgoers who know the quality of her work in pictures will appreciate this, for she plays exotic types, which usually lead the hero of the searing tropic or East-of-Suez drama to destruction. She promises, however, that her stage turn will be different. 'It is a potpourri of elocution, a little singing and perhaps a mild venture into dramatics,' she said."[71]

The Show

Australian audiences really only knew Anna May Wong through her movies, so there was some early conjecture about what she might do on stage in Melbourne and Sydney. For example, three months before the film star arrived in Australia, *The Sydney Morning Herald* reported: "The engagement of Anna May Wong by Mr. Frank Neil was the only interesting theater news of a quiet week. She will arrive late in May [sic], commence her tour of the Tivoli Circuit in June, and will appear in Sydney in July. There will be speculation as to the form Miss Wong's act on the vaudeville stage will take. The memory of filmgoers recalls only vivid and occasionally sinister Oriental portrayals, stilettos, and dealing with gangsters as her contribution to the cinema. One cannot remember having seen her in any sort of light role. Does Mr. Neil plan some miniature drama as part of the revue in which he places her? We must wait in patience until Miss Wong appears."[72]

However, Anna May Wong had been doing vaudeville in Europe, England and America since 1933, and her repertoire was actually quite well known. "In her stage appearances [in Australia] she will sing in Chinese, French, Italian, and English," reported Lon Jones from *The Sydney Morning Herald*. "She will do short dramatic monologues and impersonations of flappers around the world. If the public demands it, she will put on a few dramatic sketches."[73] It was also reported that, "in addition to her routine act, [in Australia] Anna May Wong will sing new numbers and use comedy material written for her broadcasts with Bing Crosby [(1903-1977), an American crooner who was one of the best-selling recording artists of the 20th century,] and [the very popular American ventriloquist, Edgar Bergen (1903-1978), and his cheeky dummy,] Charlie McCarthy."[74] In 1938, Wong guest starred on two popular U.S. radio shows, *The Kraft Music Hall*, which was hosted by Crosby, and *The Edgar Bergen & Charlie McCarthy Show*, which featured Bergen and Charlie.[75]

The cast of *Highlights From Hollywood* had only six days to rehearse (since almost nobody in Australia worked on Sundays in 1939) before the show premiered in Melbourne on Monday the 12th of June 1939. Jonathan Swift, a journalist from *The Sun News-Pictorial*, "drifted into the comparative calm of a final rehearsal for Anna May Wong before the Tivoli matinee [which started at 2.15 p.m.]. While her dresser was giving an array of costly frockings the final once-over with an iron, I exchanged a few words with the film star, and she mentioned her appearances in Vienna. Naturally, I asked about Franz Lehar [(1870-1948), an Austrian composer,] and she mentioned how he had sought her to play the sister role in *The Land of Smiles* before it was produced in Berlin [in 1929]. Other engagements at the time prevented her accepting the part, but she was present at the first night. Anna May speaks both German and French fluently and, above all, she has a keen sense of humor. One question she asked was what I thought would happen if she sang something from Puccini's opera, *Madame Butterfly* [(1904)], in German? Fancy a Chinese singing a song in German from an opera written by an Italian around a Japanese story!

That would just about upset the Berlin-Rome-Tokyo axis altogether."[76]

Merrill La Fontaine, who had once been "considered a musical prodigy," accompanied Wong on the piano.[77] Unfortunately, the *Highlights From Hollywood* theater program did not specify exactly what Wong did in the show, while the only review of the opening night in Melbourne was rather vague: "Charming, talented, and entertaining in the many screen roles in which she has appeared, Anna May Wong, the American-born Chinese film star, is equally attractive in vaudeville," reported *The Argus* on Tuesday, the 13th of June 1939. "She proved a first-rate entertainer yesterday, when she began her Australian season at the Tivoli Theater. There is an atmosphere of brightness about her 'turn,' which is easy to look at and to hear. A song number in Chinese, [possibly "Mo Li Hua" ("The Jasmine Flower"),[78] a French chanson, [possibly "Parlez-Moi d'Amour" ("Speak to Me of Love"),[79]] and a dramatic monologue [possibly from *Shanghai Express*,[80]] showed her versatility and met with hearty approval. Her presentation is original and 'color' is added by the many beautiful Chinese costumes she wears."[81] Indeed, on Thursday the 15th of June 1939, *Table Talk* published a photograph of Wong as she "unpacks her wardrobe of national Chinese costumes which she wears in her stage appearance at the Tivoli Theater and decides that her first job in Melbourne is to ring for help in pressing out the creases. Many of these fashions are of her own creation and, although Eastern in origin, are blended with Occidental and European design."[82]

At the conclusion of the first performance of the Tivoli show in Melbourne, Wong received a bouquet of flowers on stage from Frank Neil, who "always ordered flowers for presentation to all the women artists on opening night and personally signed each card."[83] Furthermore, an advertisement in the *Highlights From Hollywood* theater program stated: "The beautiful floral tributes handed out to the Tivoli artists on every opening night of new companies are from Miss R. Floyd,"[84] who owned a florist shop at the Eastern Market, which was located on the corner of Bourke and Exhibition streets, Melbourne. Hopefully, she did not wire the stems of Wong's flowers, which was one of the film star's pet hates, according to Mayfair from *The Sydney Morning Herald*: "I heard an interesting appeal from Anna May Wong, the American-born Chinese actress," the columnist wrote. "She does hope that nobody who sends her flowers will send her wired flowers—and she has a reason [...] 'I love flowers and I can't bear them to be wired,' she told me. 'But I can't leave the flowers wired either. Sometimes, I've sat up all night unwiring them. You've such beautiful flowers in Australia, too,' she added."[85]

The other performers in *Highlights From Hollywood* were acrobats, comedians, dancers, and singers. The American "light comedian,"[86] Jack Lane, "whose invigorating style of comedy has made him one of America's favorite young stars,"[87] was only 23 years old when he performed in Australia. However, he became much better known as the quick sketch artist at the Brown Derby restaurant in Hollywood, where he worked between 1947 and 1985,[88] although it seems that he never drew Wong for its "Wall of Fame."

The Argus reported that the American actors and dancers, Betty Burgess and Sonny Lamont, presented "some quaint humor, interspersed with dancing."[89] Burgess was a platinum blonde starlet, who made a handful of films in the 1930s. In 1960, she married the wrestler, George Zaharias, who she had first met onboard the *Aorangi* while sailing to Australia in 1939[90] (Fig. 3). Lamont was a chubby tap-dancer, who made several films during the 1930s and 40s, including *The Story of Vernon and Irene Castle* (1939), starring the most famous Hollywood dance team, Fred Astaire (1899-1987) and Ginger Rogers (1911-1995), which was released in Australia while Lamont was performing in Sydney.[91] He and Burgess had previously both appeared in the B-grade Western, *The Adventures of the Masked Phantom* (1939).[92]

The American impressionist, Bugs Wilson, took off "several leading film

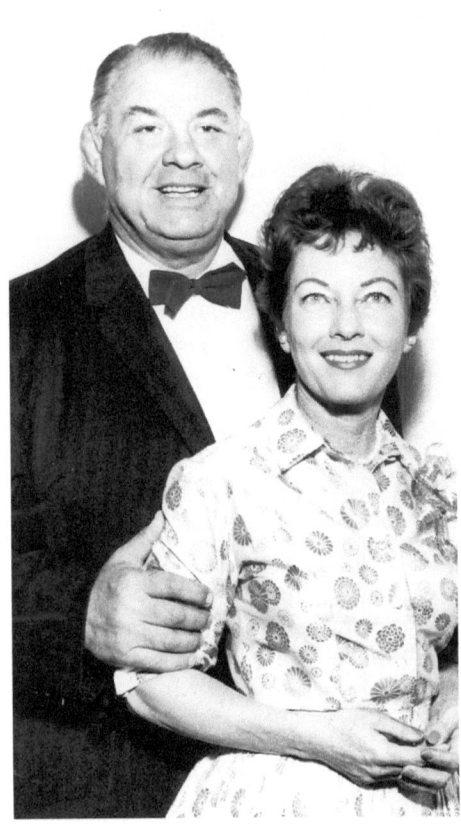

Fig. 3: George Zaharias and Betty Burgess on their wedding day, the 5th of January 1960. (Derham Groves' collection.)

stars."[93] Wilson was particularly good at impersonating the American comic genius, W.C. Fields (1880-1946), and had even doubled for him in the film, *The Big Broadcast of 1938* (1938).[94] However, in both the *Highlights From Hollywood* theater program and the Australian press, Wilson was billed as "the original voice of Grumpy in [the 1937 Walt Disney film] *Snow White and the Seven Dwarfs,*"[95] even though Pinto Colvig (1892-1967), the original voice of Goofy, had actually pro-

vided it.[96] Why did Frank Neil make this blatantly untrue claim about Wilson? The best reason that I can think of is that he wanted to link in people's minds *Highlights From Hollywood* to the Tivoli Circuit's popular *Xmas Extravaganza* (1938) of the previous year, which starred Adriana Caselotti (1916-1997), an American actress and singer who had indeed provided the voice of Snow White in the Walt Disney film.[97] It was also reported that Wilson would introduce *Highlights From Hollywood,*[98] however it seems that Sonny Lamont did this instead.[99]

A number of acts in the show reflected the general public's fascination with Latin America at the time. The Mexican crooner, Joaquin Garay ("pronounced Waukeen Gah-ray,"[100] according to the *Highlights From Hollywood* theater program), sang three "virile"[101] songs: "The Daring Young Man on the Flying Trapeze," which he had introduced in the 1934 movie, *It Happened One Night,* starring Clark Gable (1901-1960) and Claudette Colbert (1903-1996); "A Gypsy Love Song;" and "Si-Si". Ironically, Garay later provided the voice of the cocky rooster, Panchito, in the Walt Disney movie, *The Three Caballeros* (1944).[102] *The Argus* described the Andrini Brothers as "clever musicians and good vocalists."[103] Frank Andrini played the harp guitar, while his brother, Lawrence, played the mandolira.[104] However, they were not

South American, as the *Highlights From Hollywood* theater program incorrectly stated, but French-Italian.[105] The Andrini Brothers went on to become a first-class nightclub act, performing on the career-making *Ed Sullivan Show* on American television in 1955.[106] The Spanish husband-and-wife Cuban-dance team, Alfredo and Dolores, together with the 16 members of the Tivoli Ballet,[107] performed "a new version of the rhumba," which was "the best seen in Melbourne for some time,"[108] according to *The Argus.*

Cath (a.k.a. Cathleen) Esler, "Australia's own soubrette," sang five songs in the show: "Streamline is Nature's Way" (sung with Sunday Wenman and Gwennie Mackintosh from the Tivoli Ballet); "The Gypsy Girl;" "While a Cigarette is Burning;" "Neath Hawaiian Skies;" and "Lights Out" (sung with Bugs Wilson and Jack Lane).[109] *The Argus* said Esler sang "pleasantly,"[110] somewhat damning her with faint praise. Previously, she had appeared in two classic Australian films, *The Squatter's Daughter* (1933) and *Gone to the Dogs* (1939), and had done pantomime, revue and vaudeville for three years in England.[111] The American husband-and-wife high-wire artists, Evers and Dolores, performed while Esler sang "Neath Hawaiian Skies."[112] *The Argus* described Evers and Delores' routine as "something to marvel at."[113] In 1936, they had performed in another variety show at the Tivoli Theater called *Radio Parade.*[114]

Last but probably not least, "Australia's own gymnasts," the Athrillos (a.k.a. the Three Athrillos), were "neat in their acrobatics,"[115] commented *The Argus*. Clearly, this type of theater was not named "variety" for nothing. "Bright vaudeville this, in which song and dance predominate,"[116] was how *The Argus* summed up *Highlights From Hollywood* as a whole.

On Saturday the 1st of July 1939, Anna May Wong's act was unexpectedly revamped, as *The Argus* announced: "A timely dramatic episode entitled 'At the Barricade,' based on an actual incident in the Eastern situation, will be introduced by Miss Anna May Wong in [the] *Highlights From Hollywood* production at the Tivoli Theater today."[117] The event alluded to was the Tientsin (a.k.a. Tianjin) Blockade, which was dramatically unfolding at the time. On the 30th of July 1937, the Japanese army invaded Tientsin in northeast China, but they continued to respect the rights of the large number of foreigners living there. However, when four Chinese nationalists accused of murdering a Japanese official on the 9th of April 1939 took refuge in the part of the city under British control, the Japanese army retaliated by turning away supplies of food and fuel for the British quarter, and also strip-searching in public anyone entering or leaving the area. For a while, it looked like there might be an Anglo-Japanese war, especially when hostile accounts of British subjects being maltreated

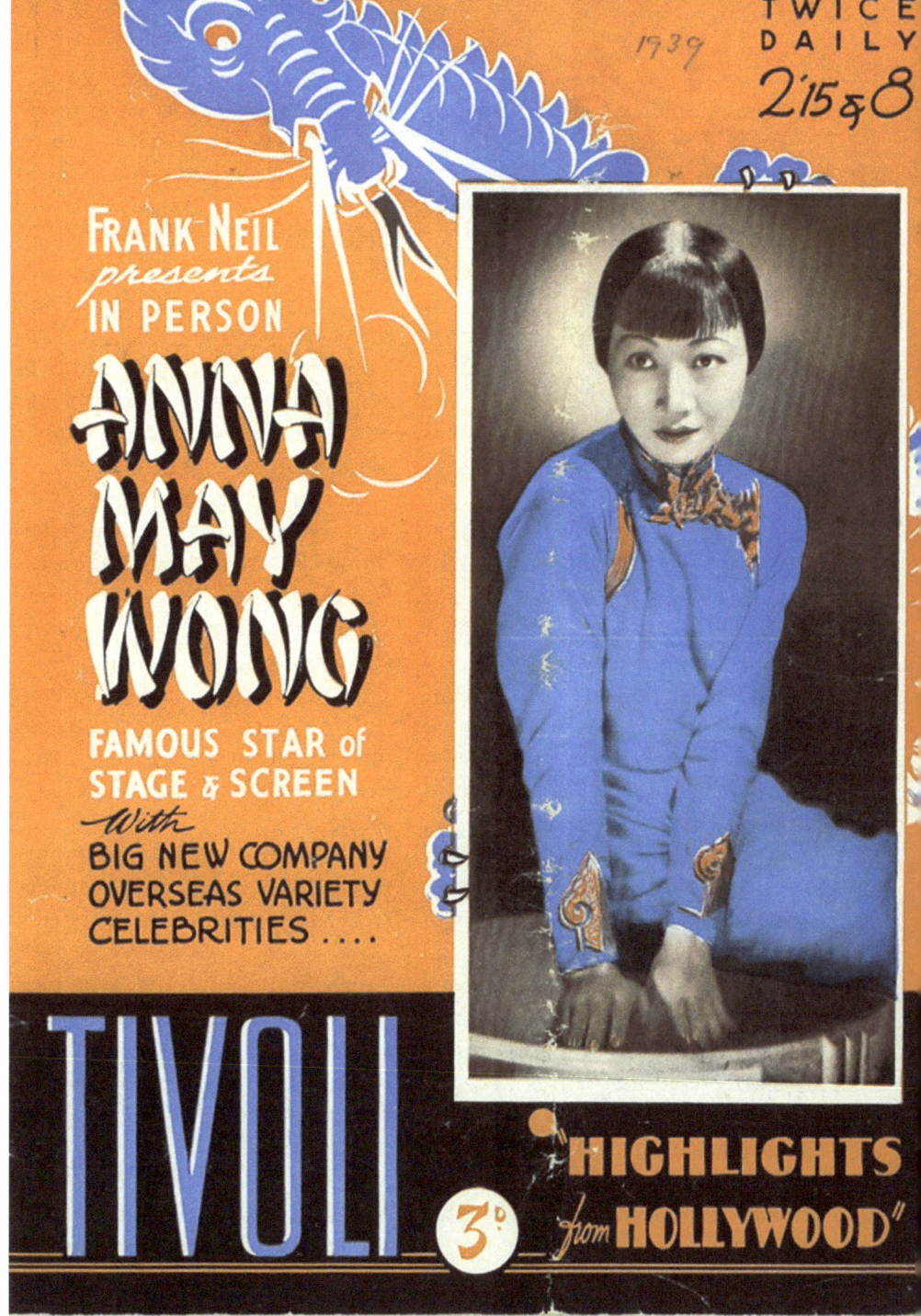

Fig. 4: The *Highlights From Hollywood* theater program. (The Performing Arts Museum.)

by Japanese soldiers were reported in England. However, the British finally backed down and handed over the four doomed murder suspects to the Japanese authorities on the 20th of August 1939, which ended the tense standoff.[118]

In "At the Barricade," Anna May Wong played Lao Chen, a Chinese woman arrested by Japanese soldiers occupying Tientsin; Bugs Wilson played General Imetsu, a Japanese commander; and Jack Lane and Sonny Lamont played American citizens living in Tientsin.[119] Firecrackers may have been used to simulate gunfire in the brief drama, because Jack Meander, the gossip columnist from *The Sydney Morning Herald* who appeared to have been quite close to the film star in Sydney, wrote: "When I called in backstage at the Tivoli last night, Anna May Wong [...] had a packet of crackers and other fireworks on her dressing table, and told me she might let them off later in the evening. In Melbourne, the fire brigade took a rather restrictive view of letting them off backstage." Meander also noticed a packet of incense or joss sticks on Wong's dressing table. "'I like them,' she said, 'they have a pleasant perfume and, apart from being heavenly incense, they are good for keeping flies away.'"[120]

"At the Barricade" focused attention on the terrible plight of the war-torn Chinese, which was something that Wong was always very eager to do, as *The Sydney Morning Herald* reported: "In New York she helped Miss Mai-Mai Sze [(1910-1992), an author, a landscape painter and the] daughter of a former Chinese ambassador, arrange a Chinese relief organization, and wherever she goes she likes to help similar organizations. It has been her custom to buy at least one of the gowns she has worn in her films and keep them as mementoes, but recently she gave the collection away to raise funds for Chinese relief."[121] Wong also attended several events in Melbourne and Sydney that raised money for occupied China (more about these later). Therefore, it came as quite a surprise to discover that "At the Barricade" was introduced into the movie star's act only because Frank Neil lost his temper. Fred Parsons (1908-1987), the Tivoli Circuit's in-house scriptwriter, who wrote "At the Barricade" especially for Wong, recalled the events 34 years later:

"Anna May Wong, that very charming Chinese film actress who had never been to China in her life [...] opened at a matinee singing several pleasant songs, including [Noel] Coward's 'Half-Caste Woman' [(1931)], but went off to lukewarm applause because the audience had been expecting an actress, not a singer. Neil was furious. As soon as the theater was empty, he called the entire company back on to the stage. Then, standing in the front stalls, he gave vent to a tirade of abuse directed against Anna May Wong. He called her 'a has-been,' 'a no-hoper' and 'a faded old bag.' With amazing dignity and control, she stood there until he had finished. Then she said, very quietly, 'Thank you, Mr. Neil,' bowed low to him and walked off. And the entire company applauded her. Wallace Parnell [(1894-1954), the Tivoli Circuit's resident producer,] called me into his office. 'We've got to do something to help Anna. Could you write a dramatic sketch for her?' I said I'd try. The Sino-Japanese war was being fought at the time, and I wrote a 10-minute playlet in which Anna, as a Chinese woman captured by the Japs, sacrificed her own life to save the village in which she lived. Parnell okayed the script, and Anna liked it. An American comic, Bugs Wilson, was pressed into service to play the Japanese officer. They rehearsed all the following day, and the sketch, 'Across the Yellow River' went on for the second night of the season. It was what audiences expected from Anna, and it went well. She thanked me very graciously, but the thanks were really due to Parnell."[122]

While Fred Parsons failed to remember the correct title of "At the Barricade," nor precisely when it was first performed—as well as the fact that Wong had visited China in 1936—I imagine that Frank Neil's fierce outburst and the film star's cool response would have been hard to forget. I do not know whether Wong and the other performers in *Highlights From Hollywood* were close and spent much time together after work, but judging by their reaction to Neil's tawdry behavior towards the star of the show, they got on quite well together as a group.

Highlights From Hollywood finished in Melbourne on Saturday the 15th of July 1939, and started in Sydney on Thursday the 20th of July 1939, with the slightly snappier title, *Hollywood Highlights*.[123] One new act joined the show, a troupe of acrobats named the Six Danwells.[124] *The Sydney Morning Herald* was unimpressed by Wong's performance, while it provided a fairly full—but patronizing—description of her act: "Anna May Wong headed the bill in *Highlights From Hollywood* [sic], the new show at the Tivoli Theater last night. The Chinese actress divided her act into four sections. First, she came in wearing an Oriental coat and a high headdress [which may have been inspired by the costume that Wong wore in *Daughter of the Dragon*] and sang a Chinese folksong. Next, she gave some 'impressions of an Australian girl.' After that came Noel Coward's 'Half-Caste Woman,' and finally a sketch entitled 'At the Barricade.' This sketch dealt with the present situation in Tientsin. It was unexceptional propaganda, but as drama it seemed very poor indeed. 'Half-Caste Woman' gave Miss Wong opportunity for some harsh and intense acting. In the rest of her material, she was agreeably decorative."[125]

With the exception of "At the Barricade," it appears that Wong performed almost the same material in Australia as she had previously done in vaudeville in Europe, England and America. She always sang a Chinese folksong; she always gave some impressions of a local girl, slightly modifying her routine each time to suit the country where she was performing; and she always sang "Half-Caste Woman."[126] Regarding the latter song, although Wong was not Eurasian, she closely identified with its soulful lyrics and its theme of placelessness:

"Drink a bit, laugh a bit, love a little more,
I can supply your need,
Think a bit, chaff a bit, what's it all for?
That's my Eurasian creed.

"Half-caste woman, living a life apart,
Where did your story begin?
Half-caste woman, have you a secret heart
Waiting for someone to win?

"Were you born of some queer magic
In your shimmering gown?
Is there something strange and tragic
Deep, deep down?

"Half-caste woman, what are your slanting eyes
Waiting and hoping to see,
Scanning the far horizon,
Wondering what the end will be?"[127]

On the other hand, *The Sydney Morning Herald* was much more upbeat about some of the other acts in the show, especially "the singing and dancing of Joaquin Garay. This 'Mexican Troubadour' showed equal facility in Spanish and English. Although the microphone amplified his voice until it became a hard blare, his gusto, his humor and his rhythm made him extraordinarily stimulating. Evers and Dolores danced with spectacular ingenuity on a tight wire and Sonny Lamont, the burly compere of the show, proved unexpectedly that he, too, could disport himself aloft. Bugs Wilson, who was the voice of Grumpy in *Snow White and the Seven Dwarfs*, made a genial singer and impersonator at the microphone. As usual, the Tivoli Ballet was young and fresh and competent to the last degree. Mr. Wallace Parnell produced *Highlights From Hollywood* [sic]."[128]

Hollywood Highlights ended on Wednesday the 23rd of August 1939, however Wong did not stay until the finish. Wong's final "gala good-bye"[129] performance occurred on Thursday the 17th of August 1939, because, as Jack Meander from *The Sydney Morning Herald* explained: "She received a cable this week offering her a part in a new film, and Frank Neil agreed to release her from her contract five days early to enable her to reach Hollywood in time."[130] However, this may have been only a story, since Wong did not make another movie until

1941. She may have simply wanted to go home sooner rather than later, especially as war with Germany looked inevitable at the time. Despite the troubles that Wong had on stage in Australia, she told Te Pana from *The Argus:* "Doing a song-and-dance and ground-and-lofty-tumbling turn in vaudeville is child's play compared with film acting."[131]

For the last few performances of *Hollywood Highlights,* Mardo and Kaye, an American husband-and-wife comedy team, took Wong's place in the show.[132] Al Mardo (born in 1894) did a funny routine with Teddy, his bone-lazy but supposedly talented bulldog, and Irene Kaye played the harmonica. They also appeared in the show that replaced *Hollywood Highlights,* which starred the "Prime Minister of Mirth," George Robey (1869-1954), a popular English comedian and renowned pantomime dame.[133] He and Wong had both appeared in the film, *Chu Chin Chou* (1934).[134]

Living in Melbourne

In Melbourne, Anna May Wong stayed at the Menzies Hotel, the best hotel in town at the time, which was located at 140 William Street, four blocks south of the Tivoli Theater. Many years later, Fred Archer, a long-serving employee of the hotel, remembered the film star staying there very well. In his memoir, *The Treasure House* (n.d.), Archer wrote: "American Chinese actress Anna May Wong [...] was strong, competent, and I think shrewd. She was giving a publicity photo to her housemaid, so I asked for one more out of politeness than anything else; on the bottom of mine she wrote words that suggested we were on the most intimate terms, then asked: 'What did you say your name was?'"[135] The other performers in the Tivoli show stayed at the far less luxurious Royal Arcade Hotel, which was located at 301-303 Little Collins Street, Melbourne, one block west of the Tivoli.[136] An advertisement in the *Highlights From Hollywood* theater program described the Royal Arcade Hotel as "the home of the Tivoli artists."[137]

On Tuesday the 6th of June 1939, Anna May Wong attended the *Gala Theatrical Entertainment,* a one-night-only variety spectacular at the Princess Theater in Spring Street, Melbourne.[138] Performing in the show were the American virtuoso harmonica player, Larry Adler (1914-2001); the Australian bass-baritone, Alan Eddy; the cast of the Melbourne University revue, *Getting the Bird;* the five-year old pianist, "Baby Moya [McCrackett]—the Australian Prodigy;" ex-members of the Russian Ballet, who were assisted by pupils from the Jennie Brenan School of Dancing; and various artists from *Broadway Hotshots* (1939), the Tivoli show that preceded Wong's.[139] The *Gala Theatrical Entertainment* was in aid of the Children's Hospital, which was unexpectedly short of funds following a recent outbreak of polio in Melbourne and an increase in nurses' wages.[140] Lady Ella (a.k.a. Eleanor) Latham (1878-1964), the president of the hospital and also the wife of Sir John Latham (1877-1964), the Chancellor of the University of Melbourne, greeted the four guests of honor at the event, namely: Wong; Adler; Arthur Coles (1892-1982), the Lord Mayor of Melbourne, who was also the managing director of G.J. Coles & Co., a successful chain of discount retail stores; and Coles' wife, Lilian, the Lady Mayoress.[141] Interestingly, the show's printed theater program noted: "Miss Anna May Wong will be present in one of the stage boxes."[142] Given that she had arrived in Melbourne only on the previous day, Frank Neil probably arranged for her to attend the event at least a week beforehand. *The Argus* reported: "Miss Anna May Wong received an ovation when she appeared in one of the stage boxes, wrapped from throat to feet in a sweeping coat of ermine, which she wore over a creamy and purple Chinese gown [a cheongsam?]."[143] The film star autographed the theater program of 12-year old Bruce McBrien (born in 1926), who attended the show with his parents (Fig. 5).

On Wednesday the 7th of June 1939, the International Club of Victoria held its annual ball at the Hollywood-inspired, Arthur Purnell-designed Palais de Danse, which was located in the Melbourne bay side suburb of St.

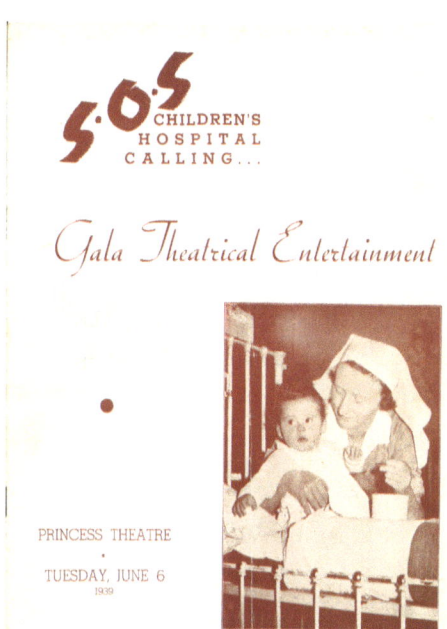

Fig. 5: Bruce McBrien's *Gala Theatrical Entertainment* theater program, which Wong autographed for him. (Bruce McBrien's collection.)

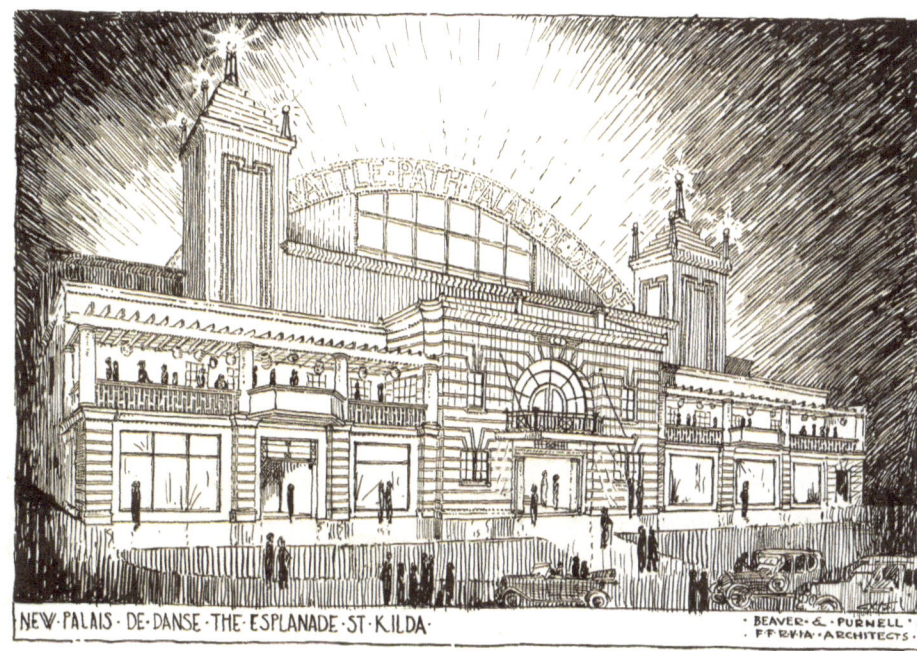

Fig. 6: The Hollywood-inspired Palais de Danse in St. Kilda. (Melbourne University Archives.)

Kilda (Fig. 6). The aims of the club were "to provide a meeting-place where residents of Melbourne may meet members of national groups either living in or visiting Melbourne; where members of individual groups may meet one another; and where distinguished visitors may be entertained with the object of promoting friendship and understanding among nationalities."[144] Over 1,000 people "representing almost all the nations of the world"[145] attended the ball, and for the second night in a row, Anna May Wong and Arthur and Lilian Coles were the guests of honor. "Miss Wong wore a national costume of chartreuse embroidered with gold,"[146] observed *The Argus*.

On Saturday the 10th of June 1939, Anna May Wong attended a dance at the Menzies Hotel, where she was staying, which had been organized by the Young Chinese League, a local Chinese social club, to officially welcome her to Melbourne. The officeholders of the league together with a group of unmarried, smartly dressed Chinese hostesses—Misses D. Chinn, P. Poon, D. Whee, and L. Young—greeted Wong when she arrived at the dance.[147] The Menzies' ballroom was very colorfully decorated for the event, as *The Argus* reported: "Pink and red carnations and snapdragons decorated the tables, and gladioli of those shades filled the bowls on pedestals around the

dance floor [...] Miss Wong wore a Chinese dress of orange crepe decorated with jade green, and the flowers which were presented to her were in red colorings, so that she made an interesting contrast to the hostesses in their Western frocks."[148] The actress inscribed a photograph of herself for Frank Chinn Tung Foo (1897-1986), the president of the Young Chinese League (Fig. 7).

After *Highlights From Hollywood* opened on Monday the 12th of June 1939, Wong had to do two shows per day—one at 2.15 p.m. and the other at 8.00 p.m.—six days per week, yet she still managed to get out and about in Melbourne. On Wednesday the 14th of June 1939, she saw *King of Chinatown* (1939),[149] a newly released film in which she co-starred with Akim Tamiroff (1899-1972), a Tbilisi-born American actor with a thick Georgian accent, at the architecturally impressive, Walter Burley Griffin-designed Capitol Theater in Swanston Street, Melbourne, which was only a few blocks around the corner from the Tivoli Theater. *The Age* published a photograph of Wong receiving a huge bouquet of flowers from a pageboy at the Capitol,[150] while a photograph in *The Argus* showed her surrounded by a large crowd of admirers in the foyer of the theater.[151] She wore a long fur coat and a light colored turban, although

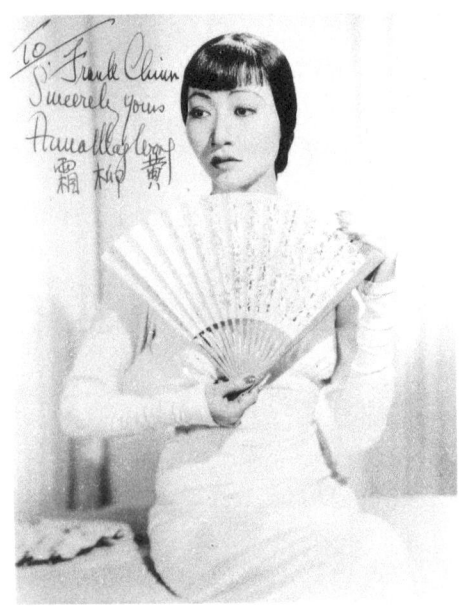

Fig. 7: Frank Chinn's photograph of Wong, which she personally inscribed for him. (The Museum of Chinese Australian History.)

for once nothing was said about her clothes in the newspapers.

In *King of Chinatown,* Anna May Wong played Dr. Mary Ling, a character based on Dr. Margaret Chung (1889-1959), the first female Chinese-American physician. To prepare for the role, Wong "arranged with the director of a big Los Angeles hospital to be present during a dangerous kidney operation," reported *The Courier-Mail.* "It was not a pleasant task she imposed on herself. First, Miss Wong had to conceal her fragile beauty beneath a surgeon's gown and a sterilizing mask, and then she had to undergo the ordeal of watching the operation itself. She absorbed the dramatic atmosphere of the operating theater so well that the corresponding sequence in the film developed into one of its biggest hits."[152]

Melbourne in 1939 was scarcely like Hollywood, so F.K.M. from *Table Talk* was understandably excited to see Wong first on screen at the Capitol Theater, and then shortly afterwards in person backstage at the Tivoli Theater. "After viewing an American talkie at a Melbourne picture house, it's not often you go 'back-stage of the film' and tell the leading actress that you thought she did a 'swell job' … but that, more or less (despite the seeming impossibility of such a procedure) is what happened to me a couple of days ago!" explained the reporter. "I'd been to the Capitol to

see Anna May Wong play an impressive part in the main feminine role in *King of Chinatown* […] and so one can well imagine the unreality of leaving that theater, wandering up to the Tivoli, and meeting the star of that film in the flesh! It all seemed so crazy and confusing that I found myself involuntarily glancing around among those present in her room at the Tivoli to see if Akim Tamiroff was also there, and I just checked myself from wishing her success with *King of Chinatown* and telling her I hoped it would have a long run!"[153] F.K.M. was also very surprised to see Wong playing a heroine instead of a villain in the film. "'You liked it?' she queried in her very clear, incisive and carefully modulated voice. 'Yes,' I told her, 'but it came as a bit of a shock to me to find you playing a straight sympathetic role, instead of one of the parts I'd grown accustomed to seeing you in—one of those—er …' 'I know what you mean,' helpfully put in Miss Wong. 'One of my usual "vamp" parts or "menace" roles.' 'That's it. I'd always seemed to remember you "slinking" around your pictures, doing a spot of spying and generally disporting yourself in a thoroughly insidious manner,'"[154] remarked the reporter somewhat unkindly.

King of Chinatown was a groundbreaking film in some respects, as Shirley Jennifer Lim, the author of *A Feeling of Belonging: Asian American Women's Public Culture, 1930-1960*

(2006), explained: "*King of China-town* not only pioneered Chinese American women's film roles; it also examined European American pre-conceptions about Chinese food and culture."[155] After waiting such a long time to play a positive role like Dr. Mary Ling, Wong would have been almost certainly disappointed at the generally lukewarm reviews the film received from Australian film critics. Typically, *The Sydney Morning Herald* commented: "The Chinese actress, Anna May Wong, now appearing at the Tivoli Theater, has the leading feminine role in Paramount's gangster story, *King of Chinatown*. Akim Tamiroff [...] plays the part of the gangster chief who fleeces Chinatown of much of its wealth while pretending to be one of its best benefactors. After he is dangerously wounded by a rival rack-eteer, the suave and heavily debonair Frank Baturin is nursed back to life and a new conception of ethics by the devotion of the Chinese woman surgeon, Dr. Mary Ling. Daughter of the patriarchal Dr. Chang Ling (Sidney Toler [(1874-1947), a white American actor who went on to play the Chinese detective, Charlie Chan, in several movies]), Mary is under the impression that it was her father who tried to kill Baturin, so she is determined to save her parent from a murder charge by saving the now infatuated gangster. As subsidiary to this main theme is the design upon Baturin's leadership by the crafty 'professor' and ex-convict employed

to look after his books. As Dr. Ling, Anna May Wong has little to do but act a mild role with dignity, plus some gentle humor. This she does, although the script makes her character a rather colorless personality. Akim Tamiroff is never at his best in such roles as Ba-turin, while his sentimental moods therein are much too studied ever to be effective. J. Carroll Naish [(1896-1973), an American actor,] is interest-ing as the scheming professor."[156]

Anna May Wong sometimes ate at the Hong Kong Café, a home-style Chinese restaurant, which was lo-cated at 212 Little Bourke Street in the heart of Melbourne's Chinatown (Fig. 8). It was popular with artists in general from the Tivoli Theater, be-cause it was nearby—the theater was virtually at one end of La Trobe Place, Melbourne, and the café was at the other end—and the Chinese own-ers of the restaurant, Lew and Nellie Boar, occasionally cooked them spe-cial dishes instead of the usual sweet and sour pork, sliced chicken breast and fried steak with vegetables.[157] The Boars' son, Raymond (born in 1934), not only remembers Wong eating at the café, but also sitting on her knee. "I must have been a cute 5-year old wanting to be nursed. Eat your heart out!"[158] Boar gleefully told me.

Anna May Wong enjoyed eating good Chinese food and described the most memorable Chinese meal that she ever had to the Australian maga-

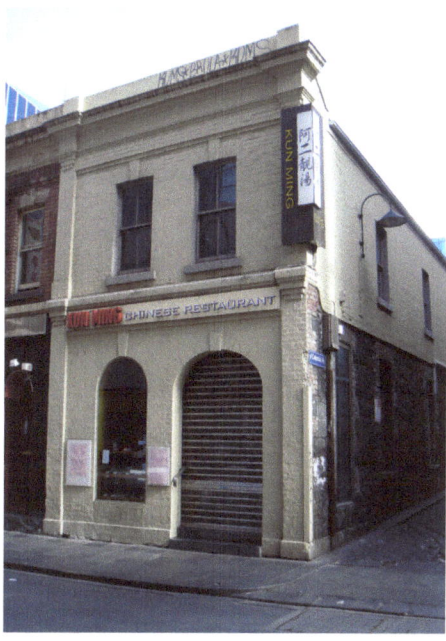

Fig. 8: The Kun Ming Restaurant, which was formerly the Hong Kong Café. (Photograph by Derham Groves.)

zine, *The Australian Women's Weekly*: "The most interesting and impres-sive meal I have ever eaten was at a restaurant in Shanghai. I was enter-taining Madame Wellington Koo, [a.k.a. Hue Lan Obi (1899-1992),] wife of the ambassador to France, and the restaurant had provided its most sumptuous meal. There were 43 courses! Most of them remain in my memory as delicious flavours. I could not tell what the dishes were made of. But three particularly stand out. They were ducks' tongues, shredded eels with sauce, and Peking duck. I have never tasted anything in the East or West so delicious as these. Every sixth course on the menu was soup, as though to encourage us to start the dinner all over again, and not one course were we allowed to miss!"[159]

Anna May Wong appeared in a newspaper advertisement for Remington noiseless portable typewriters, which was first published in *The Sun News-Pictorial* on Thursday the 15th of June 1939.[160] It featured a very good close-up photograph of the film star, dreamily looking into space while resting her chin on her folded arms; a handwritten note by Wong bearing her name in both English and Chinese, which was above the words, "Tivoli Theater;" and the following personal testimonial: "Miss Anna May Wong writes about her Remington Portable. 'I have always used a Remington portable typewriter for my personal correspondence and am delighted with your new noiseless model recently delivered to me.' Miss Wong prefers a Remington portable for it has all standard typewriter features. You, too, should use the best."[161] The typewriters were sold locally by Chartres Pty. Ltd., which was located at 375 Collins Street, Melbourne. No doubt Frank Neil charged the company a hefty fee to use Wong in the advertisement (Fig. 9).

Ironically, Anna May Wong wrote very few letters while she was in Australia, because it "seemed so far away, and by the time one's friends receive one's letter the news is no longer news."[162] She wrote one letter to Lin Yutang (1895-1976), who wrote many very popular books in English about Chinese culture (and, coincidentally, also invented a Chinese typewriter), and his wife, Tsui-feng, who wrote a number of best-selling Chinese cookbooks in English.[163] However, the actress communicated with her family in Los Angeles mostly by telephone, as Jack Meander from *The Sydney Morning Herald* reported: "Anna May has kept in touch with her family while she has been here, speaking to them on the phone on Sundays and hearing all the latest from Hollywood."[164]

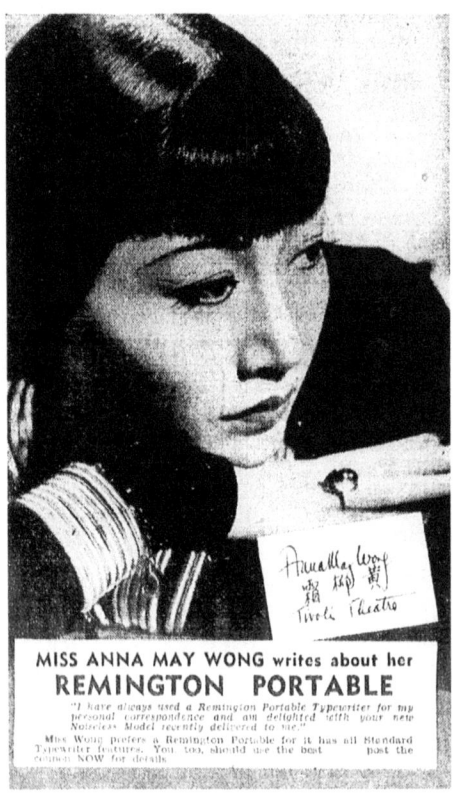

MISS ANNA MAY WONG writes about her
REMINGTON PORTABLE

"I have always used a Remington Portable Typewriter for my personal correspondence and am delighted with your new Noiseless Model recently delivered to me."

Miss Wong prefers a Remington Portable for it has all standard Typewriter features. You, too, should use the best. Post the coupon NOW for details.

Fig. 9: Anna May Wong advertising Remington noiseless portable typewriters. (The Baillieu Library, the University of Melbourne.)

On Friday the 16th of June 1939, Anna May Wong bought some new shoes from Foy's Fashion Corner (a.k.a. Foy & Gibson Pty. Ltd.), which was located at 246 Bourke Street, Melbourne, diagonally opposite the Tivoli Theater. A photograph of a lucky male shop assistant easing the movie star's dainty foot into a high-heeled shoe—Prince Charming-like—was published in *The Argus* the next day.[165] It appears that Wong's presence at the department store caused a commotion in the street, because Te Pana from *The Argus* wrote: 'The footpath was crowded outside a business house in Bourke Street. Women were breathless, and there was a decided mass movement toward the doorway. One little old woman, on her way to Swanston Street, was forced on to the roadway. 'What is all the excitement?' she asked a friend, who was waiting with 'copy' paper and pencil. 'Why, don't you know?' was the answer. 'Anna May Wong, the film star, has just arrived.' 'Goodness me,' replied the little old woman. 'Where has she been?'"[166] Certainly, Wong's ability to attract a crowd reflected her popularity with Australian filmgoers, even though it sometimes took unusual forms. For example, the film star was a favorite subject at fancy dress balls,[167] and a number of people named their pet Pekinese and Pomeranians after her.[168]

Before Anna May Wong visited Australia, she told Lon Jones from *The*

Sydney Morning Herald that she was "anxious to get a look at the bush and outback [...because she did not] want to return [home] with only visions of cities in her mind."[169] However, it appears that the furthest she got was Healesville, a small country town 52 kilometers northeast of Melbourne. On Sunday the 18th of June 1939, George Fitzwater, the manager of Neal's Motors Pty. Ltd., which was located at 134 Exhibition Street, Melbourne, took Wong to Healesville, where they ate lunch at the Grand Hotel[170] in the main street and visited the nearby Sir Colin Mackenzie Sanctuary, an Australian native fauna park.[171] They probably drove there in a Hudson Country Club 8 Series 95, which was the best and latest model car that Neal's Motors sold. A photograph of Wong cuddling a koala appeared in *The Age*. "Miss Anna May Wong found this baby koala a quaint companion when she visited the sanctuary at Healesville yesterday," read the caption of the photo (Fig. 10).[172] However, it seems that once was enough for the actress, because when *Highlights From Hollywood* opened in Sydney, she told Jack Meander that she had "no intention of paying the traditional visit to see the koalas"[173] at the Koala Park at West Pennant Hills, 25 kilometers northwest of Sydney.

One of the biggest local theatrical events in Melbourne in 1939 was the homecoming tour of the celebrated Australian soprano, Marjorie Lawrence (1907-1979), the prima donna of the Metropolitan Opera House in New York, who was born in Winchlesea, a small town 112 kilometers southwest of Melbourne. On Thursday the 22nd of June 1939, Wong attended Lawrence's first recital in Melbourne at the Town Hall in Swanston Street, which was located just around the corner from the Tivoli Theater, as *The Argus* noted: "In the audience was the Chinese film star Miss Anna May Wong, who wore a cape of silver fox fur over a vermilion and gold embroidered Chinese gown slashed with white."[174]

On Friday the 23rd of June 1939, Anna May Wong toured the University of Melbourne, located in the leafy Melbourne suburb of Parkville, before eating lunch at Union House on the university campus. "At the invitation of Lady Latham, wife of the Chancellor, guests who included several of the

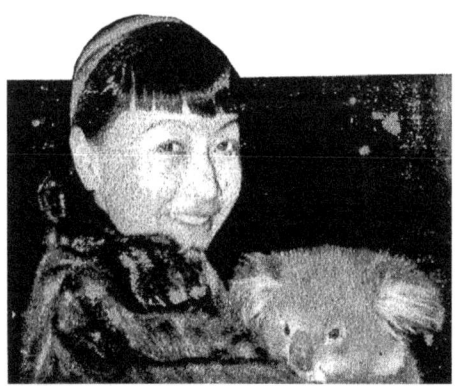

Fig. 10: Anna May Wong cuddling a koala at the Sir Colin Mackenzie Sanctuary at Healesville. (The Baillieu Library, the University of Melbourne.)

helpers at the recent theatrical performance which she organized for the Children's Hospital [i.e. the *Gala Theatrical Entertainment* at the Princess Theater, mentioned earlier], gathered to meet Miss Anna May Wong, who is appearing at the Tivoli Theater,"[175] reported *The Argus*. In appreciation of the film star's support for the hospital, Lady Latham presented the film star with a basket of violets.

Anna May Wong was certainly in great demand. On Thursday the 29th of June 1939, she planned to attend a concert at the Old Players and Playgoers Association, which had its clubrooms in the Nicholas Building at 21-47 Swanston Street, Melbourne, but she suddenly pulled out at the last minute. *The Argus* reported: "Flowers which were to have been presented to Miss Anna May Wong in person by the Old Players and Playgoers Association [...] were sent to the Tivoli Theater when Miss Wong was unable to attend the association's musical afternoon."[176] (Not wishing to disappoint anyone, the actress attended the association's meeting at 2.00 p.m. on Wednesday the 12th of July 1939.[177] Given that *Highlights From Hollywood* started at 2.15 p.m., Wong evidently skipped the first half of the show in order to go.)

On Friday the 30th of June 1939, Anna May Wong was due to "give a talk on her experiences at Hollywood and in the films"[178] to another theater group, the Theater Lovers' Club, which met in Clyde House at 182 Collins Street, Melbourne, but she cancelled this as well. Fortunately, the Andrini Brothers were able to take the film star's place at short notice.[179] What caused Wong to suddenly cancel two engagements on consecutive days? I believe that she needed the time to rehearse "At the Barricade," which was due to be performed for the first time on Saturday the 1st of July 1939.

Despite cancelling her talk to the Theater Lovers' Club on Friday afternoon, Wong was able to attend the *Golden Gate Fiesta* at the Palais de Danse in St. Kilda on Friday night, which was a truly spectacular event, as *The Argus* reported: "Replicas of the Sun Tower, which is the theme structure of the San Francisco Exposition [which ran from Saturday the 18th of February 1939 until Sunday the 29th of October 1939], were the predominating decoration at the Palais de Danse last night for the Golden Gate Fiesta— this year's annual ball arranged by the American women's auxiliary for the Children's Hospital. Each table was centred with a model 2-ft. high of the tower, which was illuminated from inside, and capped with small American and Australian flags […] At one end of the ballroom a model of the Statue of Liberty was erected and at the other the Stars and Stripes was visible through a gauze curtain bearing a spangled silver representation of the Mayan-Oriental tower with a model of the Golden Gate Bridge on each side, and the green waters of San Francisco harbor in the foreground. Large American flags hung from the ceiling above the official table, where on a mirror bordered with low greenery and orange berries stood a tall model of the tower […] Green candelabra bearing long pale green candles and low bowls of flowers in pink and yellow tonings were also set on the table. In an adjoining red and white striped marquee various stalls were arranged, one of the most attractive being hung with gay Oriental pennants and labeled 'San Francisco Chinatown.' Here many gay articles, including souvenir scarfs gaily printed with buildings at the San Francisco Exposition, were sold […] The most entertaining novelty of the evening was the appearance in the ballroom of two elephants, who gave an amazing performance, including the playing of mouth organs […] Miss Anna May Wong, who came on after her theater performance […] spent some time at the souvenir booth in the marquee."[180] Interestingly, the *Golden Gate Fiesta* was the third event in aid of the Children's Hospital that Wong attended while she was in Melbourne.

In late June or early July 1939 (the exact date is unknown), Wong was the guest of honor at a cocktail party (the location of which is also unknown), hosted by a group of Victorian women radio announcers.[181] As mentioned earlier, despite Frank Neil's best efforts, the actress did not perform on radio in Australia. However, the wireless was not really Wong's medium. Only three weeks before sailing to Australia, she played the small part of Peony, a Chinese slave-girl who eventually goes on the Long March, in an American radio production of Pearl S. Buck's latest novel, *The Patriot* (1939).[182] Characteristically, Wong sounded very wooden over the air, and to make matters worse, she also fluffed her lines. The multi-talented American actor and director, Orson Welles (1915-1985), not only played the main part of I-wan, a Chinese revolutionary who was sent to Japan by his father, but he also produced the hour-long radio drama.

What did Anna May Wong think about Australia? F.K.M. from *Table Talk* was on the verge of asking her when she almost instinctively said: "If you'll pardon my interrupting […] there's one very commendable point I've noted about all you Australian newspapermen: not one of you has asked me what I think of your country, and how I like being here."[183] This stopped F.K.M. dead in his tracks and abruptly ended the interview. But the reluctance of the Australian press to ask Wong these standard questions means that we do not know what she truly thought about the country, apart from relatively trivial details, such as telling Jack Meander from *The Sydney Morning Herald* "that she liked Melbourne, but found it very cold."[184]

Comparing Melbourne of 1939 (population 1,035,600) to the city that it is today (population 4,084,700), many of the buildings that Wong frequented while she lived there have been either demolished or rebuilt over the years, such as Foy's Fashion Corner; the Palais de Danse; the Menzies Hotel; Spencer Street Station; the Tivoli Theater; and Union House. On the other hand, a surprisingly large number of places still look or feel the same, including the Capitol Theater; the Grand Hotel; the Healesville Sanctuary (although cuddling the koalas is no longer permitted!); the Hong Kong Café (which is now named the Kun Ming Restaurant); the Melbourne Town Hall; the Nicholas Building; and the Princess Theater.

Living in Sydney

On Monday the 17th of July 1939, Anna May Wong and the rest of the cast of *Hollywood Highlights* (to use

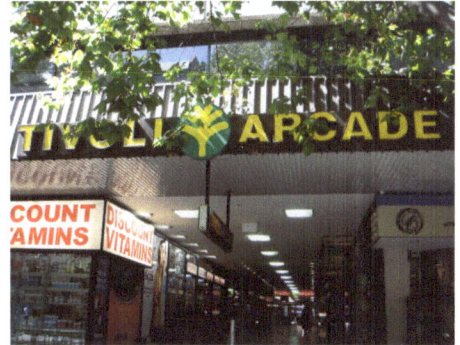

Fig. 11: Tivoli Court, the office building that replaced the Tivoli Theater in Melbourne. (Photograph by Derham Groves.)

the show's snappier new name in Sydney) arrived in Sydney by train. However, after the 13-hour 45-minute journey from Melbourne, she did not look her usual glamorous self. Wong had on a full-length fur coat, which was buttoned to the neck and concealed her dress underneath, a pair of wrist-length white gloves and a most unflattering hat (Fig. 12). Many members of the local Chinese community welcomed her at Central Station, including Dr. Chun-Jien Pao, the Consul-General of China, and his wife Edith, and Mrs. Frank (Amelia) Quan Mane, who presented the actress with a bouquet of red roses on behalf of the New South Wales Chinese Women's Relief Fund. The Hobart (Tasmania) newspaper, *The Mercury*, and the Adelaide (South Australia) newspaper, *The Advertiser*, both published photographs of Wong receiving the flowers from Mane,[185] while a photograph in *The Sydney Morning Herald* showed the film star waving to the crowd at the station.[186] "The visiting actress is delighted by the fact that members of Australia's Chinese community have given her such a whole-hearted welcome," reported *The Sydney Morning Herald*. "She has had many letters from them and yesterday when the train arrived in Sydney deputations from the New South Wales Chinese Women's Relief Fund and the Young Chinese League were there to meet her."[187] Wong must have seemed like a breath of fresh air to many Chinese-Australians. In 1939, they

were routinely subjected to racial discrimination, while Chinese-Australian women had to cope with sexual prejudice as well. By comparison, Wong's life must have seemed perfect, even though this was not exactly the case.

It seems that Anna May Wong was still in the process of re-evaluating her acting career, because on her arrival in Sydney she told *The Sydney Morning Herald* that she was "pleased with the mental relaxation which this country has given her. 'It's given me what I sought for two years in the "hectivity" of Hollywood—tranquillity and serenity of mind. Having come so far, I see my home in its true perspective,' said Miss Wong. 'But I've had a very enjoyable time in a quiet way,' she added hastily. 'I enjoy "hectivity" occasionally, perhaps for a fortnight once a year, but I'm here to work and to meet the Australian public. I like talking to people—porters and taxi-drivers and others—they often have an interesting slant on things. I like

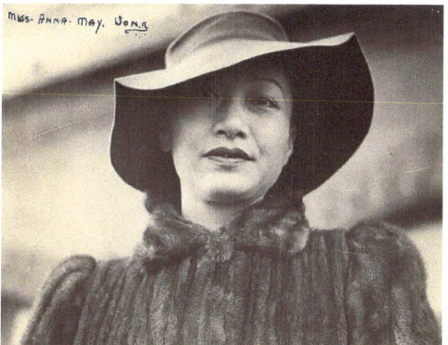

Fig. 12: Anna May Wong on arrival in Sydney. (The State Library of New South Wales.)

people who respond to life with enthusiasm—not dead people—that's why I like myself so much, I guess!' she remarked with a smile. 'I don't get lonely. I think the whole trouble is that without any quiet periods for reflection we can't "re-charge" ourselves for the next day.'"[188] However, I get the impression that she was missing Hollywood.

On Tuesday the 18th of July 1939, the Paos hosted a dinner party for Wong at their house at 29 Wunulla Road in Point Piper, one of Sydney's most exclusive and expensive harbor side suburbs. The table decorations were lavish, as *The Sydney Morning Herald* reported: "Red candles and red camellias decorated the table when Mrs. C.J. Pao, wife of the Consul-General for China, entertained at a dinner party at her home [...] last night in honor of Miss Anna May Wong. A pailou [i.e. a traditional Chinese gateway] made of sugar by her chef stood on another table, and she used some lovely embroidered silk Chinese mats more than 100 years old."[189] The guests included the Australian painter, Adrian Feint (1894-1971); Dr. G.L. Host, the Consul-General for Denmark; Mr. M.F.F.A. Jansen, the Consul-General for Belgium; Mrs. Malcolm Mackellar, a member of Sydney's aristocracy, who was also the sister-in-law of the popular Australian poet, Dorothea Mackellar (1885-1968), who wrote "My Country" (1911); and the Australian artist and publisher, Sydney Ure Smith (1887-1949).

In 1916, Sydney Ure Smith in partnership with his brother-in-law at the time, Charles Lloyd Jones, who Wong had met on the voyage to Australia, and Bertram Stevens (1872-1922), an Australian editor and writer, founded the *Vogue*-style, Australian quarterly journal, *The Home*. Coincidentally or not, the August 1939 edition of the magazine contained a number of glamorous photographs of the Chinese-American film star by Athol Shmith (1914-1990), a leading fashion and portrait photographer from Melbourne. Wong was shown dressed in Western-style day clothes and holding two flowers in two photographs and the Chinese coat and headdress that she wore in her vaudeville act in three photographs (Fig. 13). The accompanying text read: "Her real name is Wong Liu Tsong—'Frosted Yellow Willow' [sic]—and she was born in the United States. At school she was always Anna Wong. Then her acting career started. 'Anna Wong was too abrupt,' she explains, 'so I put in the name of my favorite month, May.' Graceful, smartly dressed and possessed of a superb sense of humour. Miss Wong is the Orient and the West in one person—one moment she will be speaking of the mystery of China's lost cities; the next moment the latest Hollywood wisecrack will cross her lips. But with it all she has an arresting personality."[190]

On Wednesday the 19th of July 1939, Anna May Wong attended the final performance of *Broadway Hotshots* at the Tivoli Theater in Sydney, which was located on the corner of Castlereagh and Campbell streets.[191] Performing in the show were the following American vaudeville artists: the singers, Carl and Leone Bonner, who figured in several duets; the comic film actor, Sammy Cohen (1902-1981), whose routine included a "farcical boxing turn;"[192] the pianist, Lee Donn, who played both classical and swing tunes on a concert grand piano and "proved himself a showman beyond the ordinary;"[193] the comic dancers and musicians, the Four Franks—two brothers and two sisters—who performed "an enjoyable turn consisting of fast dancing and musical numbers by trombones and trumpets;"[194] the juggler, Joe Melvin, who "achieved several almost uncanny feats with four hats;"[195] the precision dancer, Mignone, who was described by one critic as "a better contortionist than she was a dancer, for she appeared in both roles, and made an unusual impression in both;"[196] the political satirist, Senator (Francis) Murphy, who "had represented Illinois [...] in the Senate for four-and-a-half years"[197] before he took up comedy; the comedy equilibrists or balancers, the Myrons, who "for spectacle [...] stole the program,"[198] according to *The Sydney Morning Herald;* "the eccentric dancers,"[199] the Stanley Brothers; and the comedian, Jack Stocks, who presented some "new satirical and inoffensive parodies on women."[200]

On the following day, *Hollywood Highlights* took over from *Broadway Hotshots.* Just prior to the first performance of the new Tivoli show, Jack Meander from *The Sydney Morning Herald* called into Wong's dressing room while she was "busy making up, a 45 minutes' proceeding, which she allowed me to watch for a while. I drew her attention to the call sheet on the wall, in which her act was numbered 13. 'Aren't you superstitious?' I asked her. 'Not a bit,' she said. 'After all, one and three make four; there are 11 letters in Anna May Wong; and my lucky number is 22; so what?'"[201]

However, despite claiming not to be superstitious, the following item in the Perth (Western Australia) newspaper, *The Western Mail,* suggests that Wong believed in astrology: "Five years ago [(i.e. in 1934)] her own horoscope was set up and it foretold that she would be of 'great service to your ancestral country during the years of 1937 and 1938.'"[202] Wong also believed in Chinese geomancy or feng-shui, as *The Western Mail* once again reported—albeit not in so many words: "Miss Wong, with many others of her race, believes that there are unseen forces that direct people and may even control the life of nations."[203] But the clincher was Wong's

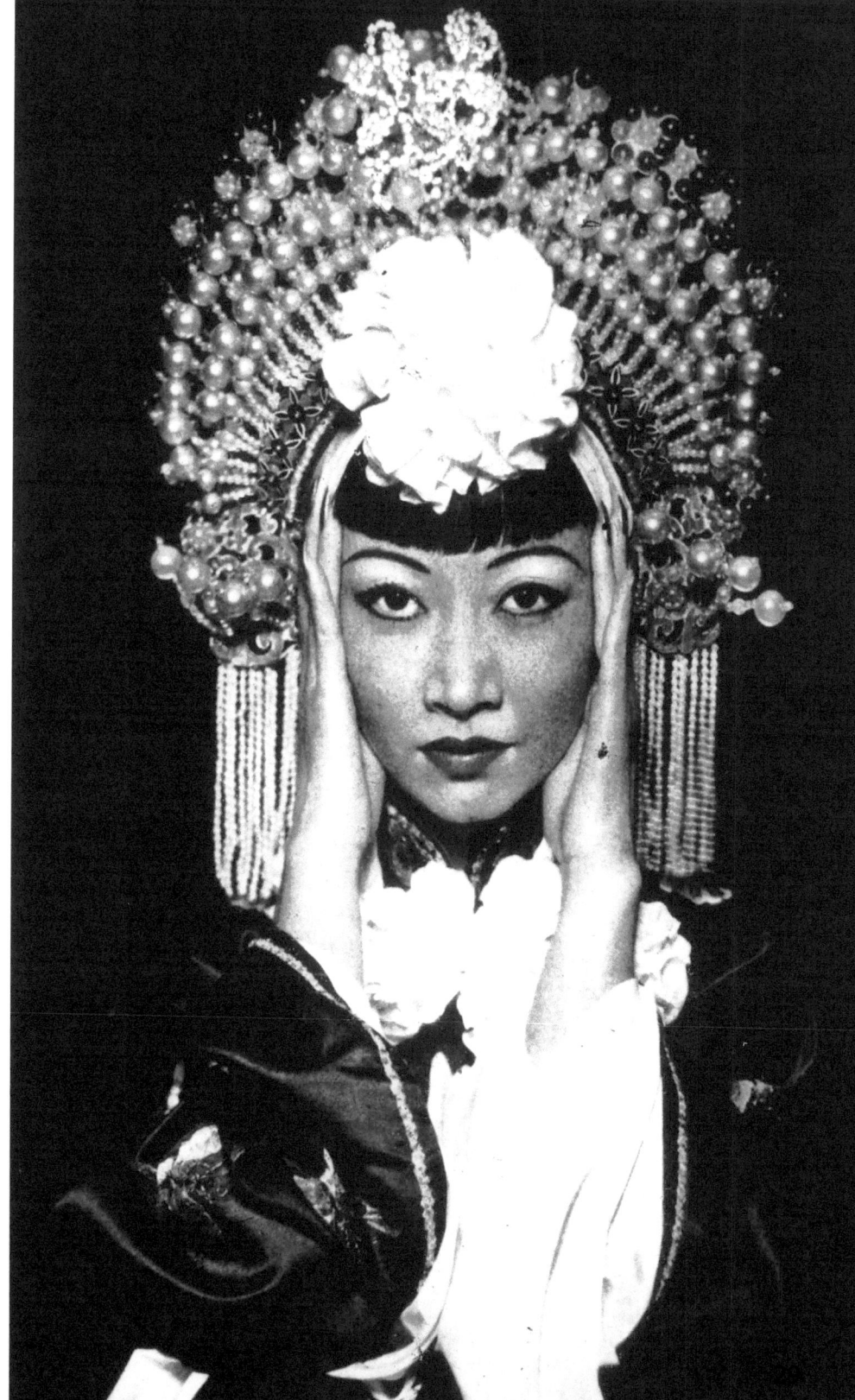

Fig. 13: Anna May Wong by Athol Shmith. (The State Library of Victoria.)

two lucky charms, which were both associated with her childhood. One was a Chinese coin, given to her when she was a child by a friend of her mother, which the film star wore around her neck on a gold chain.[204] The other was a pincushion, made from a shoe that Wong had worn as a young girl, which she kept in her dressing room at the Tivoli Theater. When Jonathan Swift, a journalist from the *Sun News-Pictorial*, "pointed out that it resembled a boy's shoe, she related the fact that, until the age of 10, she was brought up as a boy. It seems the first child in the family was a girl [i.e. Lulu Wong Lew Ying (1902-1995)] and then Anna May arrived. Her father [Wong Sam Sing (1860-1949)] was so annoyed because he had no heir to his name that he ordered Anna to be considered as such for nearly 10 years. It was her sister [i.e. probably Lulu] who kept Anna's first shoes, and today she keeps the other one of the pair as a luck-bringer."[205] Swift's article was illustrated with a tiny photograph of Wong's shoe-cum-pincushion-cum-lucky charm.

While the Chinese custom of dressing girls as boys was not unique to the Wong family, it still seems ironic—not to say more than a little strange—that Anna May Wong, a genuine motion picture diva of the 1920s and '30s, who was widely admired around the world for her beauty and femininity both on and off the screen, was dressed as a boy by her parents for the first decade of her life. Apparently, it did not do the actress any psychological harm, because she credited her later confidence in public to this early masculinizing effect.[206]

On Saturday the 22nd of July 1939, Anna May Wong hosted a Chinese dinner party at Prince's, a fashionable new French restaurant in Martin Place, Sydney. Among those present were Mr. and Mrs. Carl O. de Dardel, the Consul-General for Sweden; Sir Henry Gullett (1878-1940), the Australian Minister for External Affairs [i.e. the Australian equivalent of the Secretary of State], his wife, Elizabeth, and their daughter, Sue; Charles and Hannah Lloyd Jones; and Chun-Jien and Edith Pao. On the menu were "prawn cutlets, chicken and crab rolls, chow mien [i.e. fried noodles], kumquats, lychee nuts and ginger, soy sauce and mustard."[207] Jack Meander reported: "The Wong party sat at a table specially set by Leo, [the Maître d',] who spent Saturday afternoon learning the art of setting tables a la Chinoise. There were pretty little blue bowls and cups, and fine ivory chopsticks."[208] *The Sydney Morning Herald* published a photograph of Wong showing Gullett "how to manage his chop sticks at a Chinese dinner at Prince's,"[209] but presumably the actress and the politician also talked about the tense situation in China. It appears that Prince's was Wong's favorite restaurant in Sydney, because on another occasion Meander spotted her there with Orry Kelly (1897-1964), the Australian-born chief costume designer at Warner Brothers studios in Hollywood, who was in town to visit his mother.[210]

In Sydney, Anna May Wong provided a number of stories for Jack Meander's gossip column, including the following one, which is also about the film star and Chinese food: "When Anna May Wong was in Peiping [a.k.a. Peking and Beijing] she met Lady Diana Fitzherbert, whom she had known for many years," wrote Meander. "'Now I wanted to take Diana to the famous 300-year old café there,' she said. 'The only trouble was that Mandarin was spoken and I only speak Cantonese. So I had the proprietor make us out a special menu in Cantonese: five courses I told him, but when we sat down I found they had written down nine. I protested to the proprietor, but he told me we would lose face if we did not eat nine. Well, the chief course was Peking duck and I didn't want to go filling up with lots of other dishes first. So I asked Diana if she minded skipping the fish and concentrating on the old duck. She said OK, so I tried to tell the waiter. He didn't understand a word. So I waved my hands and said, 'Quack, quack.' The waiter immediately started rushing round, and brought in the fish double quick. I discovered afterwards that in Mandarin, the word for quickly is very much like quack.'"[211]

Kerwin Maegraith (1903-1970), an Australian maverick quick sketch artist and writer,[212] drew Wong's portrait at the upmarket Wentworth Hotel in Lang Street, Sydney, where she was staying. "I sat Anna May Wong with her eyes glued outside the window of her hotel," he wrote. "She sat as still as a statue. I showed her my drawing. She did not like it, and told me so."[213] Maegraith did another drawing of the film star and fortunately it "was a success. Would you be interested to know that one side of Miss Wong's face is entirely different from the other?"[214] he observed. Maegraith did three sketches of the actress that she signed in both Chinese and English, which appeared in *The Sydney Morning Herald* on Monday the 24th of July 1939 (Fig. 14). Intriguingly, one of them looked like a copy of the photograph of Wong that was used in the typewriter advertisement, described earlier. Maegraith noted that her "perfectly groomed figure, the force of personality written all over her face, light brown complexion, and expressive dark eyes have intrigued many world-famous artists. James Montgomery Flagg [(1877-1960), an American artist,] has drawn her portrait, and so has Willy Pogany [(1882-1955), a Hungarian artist]. Joseph Oppenheimer [(1876-1966), a German artist,] described her as a perfect model, and among the other noted brush-wielders, Olive Snell [(died in 1962), an English artist,] did a prominent picture of the Oriental actress a couple of years ago in England."[215]

Indeed, Anna May Wong is still a fascinating subject for many artists around the world, such as Hannah Hall (born in 1967) from Sydney. In 2006, she painted the film star on black velvet for an exhibition about death and remembrance. "I was drawn to Anna May Wong by her beauty captured in still photographs," Hall told me. "I realized that part of Anna's beauty and attraction is due to a sadness or melancholy in her eyes. This reveals an emotional state that depicts a silent truth. It is rare to see this kind of truth in actors and probably rarer for this type of sadness to be portrayed as profound beauty."[216]

On Wednesday the 26th of July 1939, Anna May Wong and her new best friend, Edith Pao, attended a luncheon hosted by the Playgoers' Club at the avant-garde Blaxland Galler-

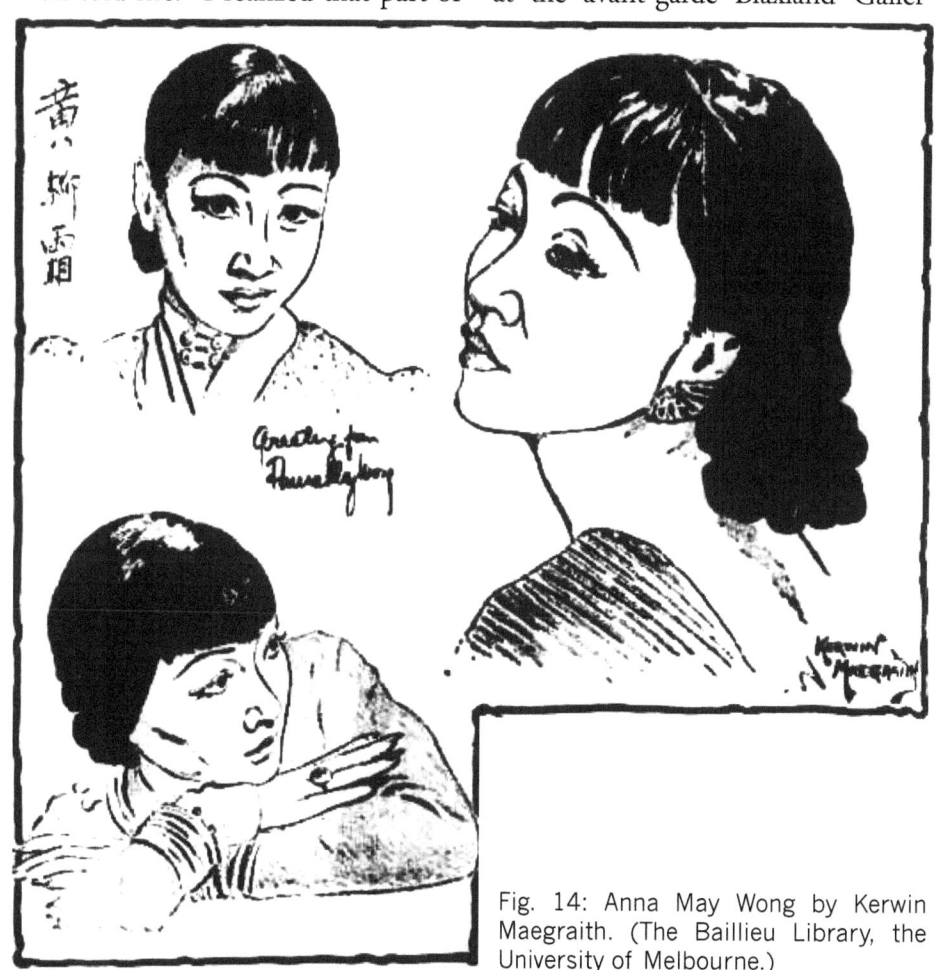

Fig. 14: Anna May Wong by Kerwin Maegraith. (The Baillieu Library, the University of Melbourne.)

ies, which was located on the eighth floor of Farmer's department store in George Street, Sydney. On the menu were "chow mien and fried rice."[217] As usual, *The Sydney Morning Herald* described Wong's glamorous outfit: "Miss Wong, who looked striking in a flame wool sheer frock, with a matching toque [i.e. a rimless hat], and silver fox cape, gave a short talk. 'The more you become keen and interested in the theater, the more good things you bring to your doorstep,' she said."[218]

On Thursday the 27th of July 1939, Anna May Wong had an early morning meeting with Edith Pao and representatives of the Young Chinese Relief Movement at the Wentworth Hotel, where she was staying, to plan the forthcoming "Anna May Wong Ball," a fundraiser for war-torn China, as *The Sydney Morning Herald* reported: "Miss Wong expressed the hope that all interested would cooperate to make the ball a great success, so that the funds to provide medical aid to the Chinese wounded and refugees would benefit considerably. Mrs Pao, who will be patroness of the ball, complimented the movement on the good work its members had already done."[219]

Later, at 5:15 p.m. on Thursday afternoon, Anna May Wong together with Ladislas De Noskowski (1892-1969), who was the Consul-General for Poland, and Clifford Huntsman, an English pianist who was on a con-cert tour of Australia, were all guests of honor at a cocktail party given by the International Society, which met in the clubrooms of the Overseas League at 28 Martin Place, Sydney. The actress wore a black frock braided in red, a mink coat and a red turban. Given Germany's increasing aggression towards Poland, De Noskowski grimly predicted: "If Poland has to fight it will be a matter of life and death, and the fight will be carried on to the last man."[220] (On Friday the 1st of September 1939, Germany invaded Poland, which triggered World War Two.) Almost certainly thinking about what was happening in China as well, "Miss Wong [...] said that she was happy to be in a peaceful country that was sympathetic to other peaceful and peace-loving countries,"[221] reported *The Sydney Morning Herald*. However, the cocktail party also had some humorous moments. De Noskowski joked that since he had once played in *Macbeth*, "I rob Miss Anna May Wong of the distinction of being the only film star present," while she responded by saying: "I only know one Polish word, and that is 'I love you,' but I will say it just the same."[222] A photograph in *The Sydney Morning Herald* showed the film star presenting De Noskowski with a flower for his buttonhole, while his Australian wife, Beatrice (died in 1960), and Mrs. Maurice Gulson, the International Club's hostess for the evening (who wore a hat in the form of a clock!), both looked on.[223]

On Thursday the 3rd of August 1939, the Broken Hill (New South Wales) newspaper, *The Barrier Miner*—normally, an unlikely source of Hollywood gossip—reported: "Anna May Wong's option has not been taken up by Paramount."[224] In other words, the film studio had sacked her. Certainly, Wong never worked for Paramount again, and she made only five more feature-length movies in her lifetime: *Ellery Queen's Penthouse Mystery* (1941); *Bombs Over Burma* (1942); *Lady From Chungking* (1942); *Impact* (1949); and *Portrait in Black* (1960). While being let go by Paramount was no doubt bitterly disappointing for the actress, given that she was in the process of re-assessing her movie career at the time, it may have just seemed like providence. On the other hand, the studio's decision may very well have been on the cards before Wong left for Australia, which was what prompted the re-evaluation of her career in the first place.[225]

On Friday the 4th of August 1939, Anna May Wong attended a welcome home party for Hubert Fairfax (1872-1950) who was a director of his family's firm, John Fairfax & Sons Ltd., which published several magazines and newspapers, including *The Home* and *The Sydney Morning Herald*—two publications that Wong would have been very familiar with in Sydney—and his wife, Ruth (1878-1948), who was one of the founders of the Country Women's Association.

They had both just returned from England, where Mrs. Fairfax had attended a conference of the Associated Countrywomen of the World in London. Wong already knew a number of people at the party, including Chun-Jien and Edith Pao; Charles and Hannah Lloyd Jones; Dr. G.L. Host, the Consul-General for Denmark, and Mrs. Host; the Sydney blueblood, Mrs. Malcolm Mackellar; and the English pianist, Clifford Huntsman.[226] Thomas Kelly (1875-1948), a wealthy businessman, and his wife, Ethel (1875-1949), a former actress, held the welcome home party at their house in the exclusive Sydney harbor side suburb of Darling Point. As it happened, he had helped to establish the Koala Park that Wong had told Jack Meander from *The Sydney Morning Herald* she had no intention of visiting.[227] However, I wonder whether she considered changing her mind after meeting Kelly?

Tuesday the 8th of August 1939 was a particularly busy day for Wong. After performing at the Tivoli Theater in the afternoon, she attended a welcome home party for Ralph Doyle (1894-1955), the managing director of R.K.O. Radio Pictures (Australia) Inc., and his brother-in-law, Devon Minchin (born in 1919), a representative of the Vick Chemical Company, who had both just returned from the United States. Doyle's wife, Patricia (1910-2002), a former actress and beauty queen, had arranged the party at the exclusive Royal Sydney Yacht Squadron,[228] which is almost next door to Kirribilli House, the official Sydney residence of the Australian Prime Minister. Coincidentally, Wong and Patricia Doyle (née Minchin) had both worked with the English actor, John Longden—the Chinese-American actress in *The Road to Dishonor,* as stated previously, and the Australian actress in *The Silence of Dean Maitland* (1934).[229] At the party were several leading members of the Australian film industry, including Ralph's brother, Stuart Doyle (1887-1945), the managing director of Cinesound Productions Ltd., which had made the newsreel that showed Wong and the other overseas celebrities arriving in Sydney onboard the *Aorangi;* Ken G. Hall (1901-1994), the general manager of Cinesound, who also directed many of the company's films, including *The Squatter's Daughter* and *Gone to the Dogs*—the two films that featured Cath Esler, the *Hollywood Highlights* singer—and *The Silence of Dean Maitland;* Herc (a.k.a. Hercules) McIntyre, the managing director of Universal Pictures Corporation (Australia); and Stanley Crick (1888-1955), the managing director of Australia and New Zealand Theaters Ltd. (Harry Hunter, the managing director of Paramount Pictures (Australia) Inc., the Australian representative of Wong's former studio, may very well have also been at the party, however he was not mentioned in the newspaper report of it.)

Then after attending the welcome home party for Ralph Doyle and Devon Minchin and performing at the Tivoli Theater on Tuesday evening, Wong attended the "Anna May Wong Ball" at the Wentworth Hotel, which she had helped to plan, as mentioned earlier. *The Sydney Morning Herald* reported: "On her arrival, Miss Wong was received by the Consul-General for China, Dr. C.J. Pao, and Mrs. Pao. On the official table where the decorations were carried out in multicolored flags, Miss Wong's name was formed with primroses and violets. During the evening, she autographed photographs of herself at a small charge, and the money was donated to the [Chinese War] relief fund."[230]

In 1938, the American biweekly magazine, *Look,* declared that Wong was "the world's most beautiful Chinese girl."[231] Towards the end of her stay in Sydney, the film star revealed some of her beauty secrets to Jesse Collings, the author of "There is No Virtue in a Shiny Nose" (1939), which was published in *The Sydney Morning Herald* on Monday the 14th of August 1939. "Anna May Wong, now in Sydney, is emphatic that it is important for a girl to look beautiful," wrote Collings. "'There are so many ugly things in the world today that beauty is always sure of a welcome, and can only be regarded as an asset!' she says. 'But beauty must be allied with personality. A girl must be individual—not cut to a pattern. In everything she must seek to express herself—in her bearing, her attitude towards life, in her clothes, and in her make-up. I do not think young girls, with fresh, youthful complexions, need any make-up at all. But when the time comes for them to use it they must learn to use it intelligently—to aid and exploit their own personality, not to imitate some reigning stage or screen beauty who may not be at all their type. Clothes, too, are very important. I choose what will suit *me*. And sometimes I find that a frock that may be several years old is not out of fashion when I wear it because it expresses *me*. Sometimes the latest fashion does not do that and I do not feel at my best when I wear it. On the other hand, sometimes it does. A woman cannot run the risk of being out of date, but she can choose what suits her and accentuates her appeal. Thus it is that in my wardrobe I have my happy frocks and my unhappy frocks.'"[232]

My impression is that Anna May Wong liked Sydney more than Melbourne. Sydney was a bit warmer, a bit larger (population 1,228,720) and—thanks to Sydney Harbor—a bit more picturesque than Melbourne. But perhaps most importantly of all, her closest Australian friends, the Lloyd Joneses and the Paos, lived in Sydney. They introduced Wong to their rather exclusive circle of friends, who included actors; artists; businessmen; diplomats; filmmakers; publishers; socialites; and writers. The film star was well and truly in her element. Nevertheless, after spending just over 15 weeks in Australia away from her family and American friends, Wong doubtlessly would have agreed with the famous line from the popular old song, "Home! Sweet Home! (1822): "Be it ever so humble, there's no place like home."[233]

Going Home

When the time finally came to leave Australia, Wong was delighted to be returning home. On Friday the 18th of August 1939 she left Sydney for Los Angeles onboard the *S.S. Monterey*, a luxury steam ship operated by the Matson Line, which sailed between Sydney and San Francisco via Auckland, Suva, Pago Pago, Honolulu, and Los Angeles (Fig. 15). Her Sydney chronicler, Jack Meander, "found Anna May Wong on 'B' deck, so excited at sailing that she could hardly speak. She ran away three paces then ran back again. 'Gee, isn't it wonderful, going home?' she said. Down in her cabin I found a large collection of souvenirs of Australia—about 150 skeins of wool (she likes to knit), rugs, blankets, [and toy] koalas."[234] (In 1936, Wong sailed the final leg of her return voyage from China—from Honolulu to Los Angeles—also onboard the *Monterey*.)

It seems that Anna May Wong gave away some of her stylish outfits to friends in Sydney before she departed for Los Angeles, because at the annual ball of the Australian-Chinese

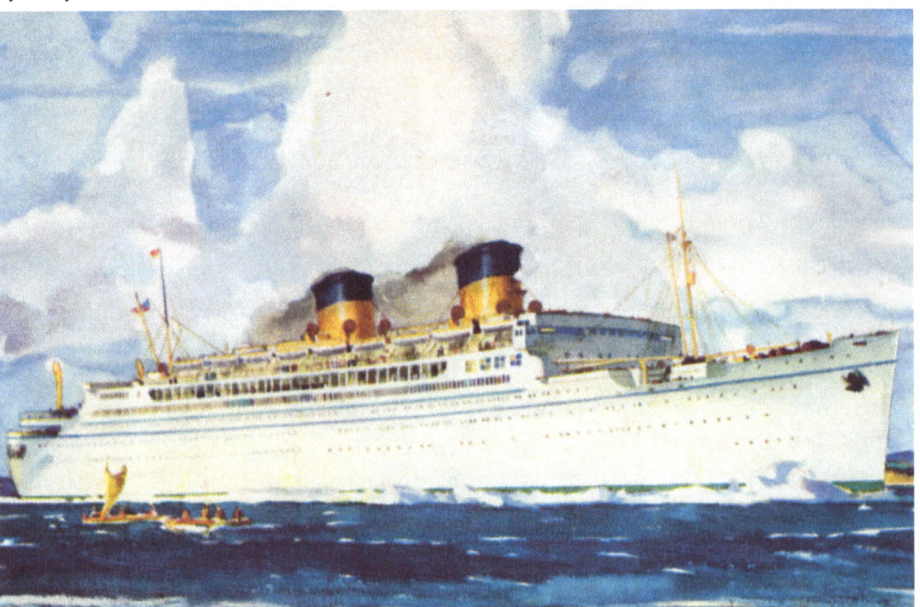

Fig. 15: The *S.S. Monterey*. (Derham Groves' collection.)

Association in 1950, "a suit originally worn in a Hollywood film by Anna May Wong was among the Chinese clothes shown at a cocktail party (with Chinese finger-food) and mannequin parade at the Nankin Café," reported *The Sydney Morning Herald*. "The suit, which had black trousers under a blue and pink satin embroidered coat, was given by Miss Wong to Sydney friends."[235]

Also sailing on the *Monterey* were the Broadway songwriter, Martin Broones (1903-1971); his wife, the talented American comedienne, Charlotte Greenwood (1890-1977), who had been touring Australia in her own production of *Leaning on Letty* (1935), a play by Norma Mitchell and William Daniel Steele; the Austrian classical pianist, Artur Schnabel (1882-1951), who had been performing a series of concerts in Australia; and Wong's former boss, the head of Paramount Pictures Inc., Adolph Zukor (1873-1976), and his wife, Lottie (1897-1956), who had been visiting Australia for 19 days on movie business.[236] As far as I can tell, Wong and Zukor did not meet while they were in Sydney, although at some time on the voyage home to America they would have almost certainly discussed why the movie star's contract had not been renewed by Paramount—but unfortunately to no avail (assuming, of course, that she still wanted to work for the studio).

Wong also socialized with some of the lesser-well-known passengers onboard the *Monterey*. On Wednesday the 4th of October 1939, *The Courier-Mail* reported: "On the voyage to America, Mrs. John Campbell, [the wife of a well-known Brisbane hairdresser,] who left Brisbane in the middle of August for a holiday abroad, encountered a number of interesting personalities among her fellow passengers aboard the *Monterey*. Artur Schnabel, the world famous pianist, who recently visited Brisbane, was among them, and so was Charlotte Greenwood, the comedienne. Mrs. Campbell had tea with Anna May Wong, the film star, one afternoon, and another film celebrity on board was Mr. Adolf Zukor, who was accompanied by his wife, and arranged for Mrs. Campbell to see through the Paramount Studios while in America—a privilege granted to few tourists. In a letter written shortly after the outbreak of war, Mrs. Campbell mentions that bookings for ships leaving America for Australia were tremendously heavy, and there were hundreds on the waiting list for every vessel."[237]

Anna May Wong arrived home on Sunday the 3rd of September 1939,[238] the same day that World War Two officially started. About a week later, she wrote to her New York friends, Fania Marinoff (1890-1971), a Russian-born American actress, and her husband, Carl Van Vechten (1880-1964), an American author and photographer who had taken some publicity shots of Wong shortly before she went to Australia. "I am so happy and delighted to be home again," Wong told her friends. "Australia seemed so far away and by the time one's friends receive one's letter the news is no longer news. In spite of a few things, all in all it was a very interesting journey, but I like the end of the journey on this side better than the other. My brother [i.e. probably Richard] forwarded your photographs to Honolulu and honestly I think they are the best pictures I have had in ages. Using the exact words of my brother when he wrote me to Australia about them—they are simply marvelous. Thanks ever so much for being so generous in sending me all the prints, which I think proves you are also pleased about the sitting. I sent a letter to the Lin Yutangs care of your address with a letter enclosed to them from Sydney. I hope you did not mind. There were quite a number of theatrical people on the return voyage home, Charlotte Greenwood and her husband, [Martin Broones,] Adolph Zukor and [Artur] Schnabel, [the] famous pianist. It seems we got home just in time. I know we all feel the same way about this new war and hope that it will be a brief business as there is enough bloodshed in the world already. I was wondering if our mutual friend, Eddie [Wasserman, a Wall Street banker], will be returning to New York. My conscience suddenly reproached me for not having written and I would like to drop him a letter. Have you his address? Had dinner at Bernadine's [i.e. Bernadine Kielty (1880-1973), an American author and critic,] last night and she is looking wonderful, simply sparkling. Did not see Rosemary [Carver, an American actress and *Vogue* model,] as she was in Laguna Beach for the day. Sorry I have not got more news of mutual friends to send you, but I have been up to my ears getting unpacked, settled and the house running again the way I like it to run. We still have summer here. Fania, why don't you come out and sun bake in our garden? All love and blessings to you both. Yours ever, Anna May."[239]

Anna May Wong's breezy letter glossed over a couple of interesting points. What did she mean by, *"In spite of a few things* [my italics], all in all it was a very interesting journey"? Did she mean Frank Neil's shameful outburst, or being sacked by Paramount Pictures Inc., or the humiliation of traveling back to the United States on the same ship with her former boss, Adolph Zukor, or something even worse than those things? Also, when Wong said, "It seems we got home just in time," she was not exaggerating. Berths on ships sailing almost anywhere were suddenly at a premium, as Mrs. John Campbell said in her letter. And to highlight the very real risk of being far away from home towards the end of 1939, the Viennese Mozart Boys' Choir, which toured Australia at the same time as Wong, was stranded in the country for the duration of World War Two. Admittedly, Vienna's close proximity to the front line was the overriding reason for the choir not going home, but even so. Olav Schappacher, one of the choirboys, recalled many years later: "Our conductor got us together and he said, 'Look, I think it would be too risky to take you back. You just don't know what's going to happen. And so we will stay here.'"[240] Like Wong, at the beginning of the war most people hoped that it would be only "a brief business."

Designing Shoes for Anna May Wong

Since design is a form of biography—or at least it is in my opinion—I wanted the 52 architecture students who did my Popular Architecture and Design course in 2010 at the University of Melbourne to use Wong's visit to Australia in 1939 as the starting point to design … what? I first considered asking them to design the film star's room at the Menzies Hotel, where she stayed while in Melbourne, however I finally settled on something a lot smaller and more personal—a pair of shoes for her to wear in Australia. The idea came from Wong's shoe-cum-pincushion-cum-lucky charm, which she brought from home and kept in her dressing room at the Tivoli Theater; and also the newspaper photograph of her buying shoes at Foy's Fashion Corner. Apparently, the actress was fond of shoes (Fig. 16). As it turned out, there were other good reasons for choosing to design shoes as well.

Anna May Wong possessed sex appeal in spades. Take for example her impromptu little dance in the kitchen in the silent film, *Piccadilly.* Wow! Therefore, it was only fitting that the architecture students designed something as highly sexually charged as shoes for the actress. Surprised by this assessment of humble footwear? Well, according to the German psychologist, Dr. G. Aigremont, the author of *Foot and Shoe Symbolism and Eroticism* (1909): "Sexual foot and shoe symbolism is very wide-spread and age-old in origin. The shoe is the symbol of the vulva and female organs, while the foot is the symbol of the penis (there are innumerable corroborations of this in ethnographic and folklore studies). One 'thrusts' the foot into the shoe or boot or slipper. These kinds of footwear have an opening, a hole, sometimes surrounded by fur or similar trimming, and this hole is filled with a human foot or flesh. The entering of the foot into the shoe simulates the entering of the penis into the vulva."[241] Furthermore, to top it all off, the side of a shoe is called a "vamp."

Nearly as surprising as the sex life of footwear is the number of connections that exist between shoes and architecture. Once upon a time, especially in England, a well-worn shoe was concealed within the structure of a new building so as to placate any malevolent spirits that happened to be present. It was actually a substitute for a human sacrifice, because in those days people believed that a shoe was synonymous with a person, as the English physician, Dr. E.T. Renbourn, the author of "The Foot and Shoe in Body and Mind" (n.d.), explained: "To the primitive mind there was a sympathetic connection between a man or his feet and his footprint—in which he believed the soul resided." [242] Furthermore, the bottom of a foot and a shoe are both called a sole; and the idea that shoes can sometimes stand-in for people is enshrined in common sayings like "Walk a mile in his/her shoes" and "I wouldn't like to be in his/her shoes."

The old English nursery rhyme, "There was an Old Woman Who Lived in a Shoe," [243] established once and for all the architectonic character of shoes. Indeed, many buildings look like shoes, either deliberately, such as the shoe-shaped guesthouse (1948) near Hallam, Pennsylvania, [244] or inadvertently, like the shoe-shaped headquarters of I.N.G. (2000) in Amsterdam. [245] A number of architects have also designed shoes, including the Pritzker Architecture Prize winners, Zaha Hadid (born 1950), who designed some women's rubberized wrap-around shoes for the French clothing company, Lacoste, [246] and Frank Gehry (born 1929), who designed some men's leather button-up boots for the French shoemaker, J.M. Weston. "It's just part of an architect's work," remarked Gehry. "Shoes are very architectural and always have been [...] and even more recently there are new shoes like Miuccia [Prada's]—they're buildings [...] You shouldn't have to differentiate between disciplines." [247]

To introduce the shoe project to the Melbourne University architecture students, I gave them a lecture on Wong's visit to Australia, and also showed them *King of Chinatown*, her film that was playing at the Capitol Theater while she was in Melbourne. My instructions to the students were very straightforward: "Create a pair of (lucky?) shoes for Anna May Wong by altering (i.e. cutting, covering, painting, re-building, etc.) an old pair of shoes purchased from an op shop. Don't hold back!" The students also received some useful tips from Andrew Robinson, a Melbourne shoe designer who teaches at R.M.I.T. University (Fig. 17). Let me briefly discuss a small sample of the students' shoe designs.

"Anna May Wong strikes me as being akin to a flower of the Orient: she is delicate, beautiful, strong, and resilient," said Alexandra Wall. "In designing a pair of shoes for her to wear,

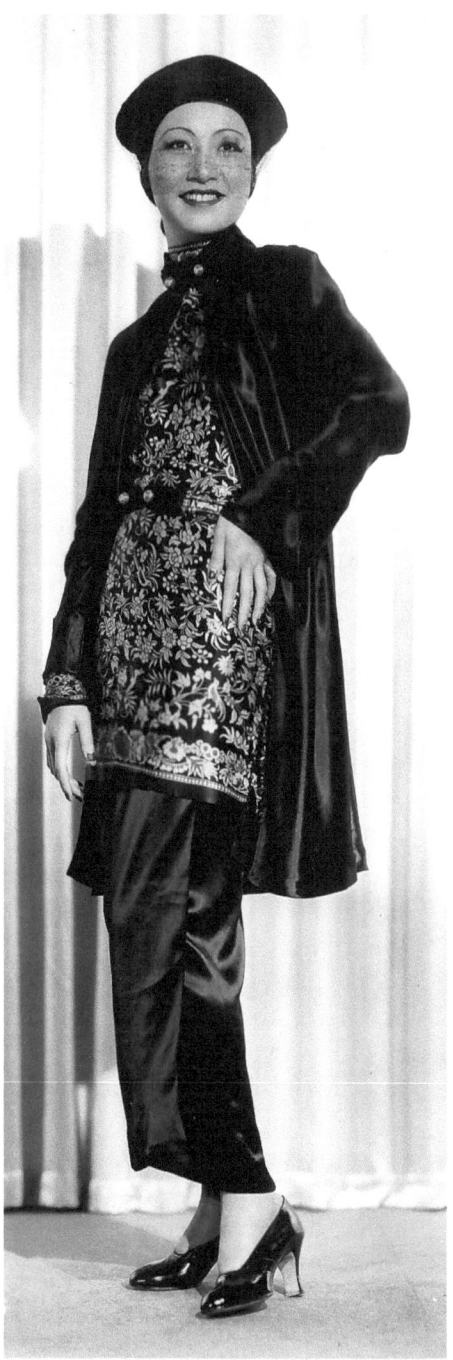

Fig. 16: Anna May Wong in high heels. (Derham Groves' collection.)

37

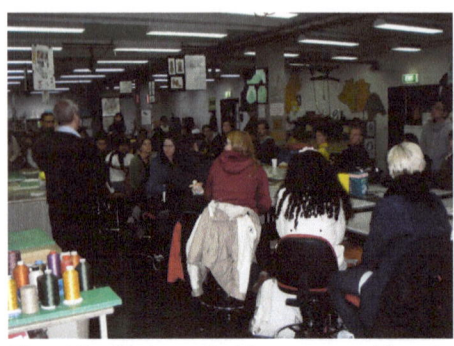

Fig. 17: Andrew Robinson speaking to the architecture students. (Photograph by Derham Groves.)

I drew inspiration from this idea and the recurring theme of flowers that seems to follow her: Wong was born on Flower Street in Los Angeles; her Chinese given names, 'Liu Tsong,' mean 'yellow frosted willows;' Wong played several characters on screen that were also named after flowers, including 'Lotus Blossom' in *Shame* (1921),[248] 'Lotus Flower' in *The Toll of the Sea*,[249] 'Rose Li' in *Drifting* (1923),[250] 'Tiger Lily' in *Peter Pan* (1924),[251] and 'A Flower of the Orient' in *Old San Francisco* (1927);[252] Wong liked growing 'geraniums, stocks, ginger, and Chinese forget-me-nots'[253] in her garden at home; in 1937, an impressive new variety of yellow gladiolus was named after her;[254] Wong's delicate complexion was once described as 'a rose blushing through old ivory;'[255] the actress liked to wear flowers in her hair; and Wong received many bouquets of flowers while she was in Australia. In addition, flowers have an honored place in Chinese culture and often appear in Chinese paintings and prints next to birds perched on branches. I replicated this in a fine, gold floral print on the insoles of Anna May's shoes: concealed beneath the movie star's feet to indicate that even when her Chinese heritage is masked and hidden from view, it is still always with her. Pearls, crystals and ribbons embellish the shoes to appeal to her love of high fashion and elegance."[256]

Discussing women's fashion in their book, *Australia 1939* (1989), Susan Johnston and Lindsay Nation wrote: "In 1939 hems were up for day wear […] Shoes were square-toed and low heels were 'smart' […] Everyone wore hats whenever they went out […] Dresses drew attention to feminine curves with their wasp waists accentuated by a belt or sash and several pleats or panels in the skirt. Bodices with puffed sleeves, bows and ruffles drew attention to bosoms and shoulders […] For day wear, women wore wrist-length gloves, while in the evenings elbow-length or longer was considered the height of fashion."[257] The Australian press rarely neglected to describe Wong's clothes, which were usually the latest Western style, but with an interesting Chinese twist, such as the full-length ermine coat and the cream and purple Chinese gown that she wore to the *Gala Theatrical Entertainment* at the Princess Theater in Melbourne.[258] This luscious-sounding outfit particularly impressed Tim Clarke, who created a pair of high-heeled shoes especially to go with it, which had purple leather pointy toecaps, cream fur-covered heel caps decorated with sprigs of purple heather, and 1930s-style straps across the insteps.

Zoe Lewis created a pair of high-heeled shoes with fur-lined cream leather uppers that looked like jiaozi or Chinese dumplings, because Wong liked Chinese food and may very well have eaten some jiaozi at the Hong Kong Café in Melbourne or Prince's in Sydney. Coincidentally, the shoes somewhat resembled the specially made bootees worn by those unfortunate Chinese women with "lotus" or bound feet (who did not include Wong, but did include my wife's grandmother, for example). According to William A. Rossi, the author of *The Sex Life of the Foot and the Shoe* (1976): "By a skilful binding process that started in early childhood, the four lesser toes were curled under the ball [of the foot] as far as they could go […] The large heel bone, which normally is in a semi-horizontal position, was pushed forward so that it was resting on end in a vertical position, much like the effect or look of a high-heeled shoe. The process ultimately reduced the foot to less than half its natural length and width and shrank it to the foot size of a small child […] The footwear designed for the lotus foot […] wasn't really a shoe in the ordinary sense […] The sole of the shoe was very soft and padded. The upper […] covered the whole foot and ankle like a bootee, for modesty's sake."[259]

Two of the Melbourne University architecture students were inspired by Wong's shoe-cum-pincushion-cum-lucky charm, which she brought to Australia and kept in her dressing room. The shoes created by Si Xiong had dressmaking pins sticking out of them on the inside; while a bed of drawing pins—like a bed of nails—covered the insoles of the shoes created by David Young. Both pairs of leather high-heeled shoes looked normal on the outside, but were unwearable due to the pins on the inside. Therefore, they symbolized Wong's calm and cool exterior on the one hand, and her painful personal inner conflicts on the other. The "pincushion" shoes also highlighted the strange relationship between fashion and pain in general. "The human desire for sex attraction is so deeply embedded that the human species is willing to undergo almost any form of 'unnatural' and even agonizing ordeal for erotic and sexual goals," wrote William A. Rossi. "And the foot and shoe have always been in the forefront of this universal psycho-sexual urge to reshape the human form."[260]

The love of Anna May Wong's life was the English lyricist, Eric Maschwitz (1901-1969).[261] When she returned to Hollywood in 1934 after living in London for several years, he wrote "These Foolish Things" (1936),

a touching song that listed the host of seemingly trivial everyday items that constantly reminded him of the actress, such as "A cigarette that bears a lipstick's traces […] Gardenia perfume lingering on a pillow […and] Silk stockings thrown aside, dance invitations."[262] The shoe designed by Steve Zhirui Yu was a very clever surrealist interpretation of Maschwitz's love song for Wong. On a horizontal board, Yu carefully arranged a number of bits and pieces that the actress probably would have carried in her handbag—including a cigarette tin; a hair band; a hairbrush; a powder compact; and a tube of lipstick—in such a way that they cast a shadow shaped exactly like a 1930s-style woman's shoe on the wall behind. Incredible!

Amanda Pei-er Tan thought that Anna May Wong's trip to Australia (a.k.a. Oz) in 1939 was somewhat akin to Dorothy's journey to the Land of Oz in the classic 1939 M.G.M. musical, *The Wizard of Oz*,[263] which was based on the book, *The Wonderful Wizard of Oz* (1900) by L. Frank Baum (1856-1919), an American author of children's stories. It was certainly an adventure into the unknown for both women. Dorothy was carried away by a fierce tornado, while Wong's mode of transport was a lot more conventional—a luxury ocean liner. Also, Dorothy left dreary Kansas for exciting Oz, while Wong left exciting Hollywood for dreary Australia—

or at least it must have seemed like that by comparison in 1939. But in the end, both women were very eager to return home as fast as possible. For Dorothy, wearing a magic pair of ruby red slippers did the trick. So Tan created an equally magic pair of ruby red and storm cloud gray boots for Wong, which were funnel-shaped like a tornado, in order to speed the actress back home to Hollywood.

Amanda Pei-er Tan's shoes represented escape from Australia, which I have no doubt was a rather dull place in 1939. The country's population was relatively small (6,927,288) and not yet very cosmopolitan, while many people were still feeling the hardships caused by the Great Depression. Nevertheless, consider the large number of overseas celebrities who visited Australia at the same time as Anna May Wong: Larry Adler; Martin Broones; Babe Didrikson; Charlotte Greenwood; Clifford Huntsman; Irene Kaye; Orry Kelly; Marjorie Lawrence; Al Mardo; George Robey; Artur Schnabel; the Viennese Mozart Boys' Choir; George Zaharias; Adolph Zukor; the American cast of *Broadway Hotshots;* and the American cast of *Highlights From Hollywood*—to name only those who I have mentioned already. Since traveling to Australia by ship took a long time and was rather expensive, what really motivated them to go? Lawrence and Kelly were visiting home, while Zukor came to learn what

Australians wanted to see at the movies (which sounds suspiciously like a junket to me). No doubt a number of American, English and European performers came to Australia because their star status had faded at home. It could be said that Wong belonged to this category, however she certainly did not consider Australia to be a destination of last resort, so to speak. However, I doubt whether the majority of overseas performers who worked in Australia before World War Two earned very much money, particularly when a skinflint like Frank Neil was paying their wages. Rather, I suspect that many overseas celebrities visited Australia because they were curious to see one of the last remaining "wild frontiers," which was how many people at the time saw the country, especially those from America.

Anna May Wong's Lucky Shoes: 1939 Australia Through the Eyes of an Art Deco Diva is a chronological account of the glamorous Chinese-American film star's 107 days in Australia in 1939, which documents her stay in Melbourne and Sydney far more thoroughly than other biographies of her have done so to date. It describes her acting career in general, but through Australian eyes; her reasons for traveling to Australia; her voyage "Down Under" and home again; her act in *Highlights From Hollywood;* her fellow performers in the vaudeville show; the personal challenges that she faced both on and off the stage in Australia; her Australian circle of friends and acquaintances; her very busy social life in Melbourne and Sydney; the haut couture outfits that she wore almost everywhere she went in the two capital cities; and her fundraising activities in Australia. Consequently, Wong's Australian story touches on various aspects of Australian everyday life—as it happened, on the eve of World War Two—including architecture; entertainment; fashion; food; and politics. The amazing pairs of shoes designed by the Melbourne University architecture students for Wong to wear while she was in Australia give a bizarre twist to my quirky little biography-cum-travelogue, by representing the movie star's curious antipodean odyssey in a totally different way. In my view, a complex and intriguing figure like Anna May Wong warrants an unusual approach such as this.

My sincere thanks go to the 52 architecture students who did my Popular Architecture and Design course in 2010 at the University of Melbourne; Raymond Lew Boar; Sophie Couchman from the Museum of Chinese Australian History; Joaquin and Val Garay, Joaquin Garay's sons; Huey Groves; Eva Guggemos and Leah Jenan from the Beinecke Rare Book and Manuscript Library; Hannah Hall; Karal Ann Marling from the University of Minnesota; Robert Mc-Bride, Merrill La Fontaine's nephew; Bruce McBrien; Lee McRae from the University of Melbourne; Mikesch Muecke from the Culicidae Press; Andrew Robinson from R.M.I.T. University; Frank Van Straten; and Elaine Mae Woo.

Dr. Derham Groves is a Senior Lecturer in Architecture at the University of Melbourne.

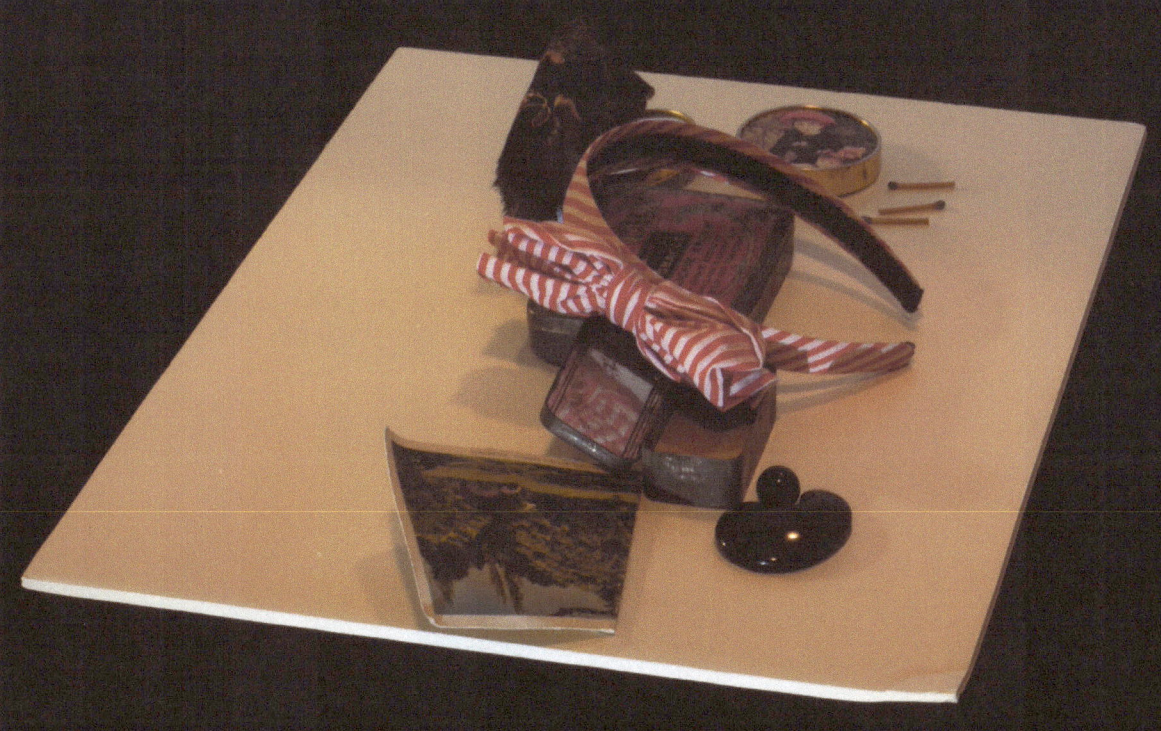

Steve Zhirui Yu

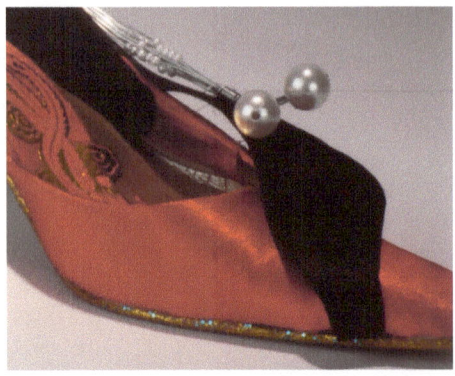

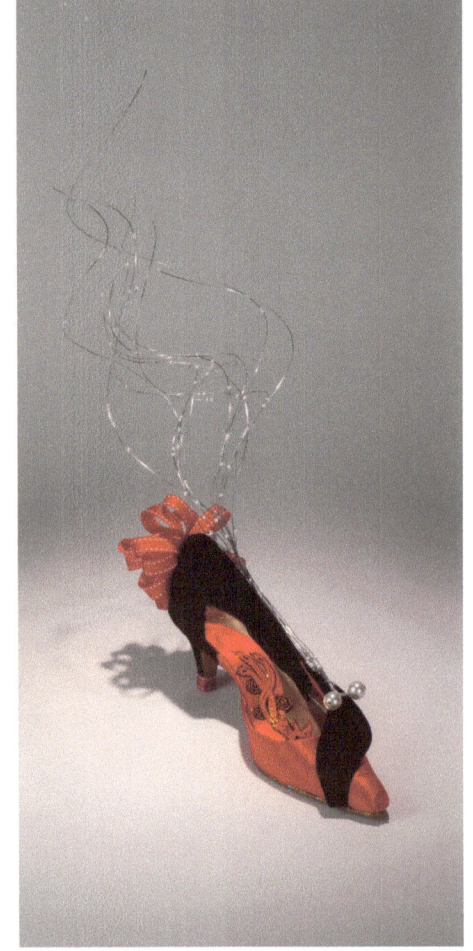

The Rise of the Phoenix

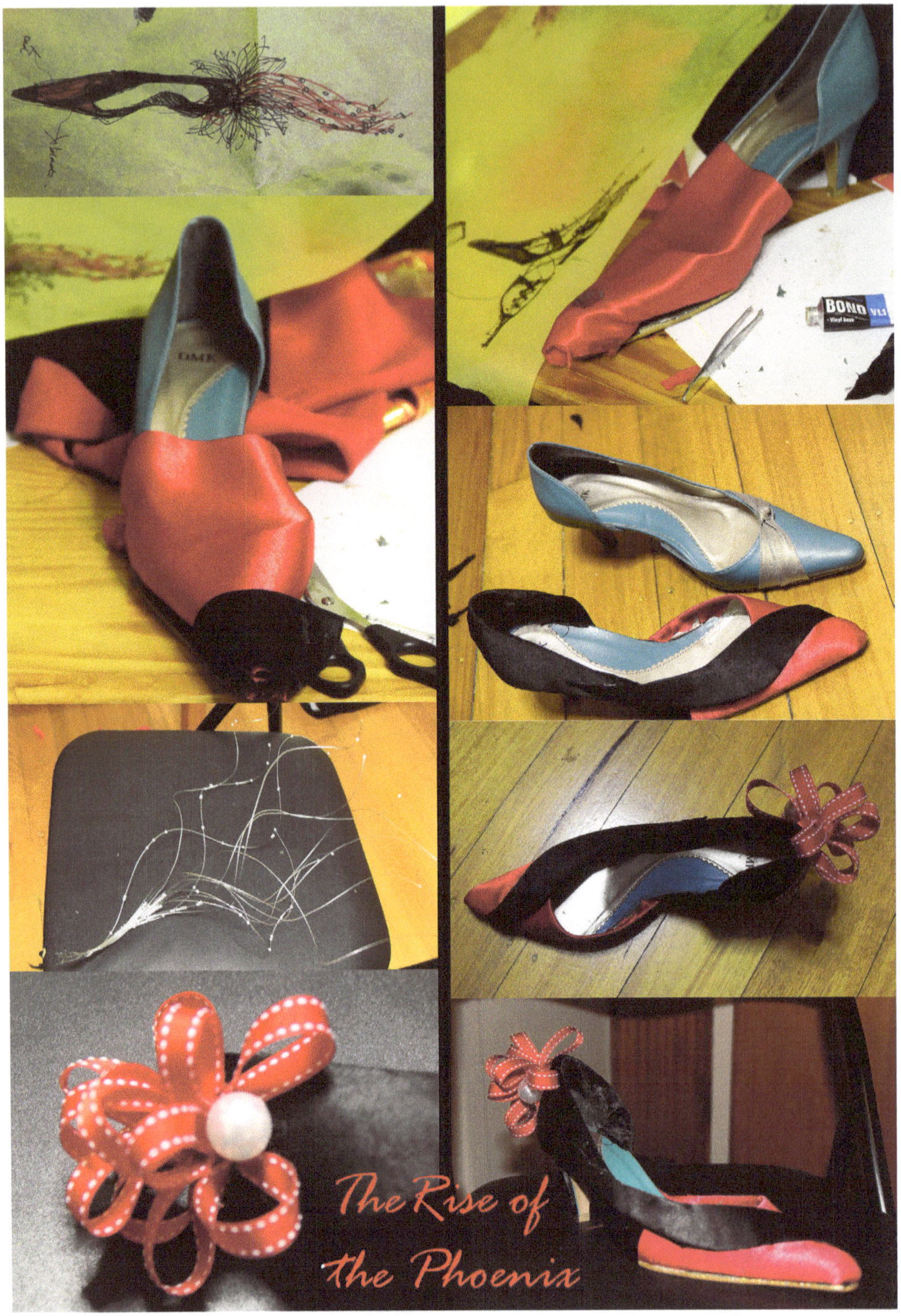

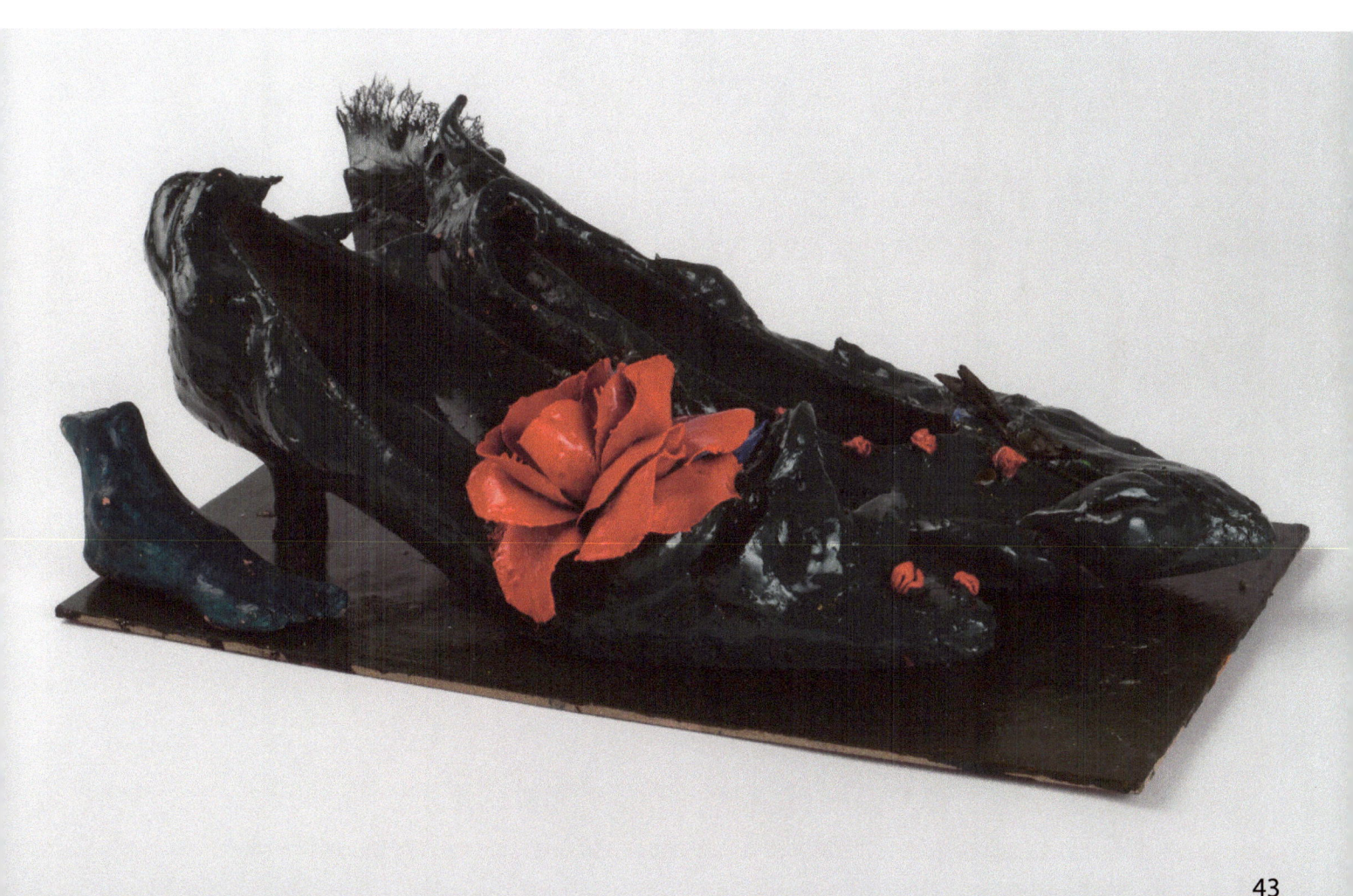

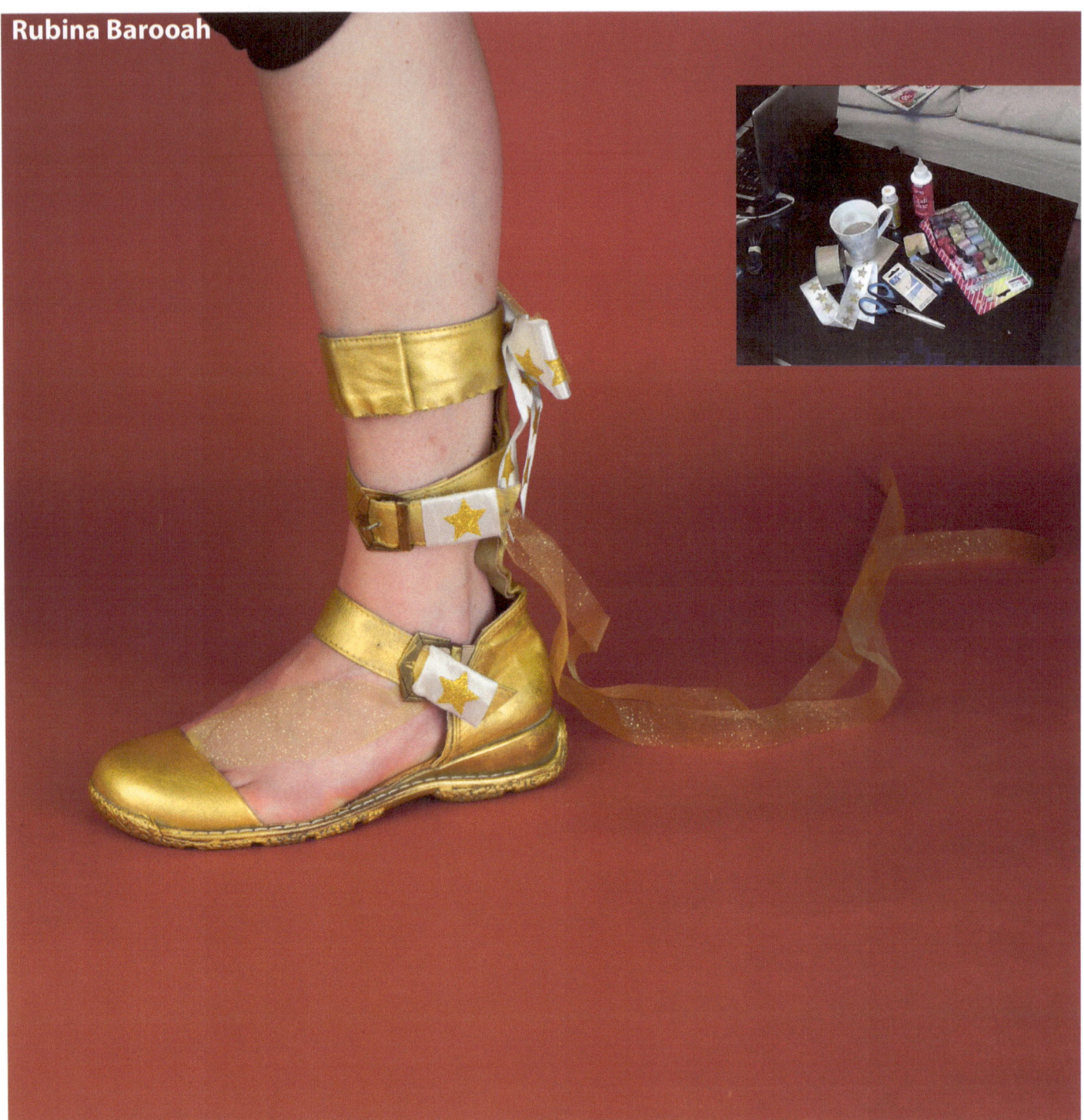

Rubina Barooah

44

THE MALE HEIR

Anna May Wong was a complex character forging a life for herself in a time and place traditionally dominated by Caucasian males. The shoes I have chosen to work with specifically relate to this. They were a pair of basic, black basketball shoes, symbolising the male lead environment surrounding Anna May Wong. Furthermore, the shoes are also a symbol of Anna May Wong's upbringing. As a child, her father was so disappointed that she was, in fact, a she and not a male heir that he brought her up as a male for the first 10 years of her life. The shoes symbolise the early years of Anna May Wong's life, and what could have been if her upbringing didn't change.

The decoration of the shoes is, in a way, a representation of Anna May Wong's 'transformation' from male to female at the age of 10. The change in style of the shoes adds a distinctly feminine touch, which was previously missing in her life. The decoration, especially the silver, draws on Anna May Wong's arrival in Australia where she wore "… smooth black turban, with a gold ornament, and a silver fox cape." (Sydney Morning Herald, 5 June 1939, p.4).

BEFORE

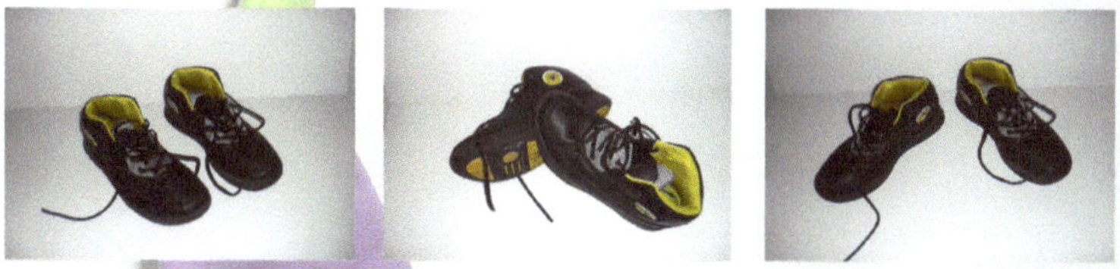

DURING

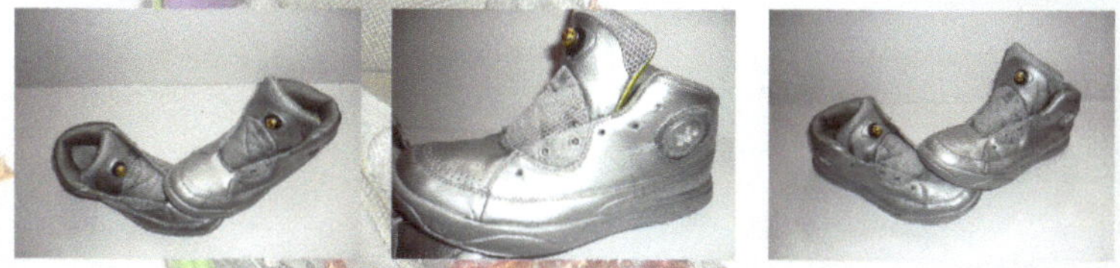

AFTER

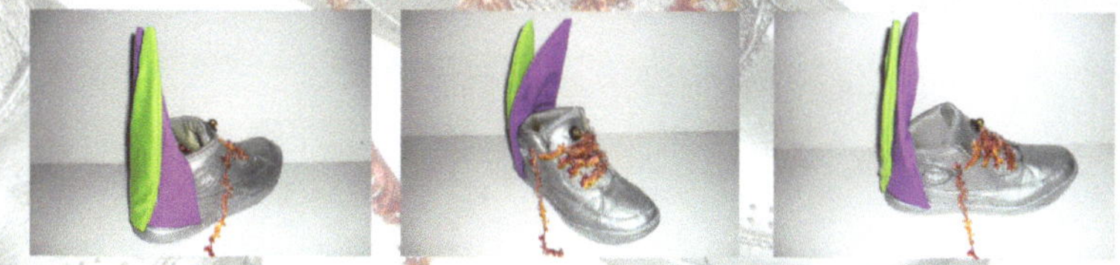

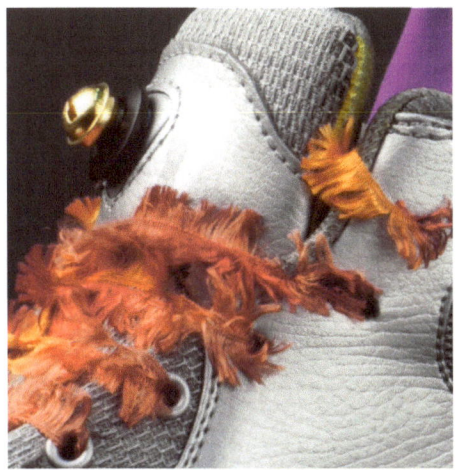

Christopher Berzins

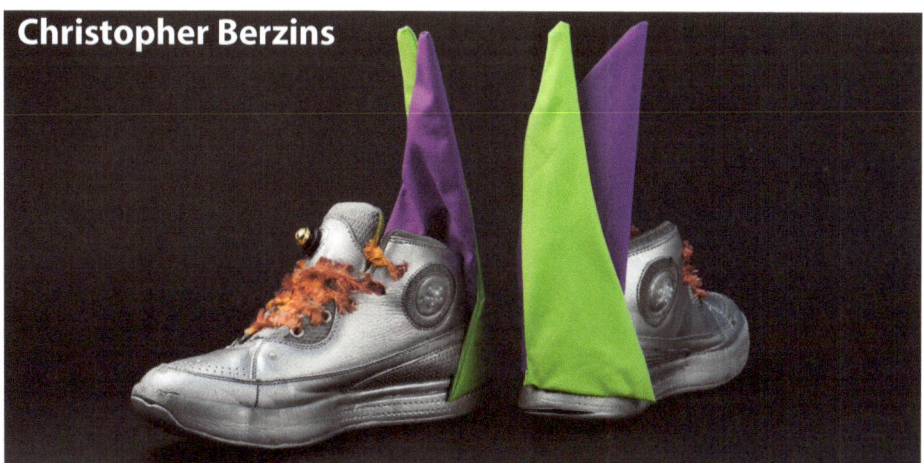

STAR BETWEEN STARS

The 'Stars between Stars' shoes for Anna May Wong reflect the challenges she faced during a period of overt racism and discrimination. Anti miscegenation laws in America prevented an Asian actor sharing a kiss with someone of European descent. This restriction resulted in a reluctance to cast Wong in leading movie roles and therefore she pursued work in both Europe and China.

The essence of this is first reflected with the embellishment of the gold star. Each star is five-pointed emulating the stars found on the American, European and Chinese Flags. The gold star colour and 'ice particle' shape are also a reference to her birth name 'Wong Liu Tsong', which means frosted yellow willows.

Each star is connected with a thin thread indicating the travel Wong encountered between America, Europe and China. The connection also expresses the form of a net, indicating the restrictions she encountered during her career.

Finally the shoes are coloured white (there are hints of the original colour below), a quip at the anti miscegenation laws and the lunacy of European actors playing Asian characters.

Justin Bolton

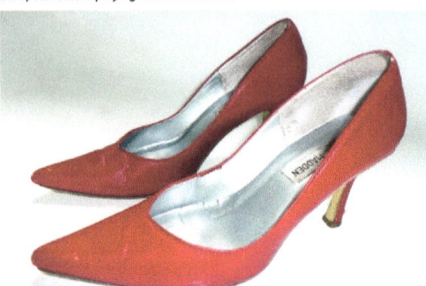

Original shoes before embellishment

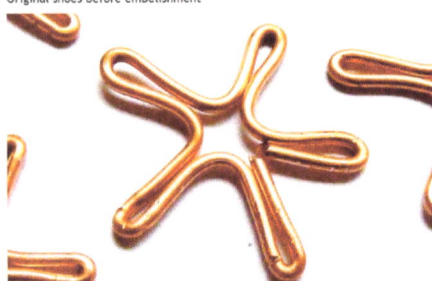

Detail of Star

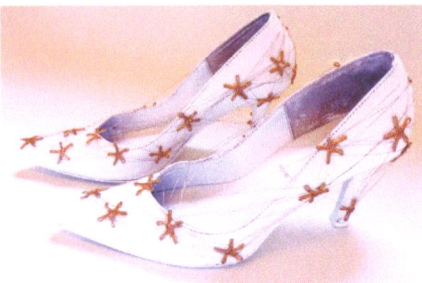

Final Shoes

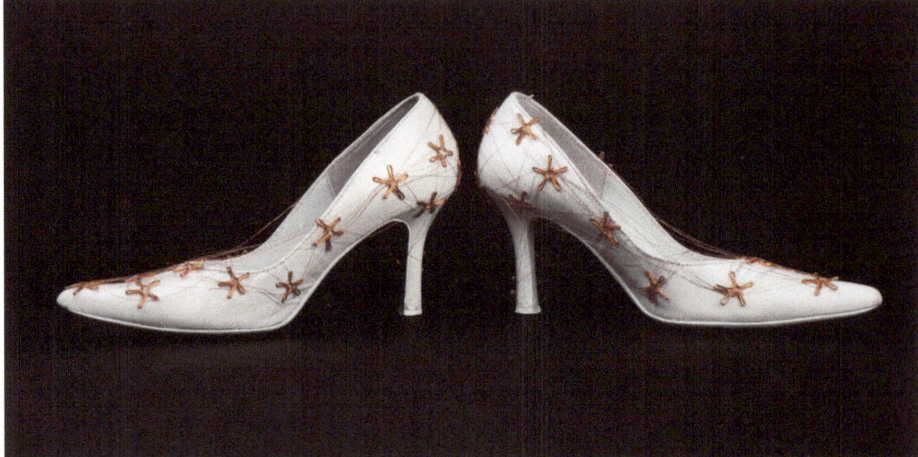

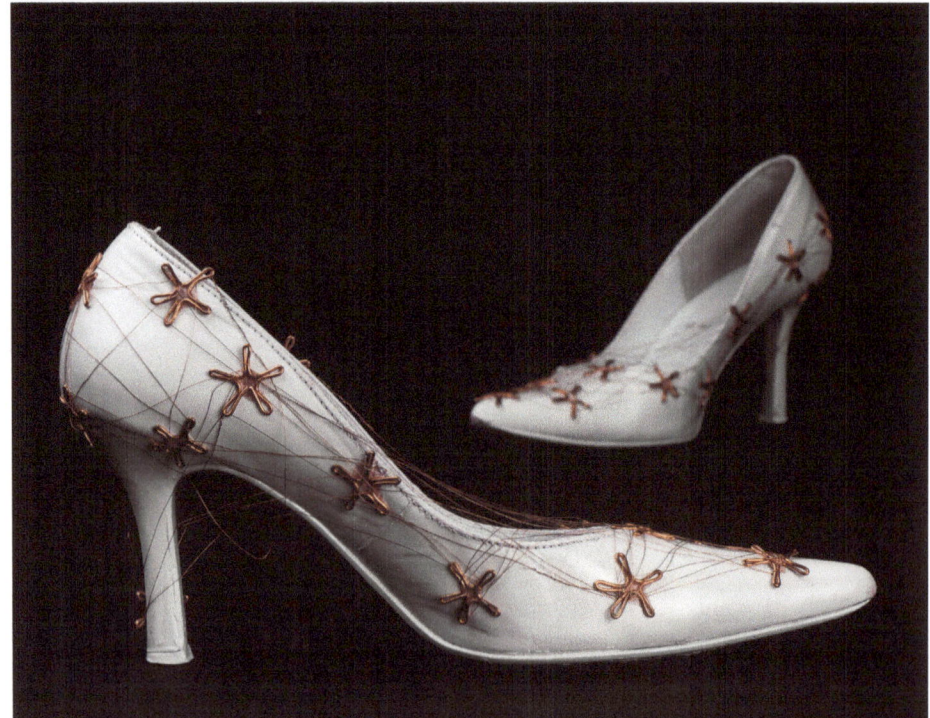

ANNA MAY WONG'S LUCKY SHOES

Tim Clarke

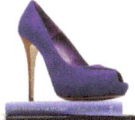

PURPLE HEELED SHOE

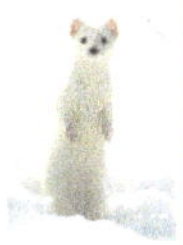

ERMINE

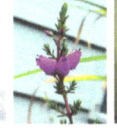

SPRIG OF HEATHER

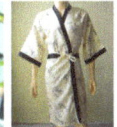

CREAM CHINESE GOWN

these influenced by garments worn by Anna May Wong and objects from her time in Melbourne.

The shoes produced take these shoes and contrast them side with a charcoal blend of shoe with the flowers and soft material inspired by the heather and ermine drawing the eye up the leg.

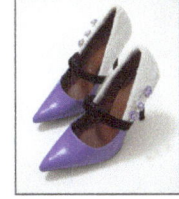

TIM CLARKE, 329140
POPULAR ART, ARCHITECTURE AND DESIGN, UNIVERSITY OF MELBOURNE
DESIGN EXERCISE 3, SEMESTER 2, 2010

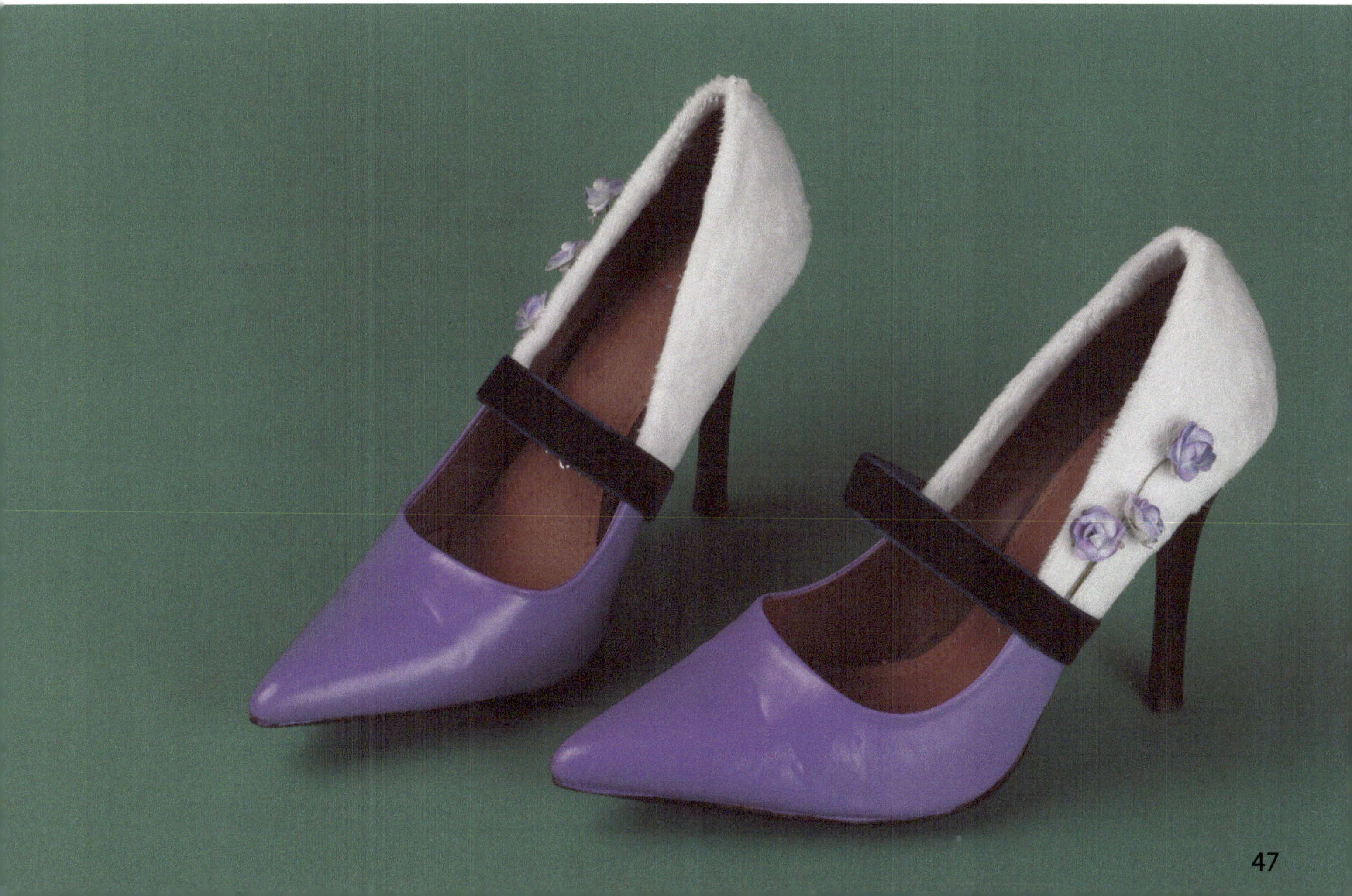

Rebecca De Haas

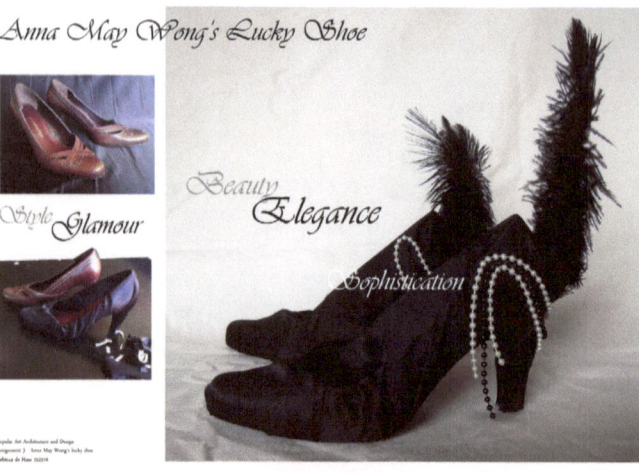

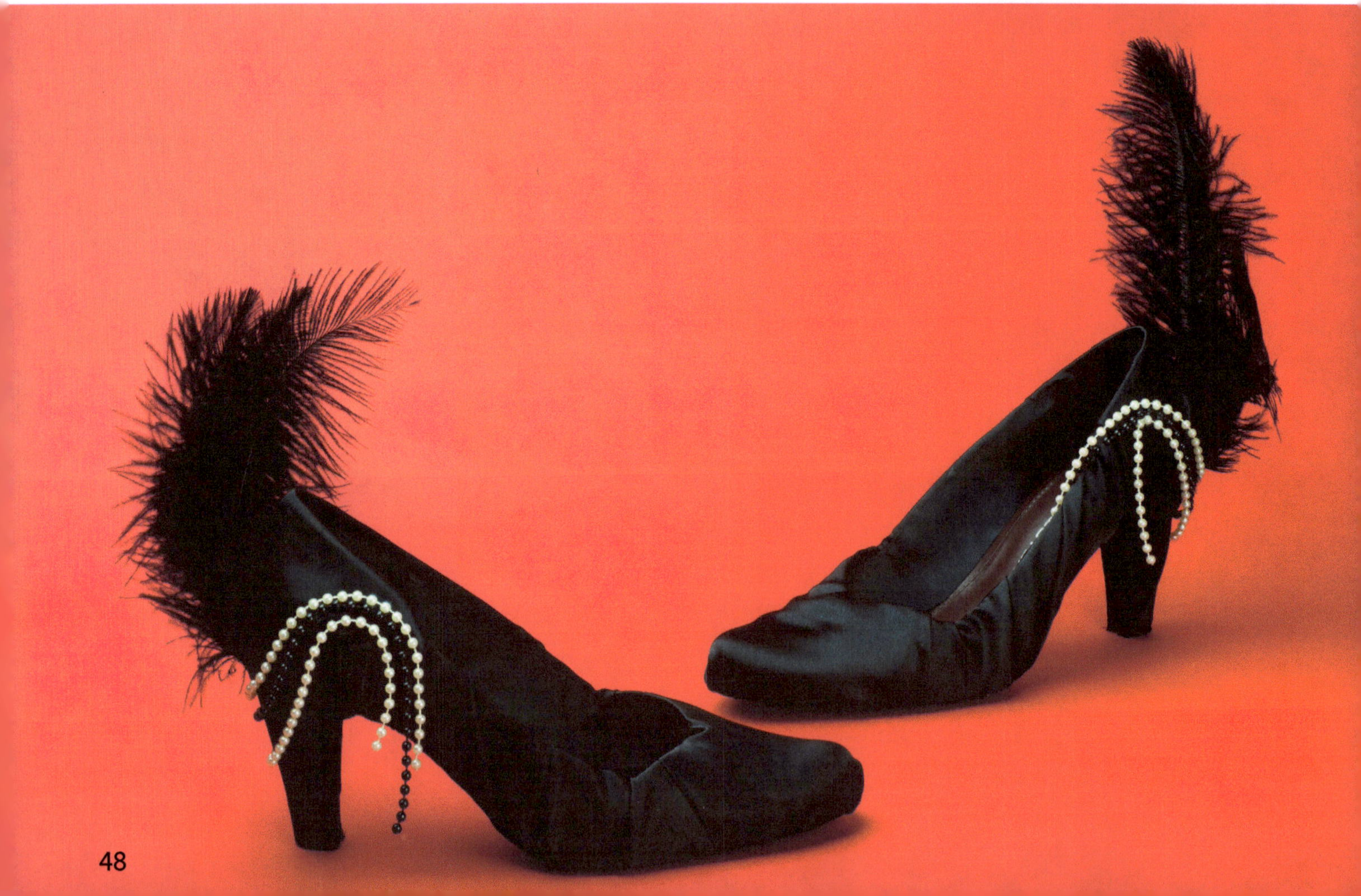

Popular Art Architecture and Design
Assignment 2 Anna May Wong's lucky shoe
Rebecca de Haas 352019

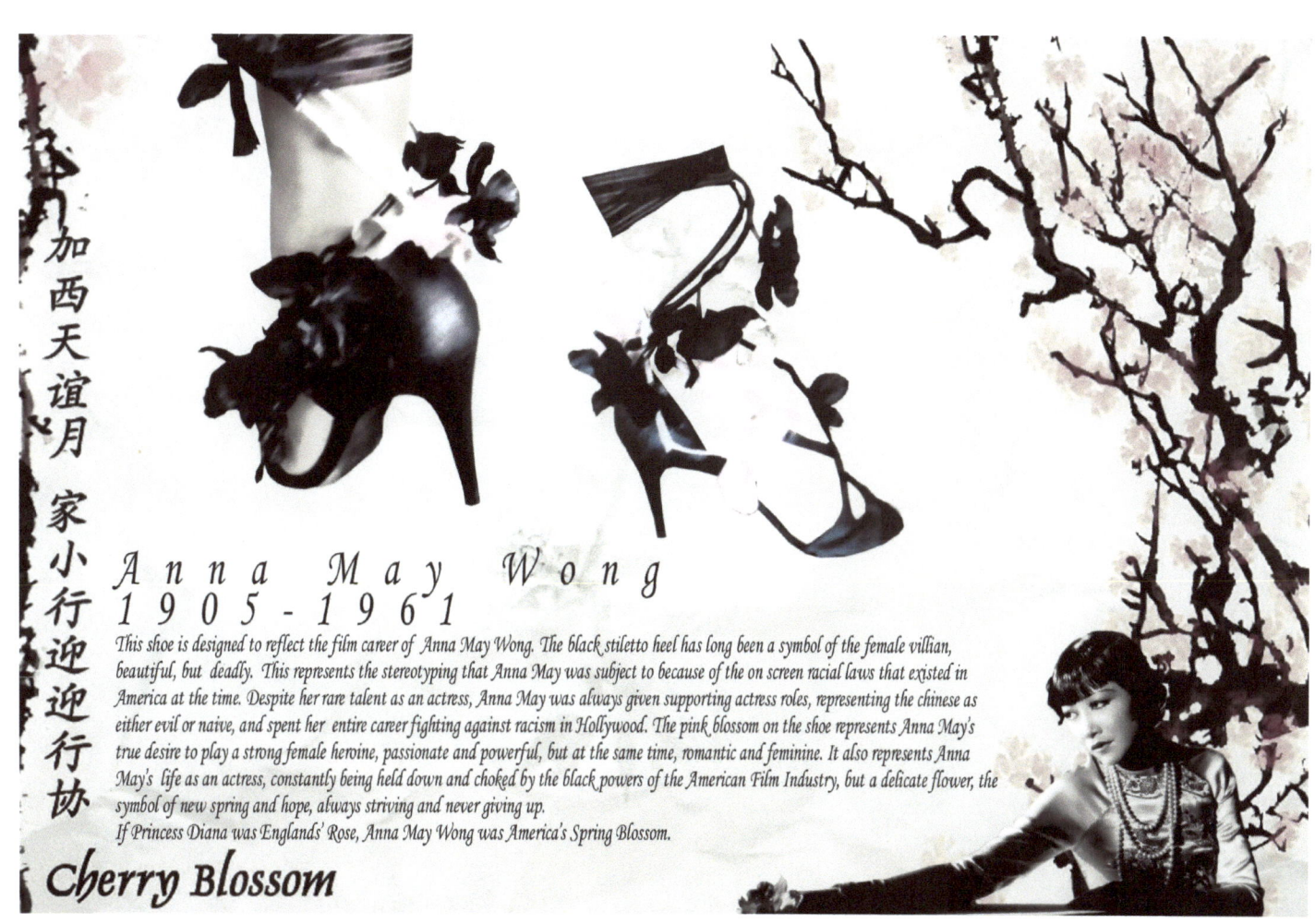

加西天谊月 家小行迎迎行协

Anna May Wong
1905 - 1961

This shoe is designed to reflect the film career of Anna May Wong. The black stiletto heel has long been a symbol of the female villian, beautiful, but deadly. This represents the stereotyping that Anna May was subject to because of the on screen racial laws that existed in America at the time. Despite her rare talent as an actress, Anna May was always given supporting actress roles, representing the chinese as either evil or naive, and spent her entire career fighting against racism in Hollywood. The pink blossom on the shoe represents Anna May's true desire to play a strong female heroine, passionate and powerful, but at the same time, romantic and feminine. It also represents Anna May's life as an actress, constantly being held down and choked by the black powers of the American Film Industry, but a delicate flower, the symbol of new spring and hope, always striving and never giving up.
If Princess Diana was Englands' Rose, Anna May Wong was America's Spring Blossom.

Cherry Blossom

Neo Fu

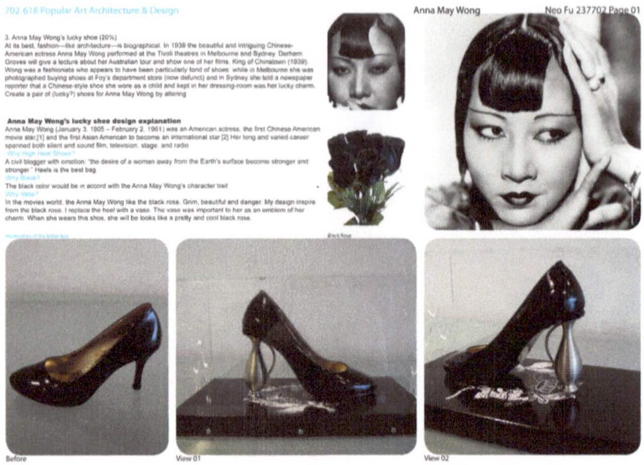

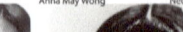

702-618 Popular Art Architecture & Design

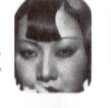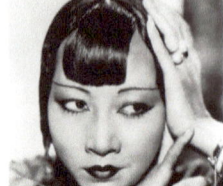

Anna May Wong   Neo Fu 237702 Page 01

3. Anna May Wong's lucky shoe (20%)
At its best, fashion—like architecture—is biographical. In 1939 the beautiful and intriguing Chinese-
American actress Anna May Wong performed at the Tivoli theatres in Melbourne and Sydney. Derham
Groves will give a lecture about her Australian tour and show one of her films. King of Chinatown (1939).
Wong was a fashionable who appears to have been particularly fond of shoes: while in Melbourne she was
photographed buying shoes at Foy's department store (now defunct) and in Sydney she told a newspaper
reporter that a Chinese style shoe she wore as a child and kept in her dressing-room was her lucky charm.
Create a pair of (lucky?) shoes for Anna May Wong by altering

Anna May Wong's lucky shoe design explanation
Anna May Wong (January 3, 1905 - February 2, 1961) was an American actress, the first Chinese American
movie star,[1] and the first Asian American to become an international star.[2] Her long and varied career
spanned both silent and sound film, television, stage, and radio.
Why High Heel Shoes?
A cool blogger with emotion: "the desire of a woman away from the Earth's surface become stronger and
stronger." Heels is the best bag.
Why Black?
The black color would be in accord with the Anna May Wong's character trait.
Why Vase?
In the movies world, the Anna May Wong like the black rose. Grim, beautiful and danger. My design inspire
from the black rose. I replace the heel with a vase. The vase was important to her as an emblem of her
charm. When she wears this shoe, she will be looks like a pretty and cool black rose.

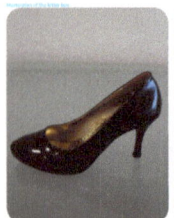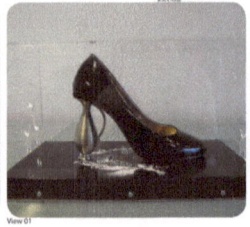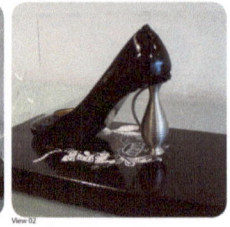

Before   View 01   View 02

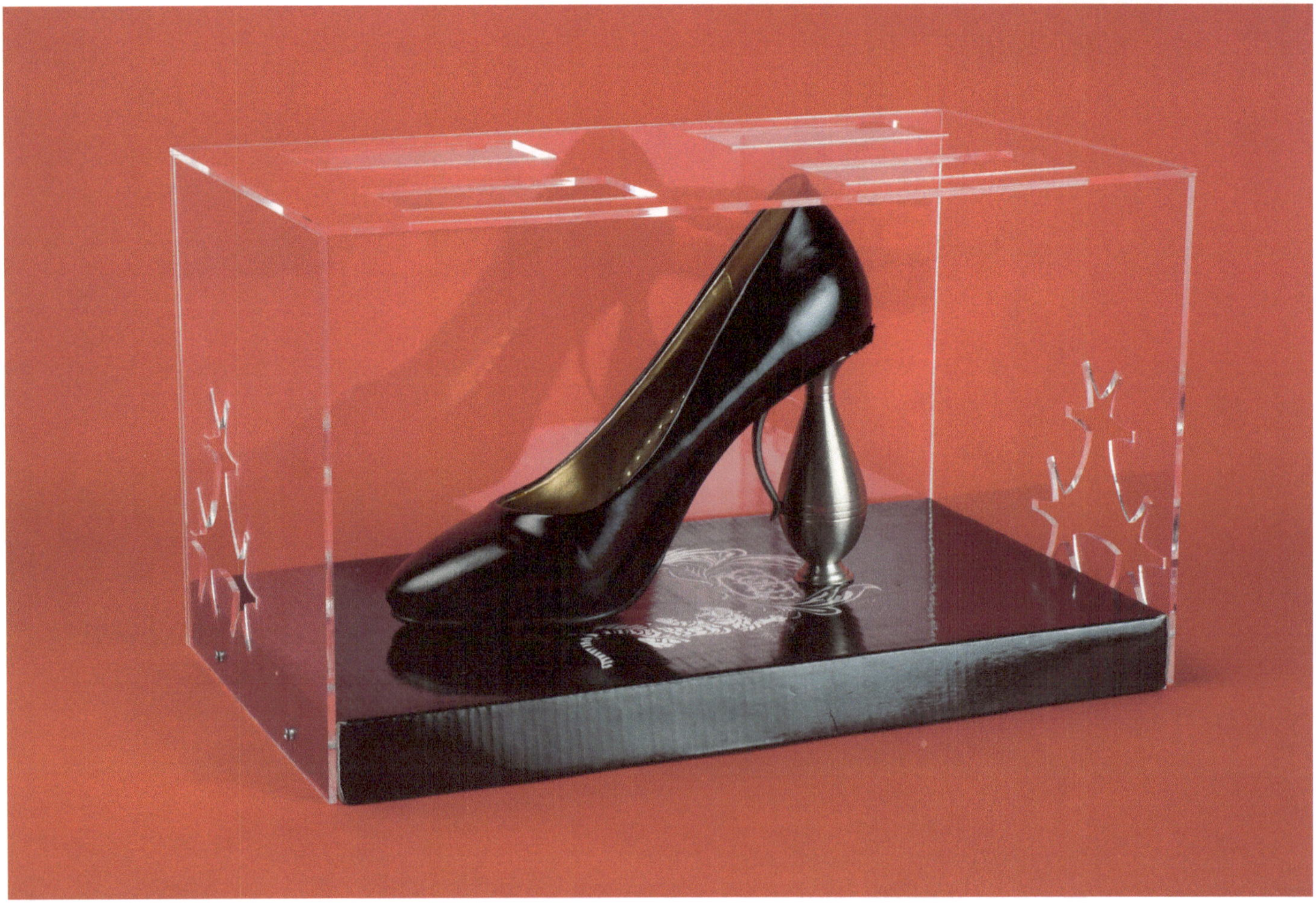

50

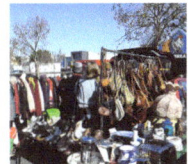 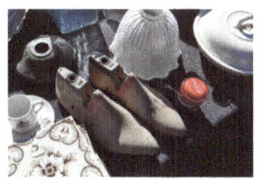 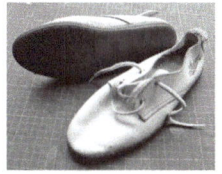 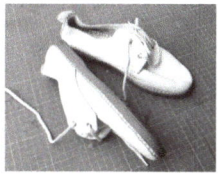 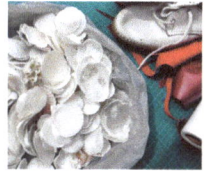 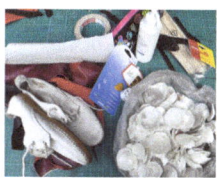

looking for the shoe   the shoe   design process

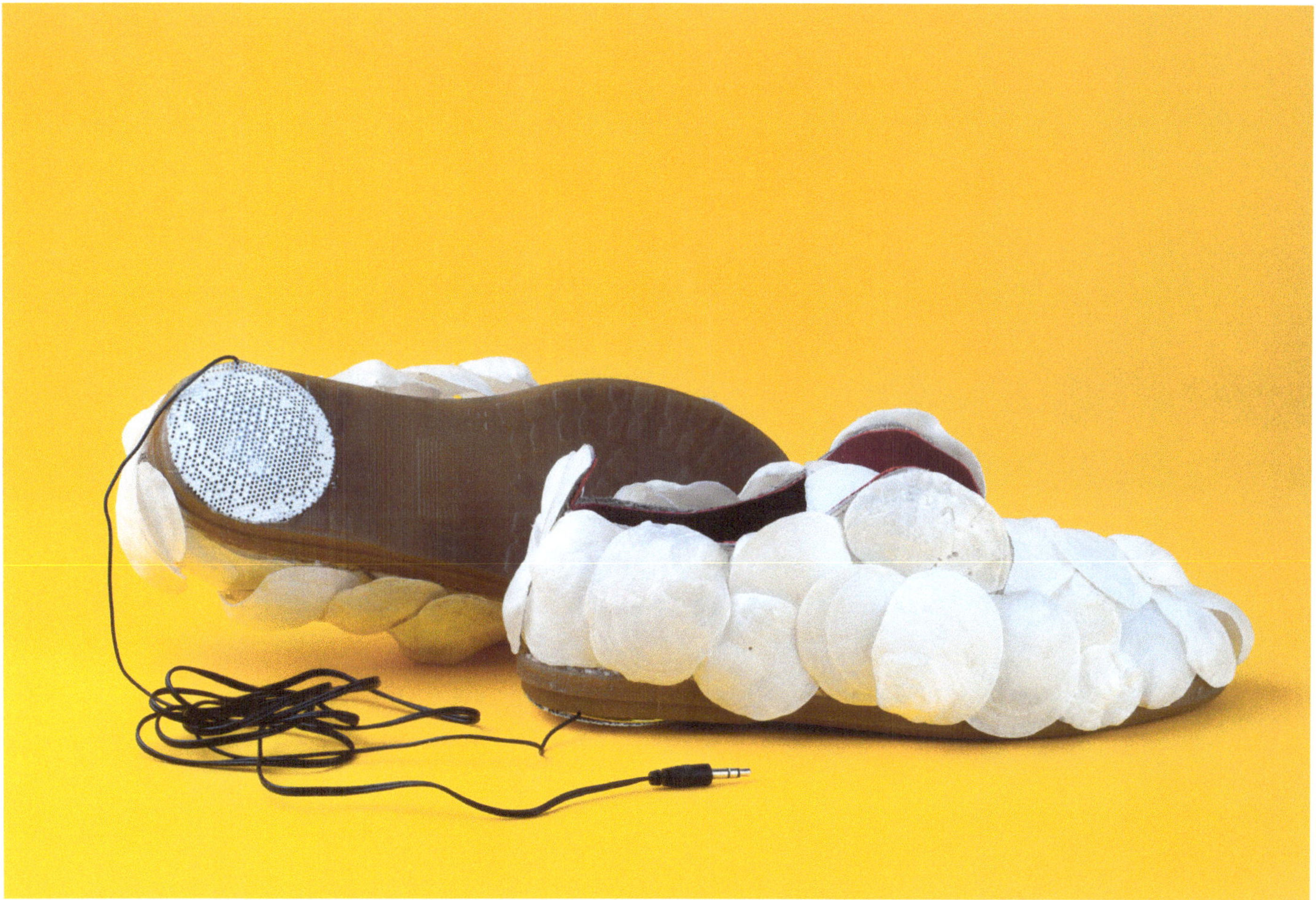

Ryan Hajeb

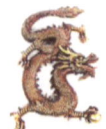

The Opressed Dragon
Anna May Wong's Lucky Shoes

Ryan Basel Hajeb - 395207
University of Melbourne

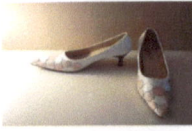

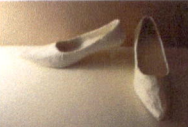

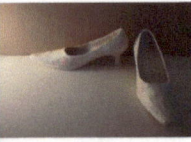

Anna May Wong, although an acclaimed Chinese-American actress, faced many instances of oppression during her long international career. These "lucky shoes" represent this oppression and struggle she faced from many European and American colleagues during that time. Like Anna May Wong, the form of the shoes is very glamorous and elegant, but this beauty has been significantly covered and masked. Examined closely, however, and a beautiful lucky Chinese dragon can be seen on the shoes dancing between the "layers of oppression". This technique of masking also alludes to the common practice of portraying Euro-American actors as Chinese characters during many mid-1900s films. In a tribute to her time spent in Australia, the dragon is created in a style hinting at traditional aboriginal design techniques.

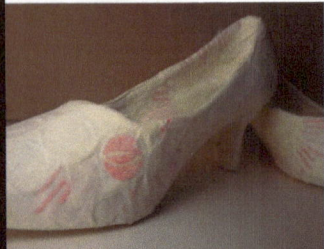

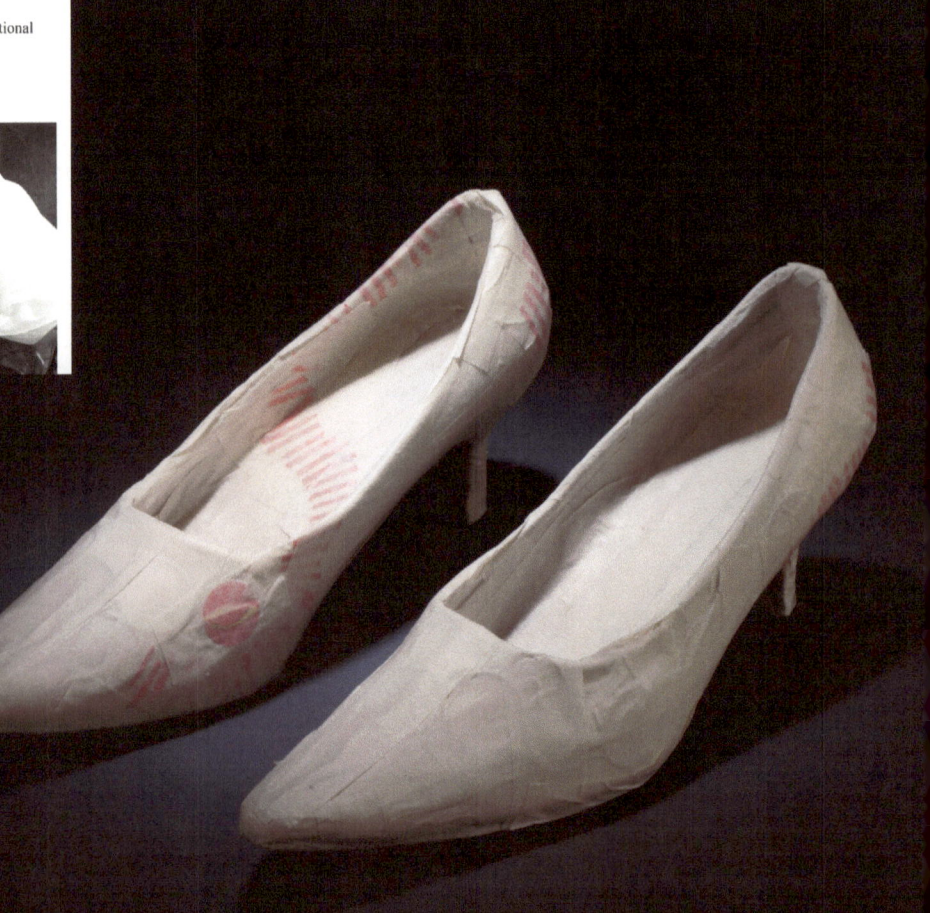

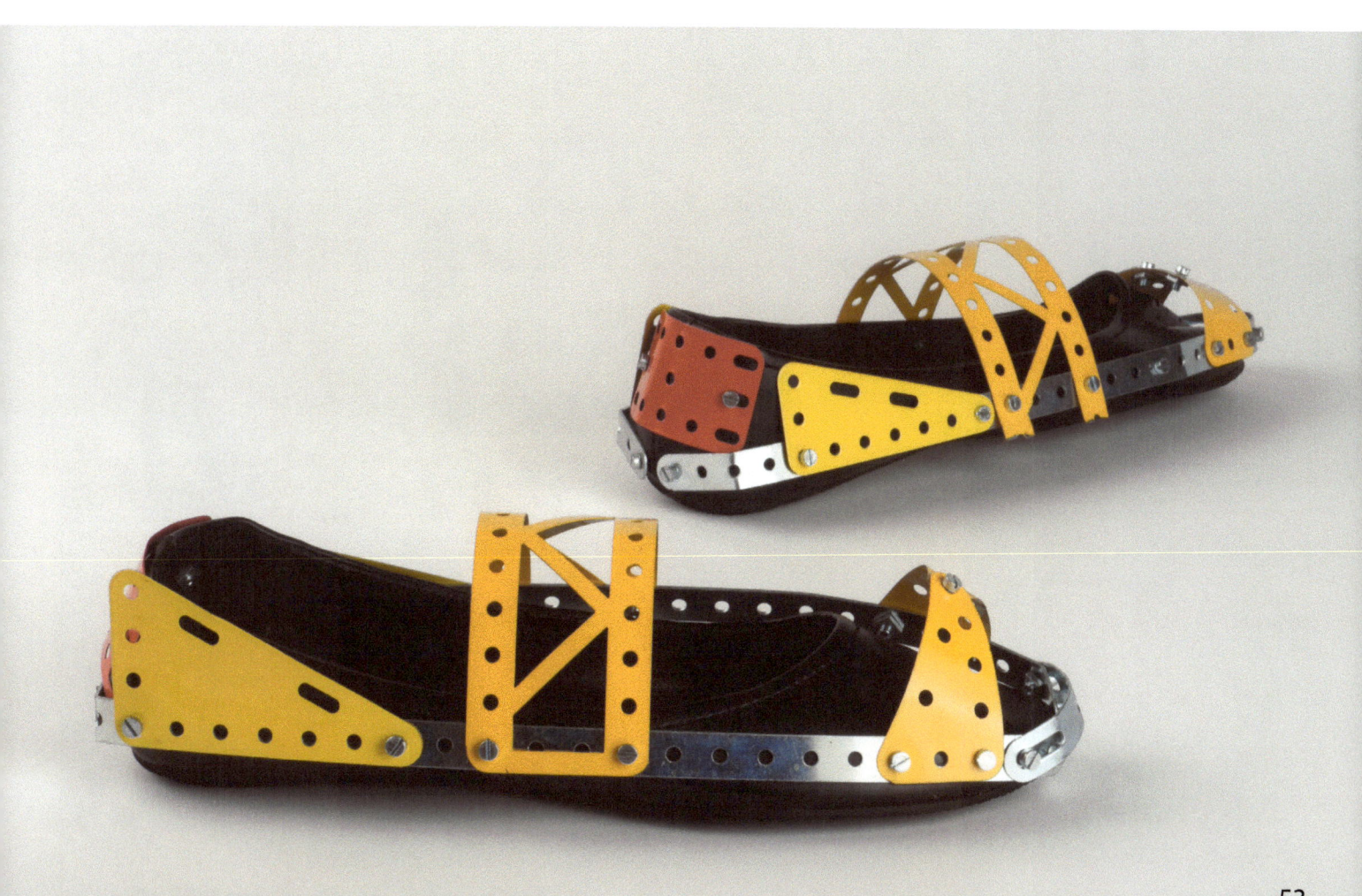

**Cheryl Siew
Wan Heap**

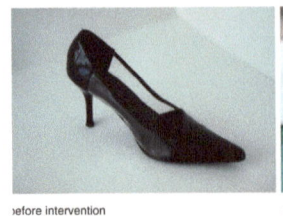
before intervention

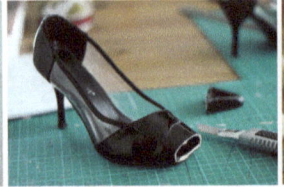
snip snip!

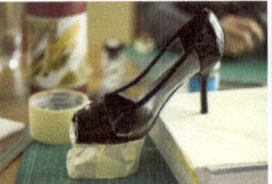
added platforms

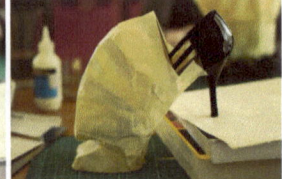
skeletal form + wrapping

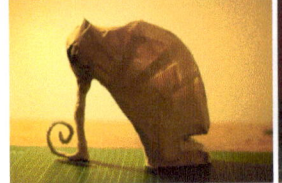
swirly tail

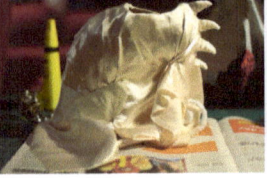
wrapping ensures

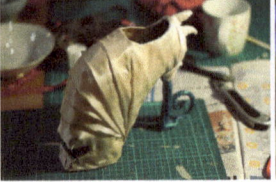
ready for beading

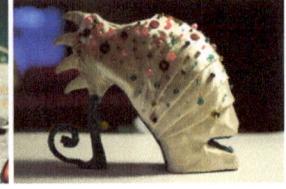
beaded!

ANNA MAY WONG'S LUCKY SHOE

(cheryl) siew wan heap 306262 13th october 2010

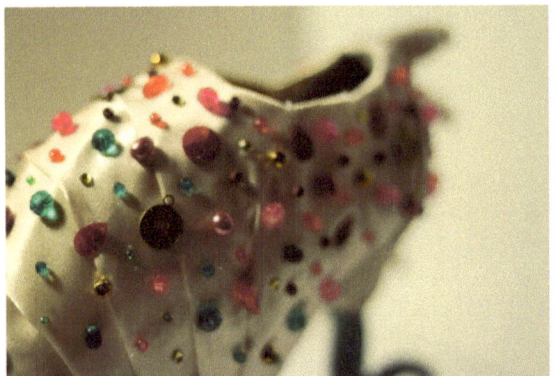

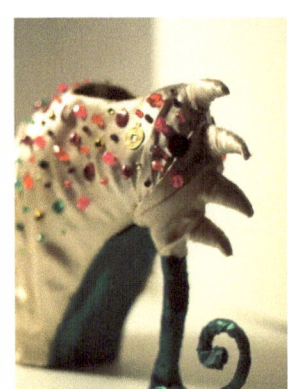

The design of Anna May Wong's shoes is inspired by her success; being one of the first Chinese American movie star, and the first Asian American to become an international star. During her time, it was very uncommon for such a Chinese actress to have such screen power, much less in a foreign country and culture. She is like a chameleon, being able to adapt herself perfectly. However instead of camouflaging herself and immerse herself with the American culture, she sets herself apart, bringing out her Chinese heritage to achieve stardom.

The shoe is a representation of Anna May Wong; glamorous and forever stylish. Beige satin wraps the shoe, as how she binds herself with her heritage. The beads change colours from green to red, a transformation to be unique. Randomly there would be Chinese coins, and one inside the front of the sole for luck. The heels ends in a swirl for its tail and the bottom of the sole in green as the hidden scales of a chameleon.

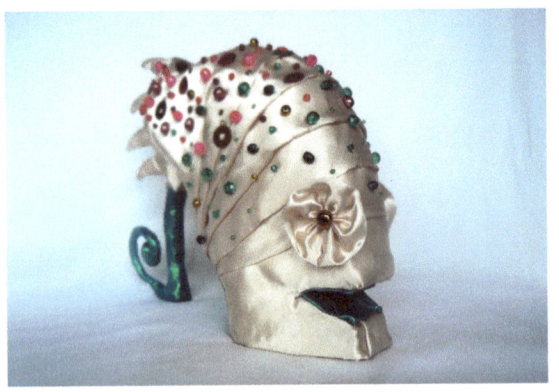

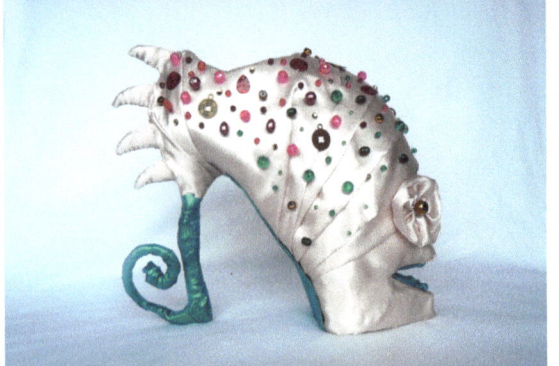

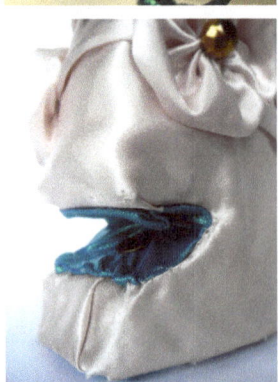

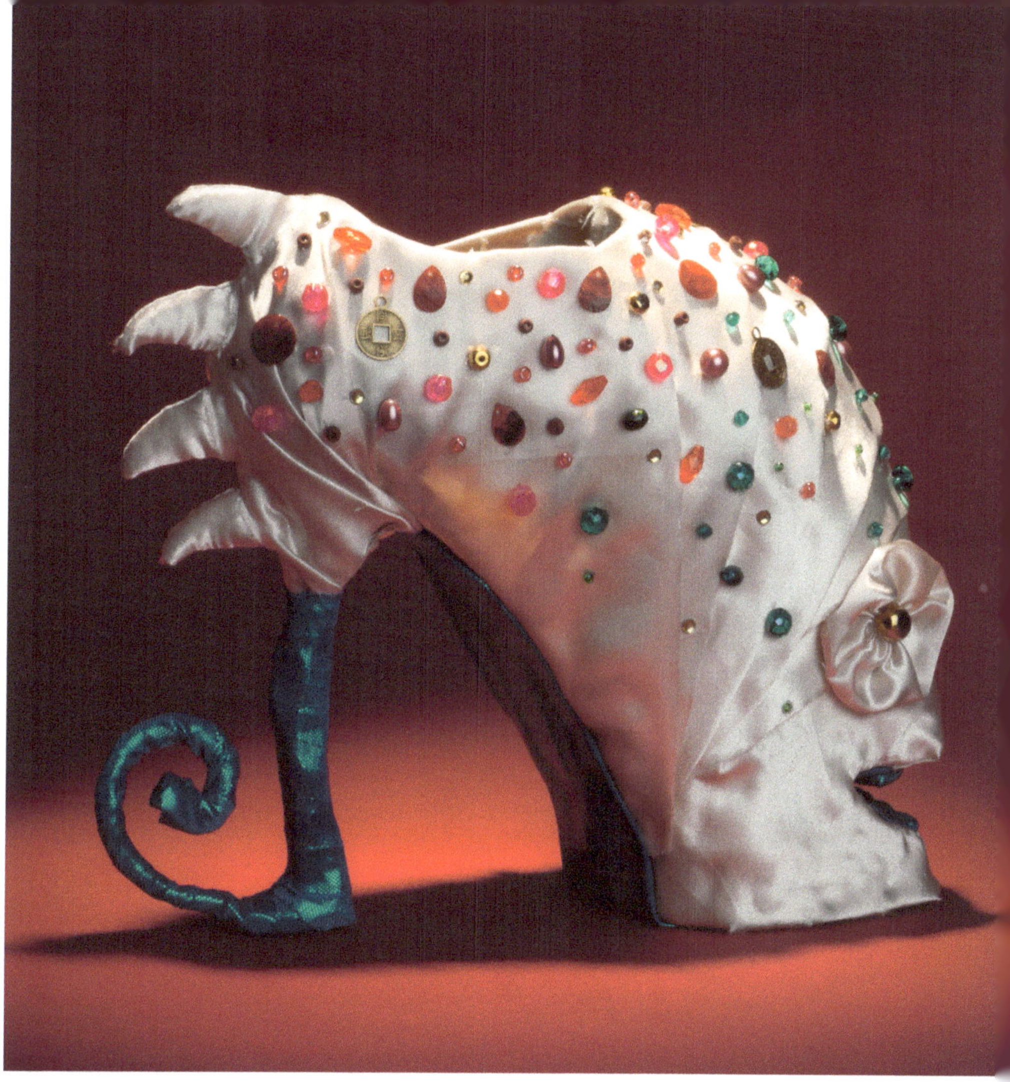

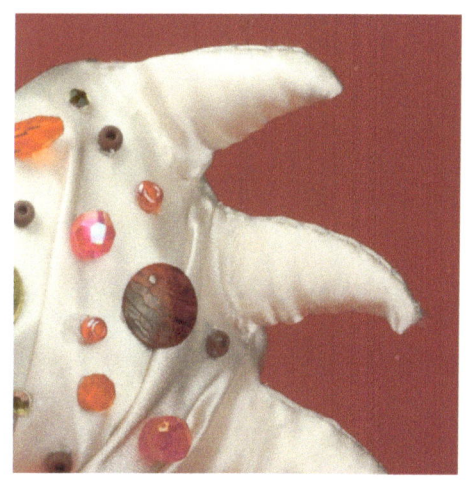

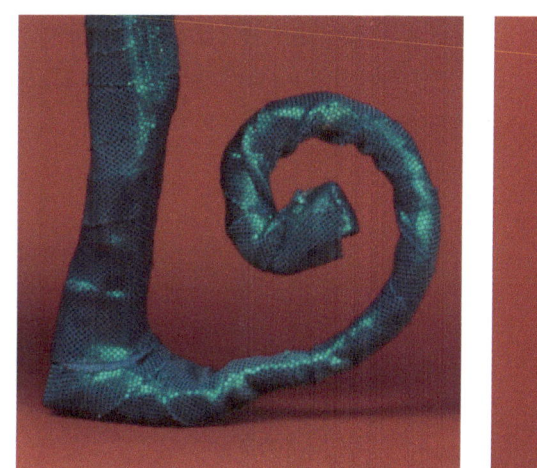

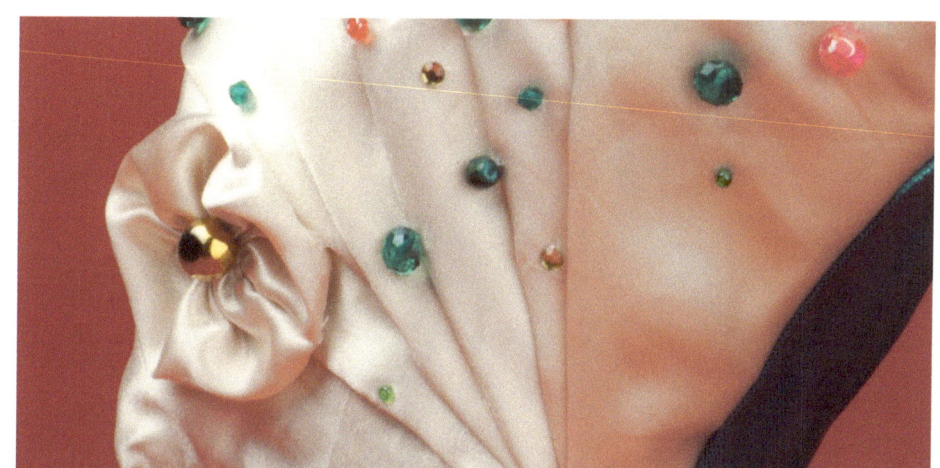

Jasmine Heo

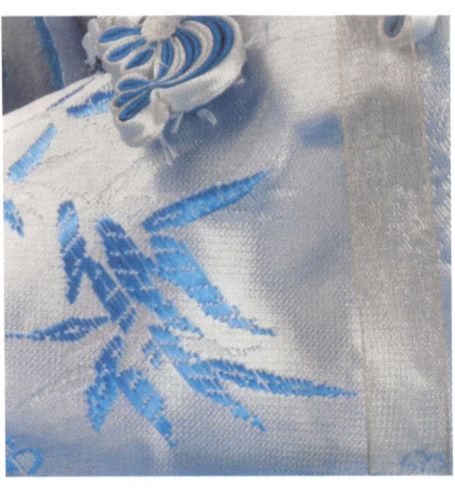

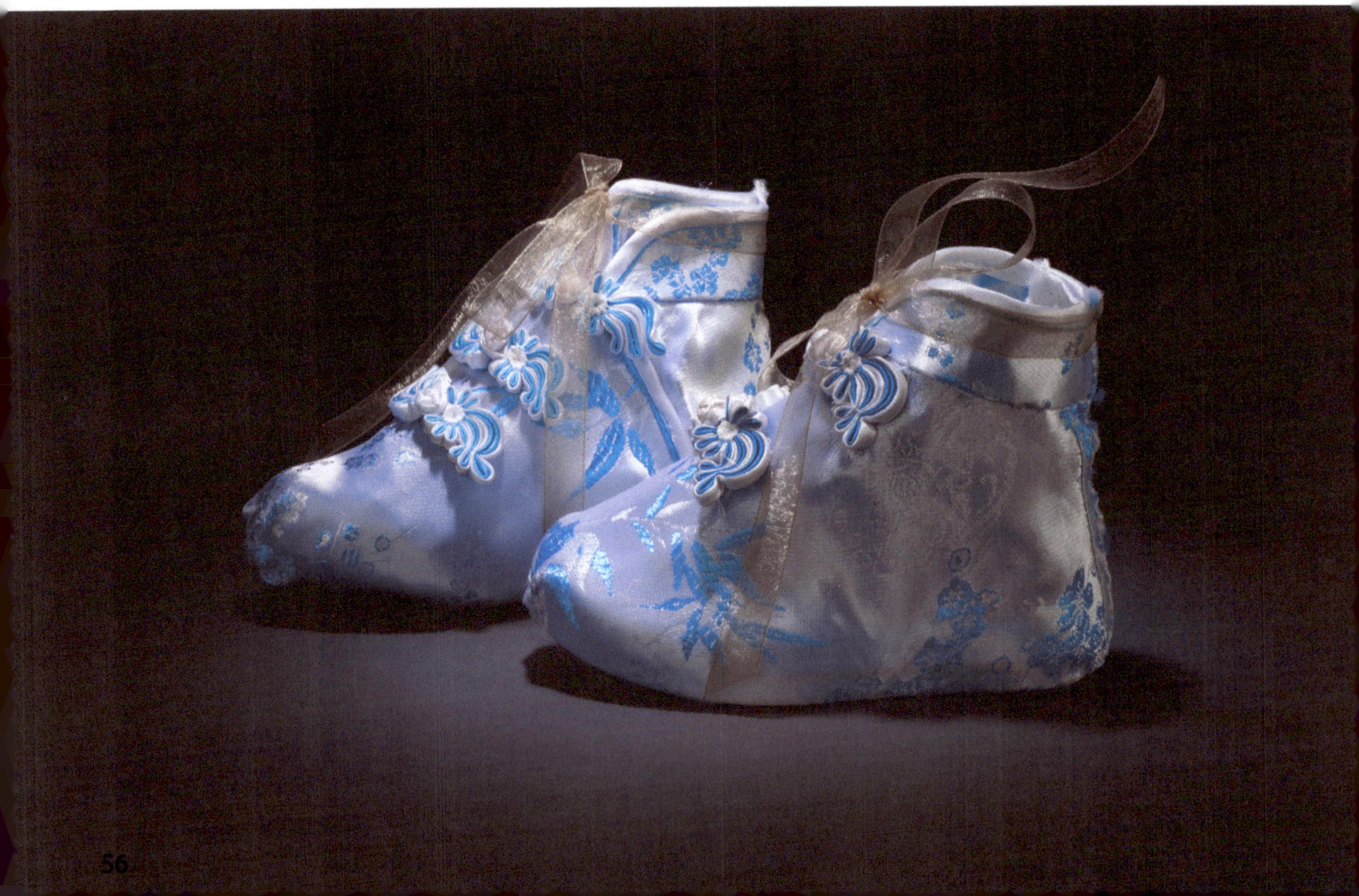

ANNA MAY WONG
FLORAL FAIRY HEELS

The shoes take inspiration from the formal American Chinese actress Anna May Wong. Anna May Wong, an ethnic Chinese actress, was born in Los Angeles. She started her acting career at the age of eight and became a well-known actress in Hollywood and then throughout the world. The shoes designed for Anna May Wong are based on her Chinese and American lifestyle. Even though she was an ethnic Chinese, she was greatly influenced by both Chinese and Western cultures while growing up and progressing through her acting careers in the United States.

In order to design a pair of lucky shoes for Anna May Wong, few aspects have taken into account such as the colour, shoe type and materials used. The colour red was chosen not only because it symbolizes good luck, blessing and prosperity in Chinese culture, but also characterizes her as a star, as an influential and fashionable actress. The heels represent the western culture, as she was born and raised in the United States. The flowers on the side of the heels embody her wideness and passion in fashion. The fabric used for the flowers is the traditional fabric for the "ChongSam" which she often wore in the films.

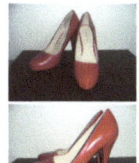
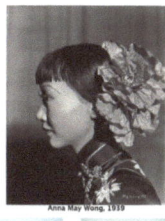

Anna May Wong, 1939

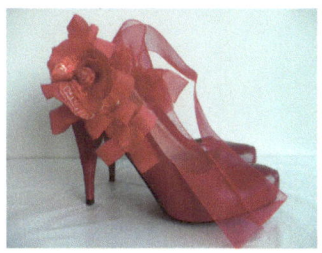
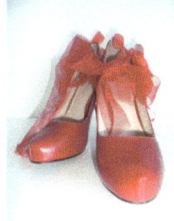
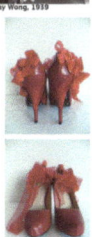

YOKE KIM LEE | 198271

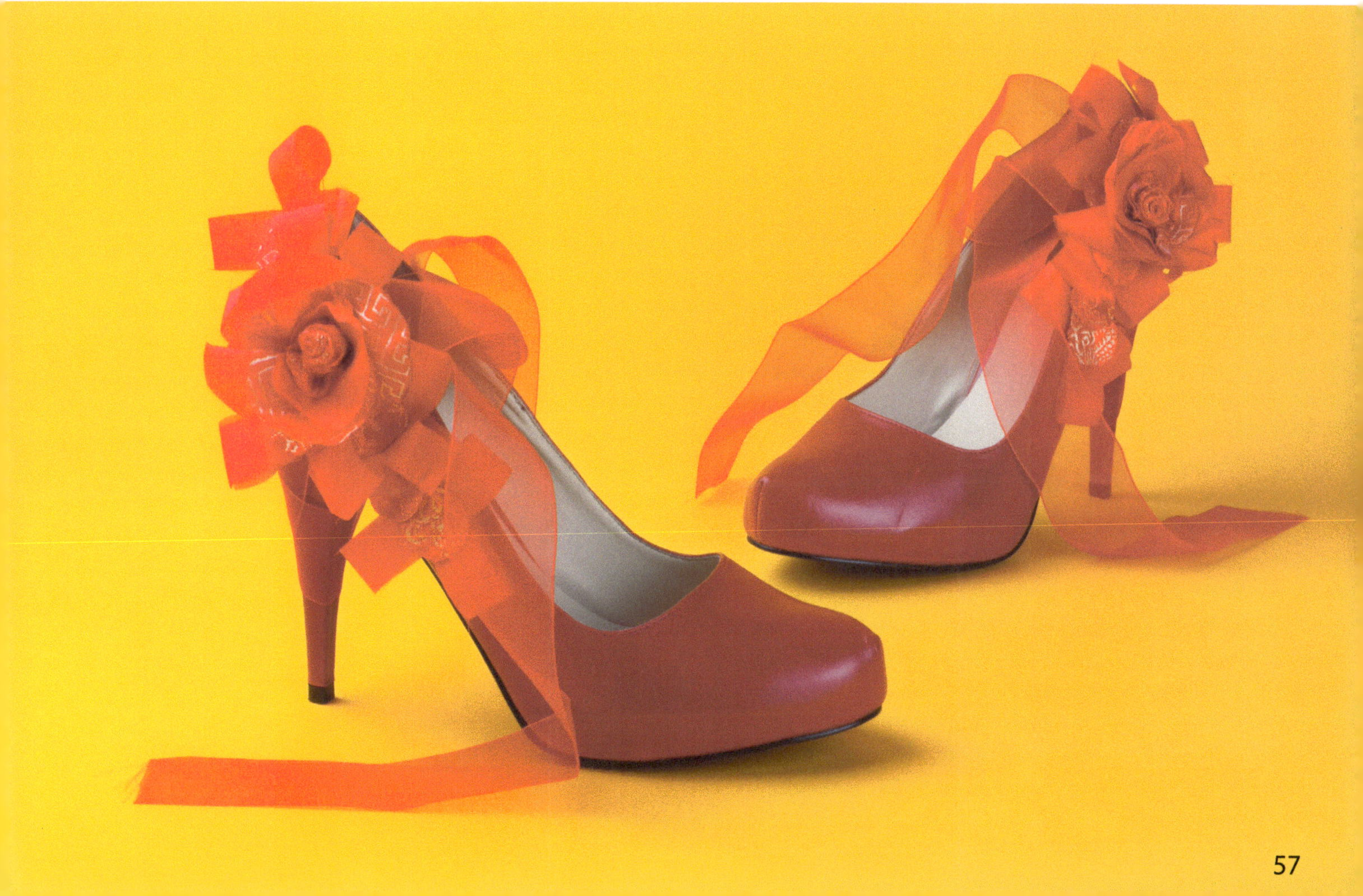

Zoe Lewis

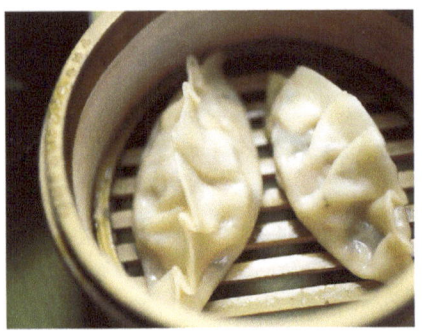

Anna May Wong's Wonton Slipper is her special luck charm. The slipper has a cream leather upper with fur lining. The wonton shape was derived for her to represent her Chinese origins. She was a 3rd generation Chinese-American, with her earliest ancestors moving to California during the mid 19th century.

Anna May was born in Los Angeles in 1905, and became a star in both silent and talking films. Although her stardom was widespread, she was held back by her Chinese origins due to America culture and the lack of acceptance of Chinese in the 1920s and 30s. In 1934, her father returned to live in China and Anna May planned a year long trip to visit him and her younger siblings in 1936. The trip was also to provide Anna May with a greater understanding of her native country for which she was much interested and involved with.

Whilst touring, Anna May Wong's Wonton slipper reminds her of her childhood where she remembers fondly making wontons with her mother and grandmother.

During her short stay in Melbourne, Anna May dined in Little Burke Street at a Chinese restaurant. Her meal there may have likely included wontons!

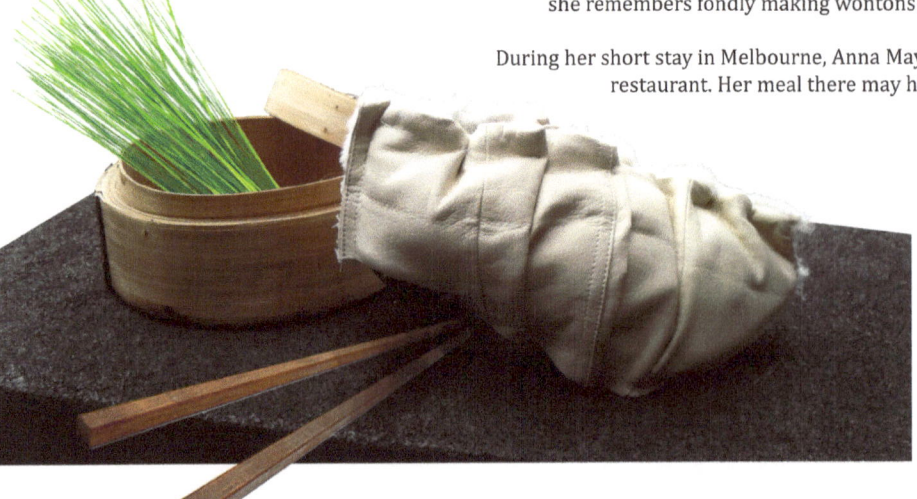

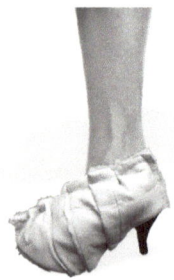

ANNA MAY WONG WONTON SLIPPER Zoe Lewis
214080

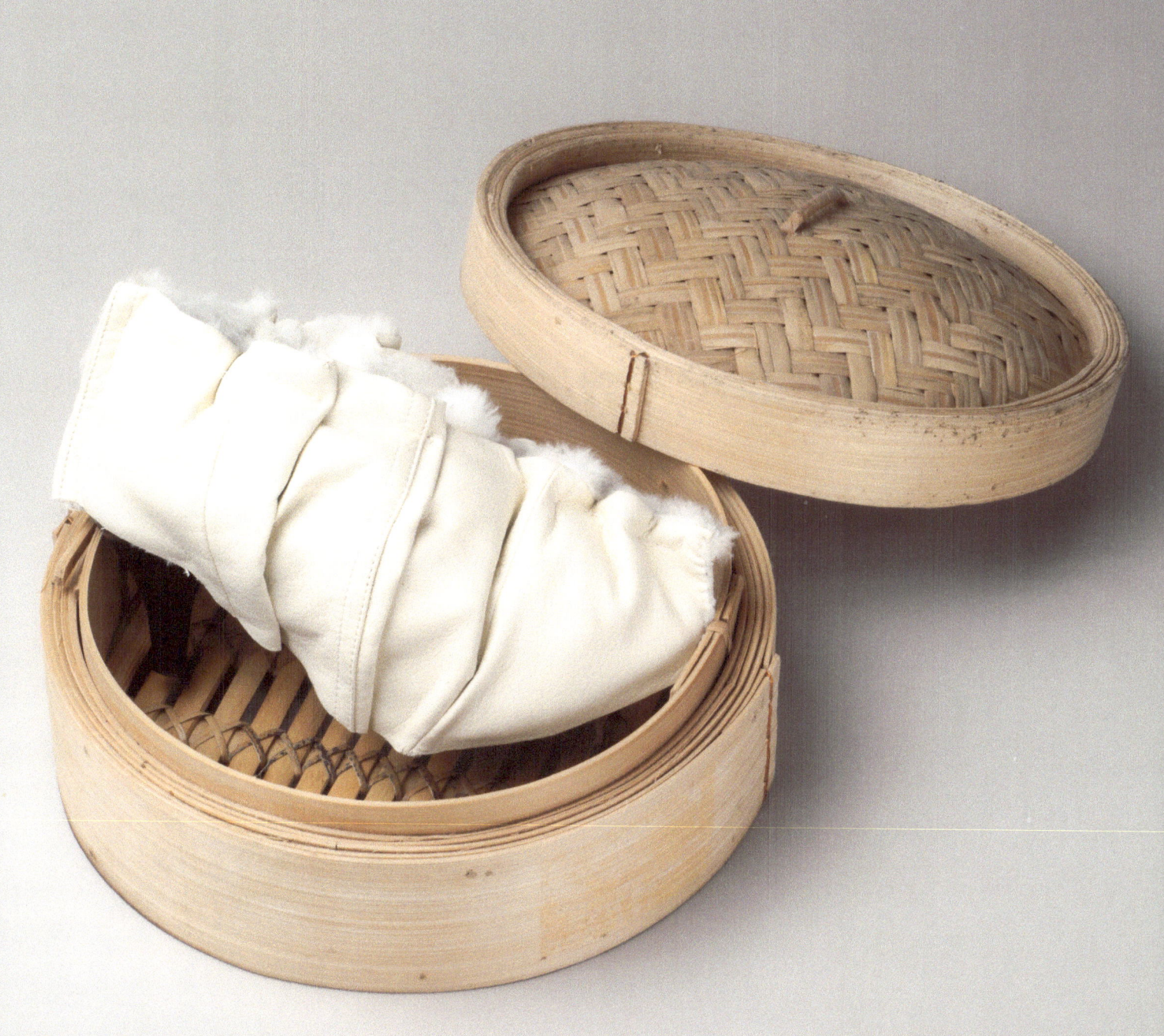

Ying Li

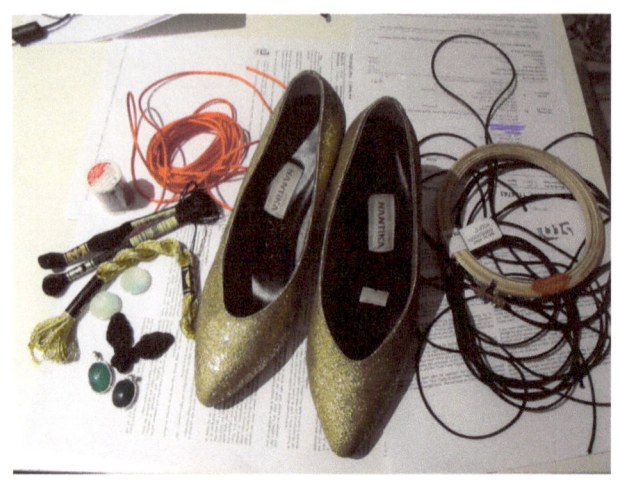

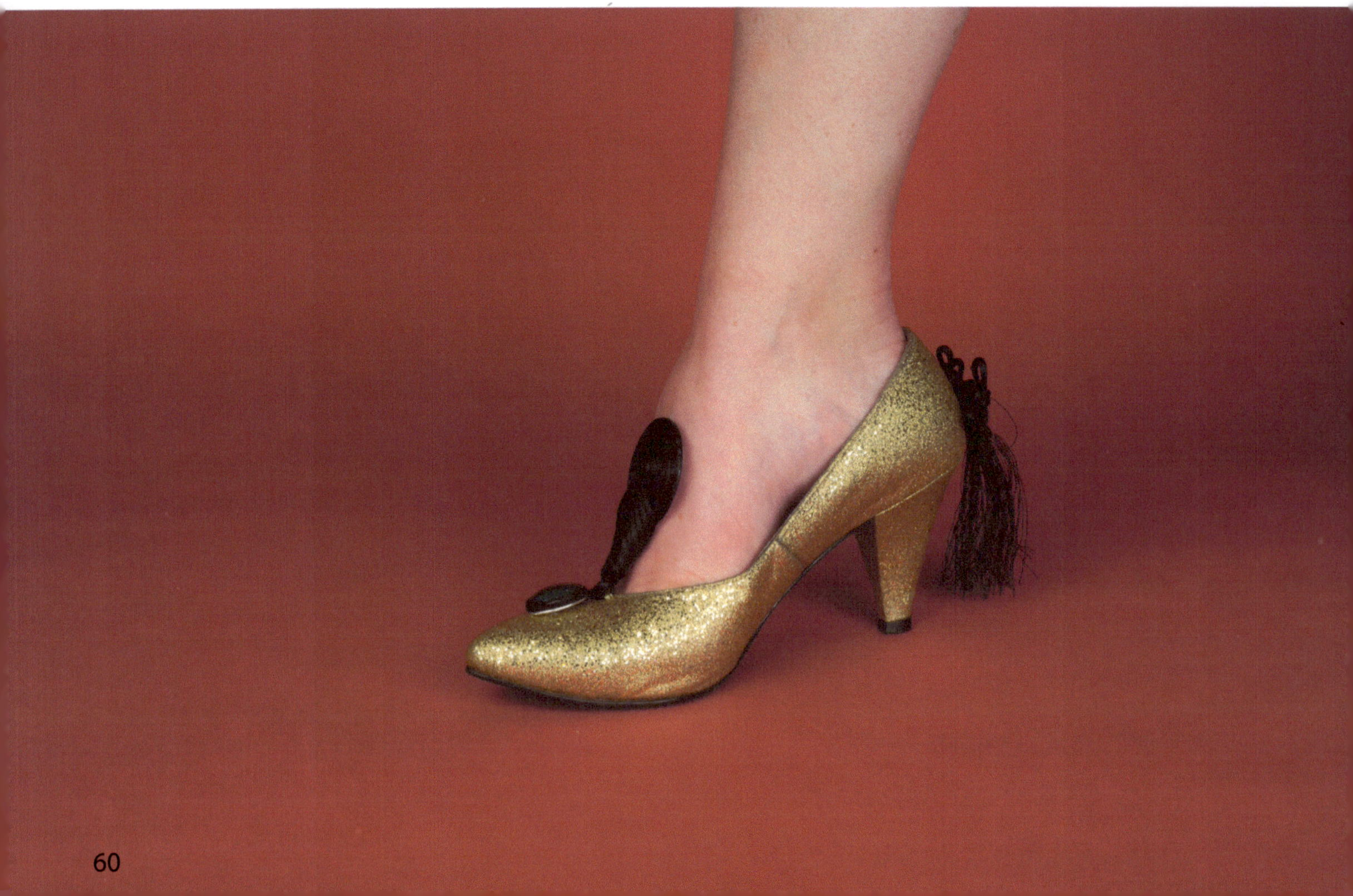

Anna May Wong growth up in a traditional Chinese family, according to the most common aesthetic of Chinese person, their idealist style should be sample but elegant. Also, as a movie star, the new shoes should adopt the fashionable elements in the 1930s, which also bring a fashion-forward spin on it. Details on the shoes may use some traditional lucky decorations.

Before:
'Classic shapes and styles' should be the principle of choosing a pair of second hand high heels. Soft texture with matt black colour also a big part of its appeal.

After:
-- A Chinese style cute peep toe will show off her pedicure, offering a feminine look and emphasis the beauty and grace of a Chinese lady.
-- Women of the 1930s returned to a more elegant, feminine look . buckles on the wrapped strap also become a feature of fashion.
-- Jewels are considered as a lucky charm for the traditional Chinese woman. People are likely wearing jewels and sometimes decorate clothes and shoes with jewels. It is designed a high wrap around ankle strap also covered in jewels adds emphasis on the design. It also brings a sex appeal to Anna May Wong.
-- There is a strip of lucky jewels around the peep toe, which well responded the jewels on the leg Wrapped Strap.
-- Repaint the heel on metallic silver, which brings contrast with the matt black and makes an artistic statement.

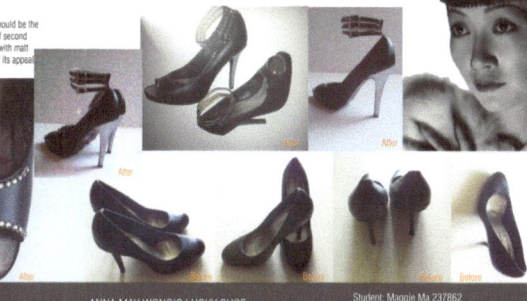

ANNA MAY WONG'S LUCKY SHOE

Student: Maggie Ma 237862
Coordinator: Dr Derham Groves

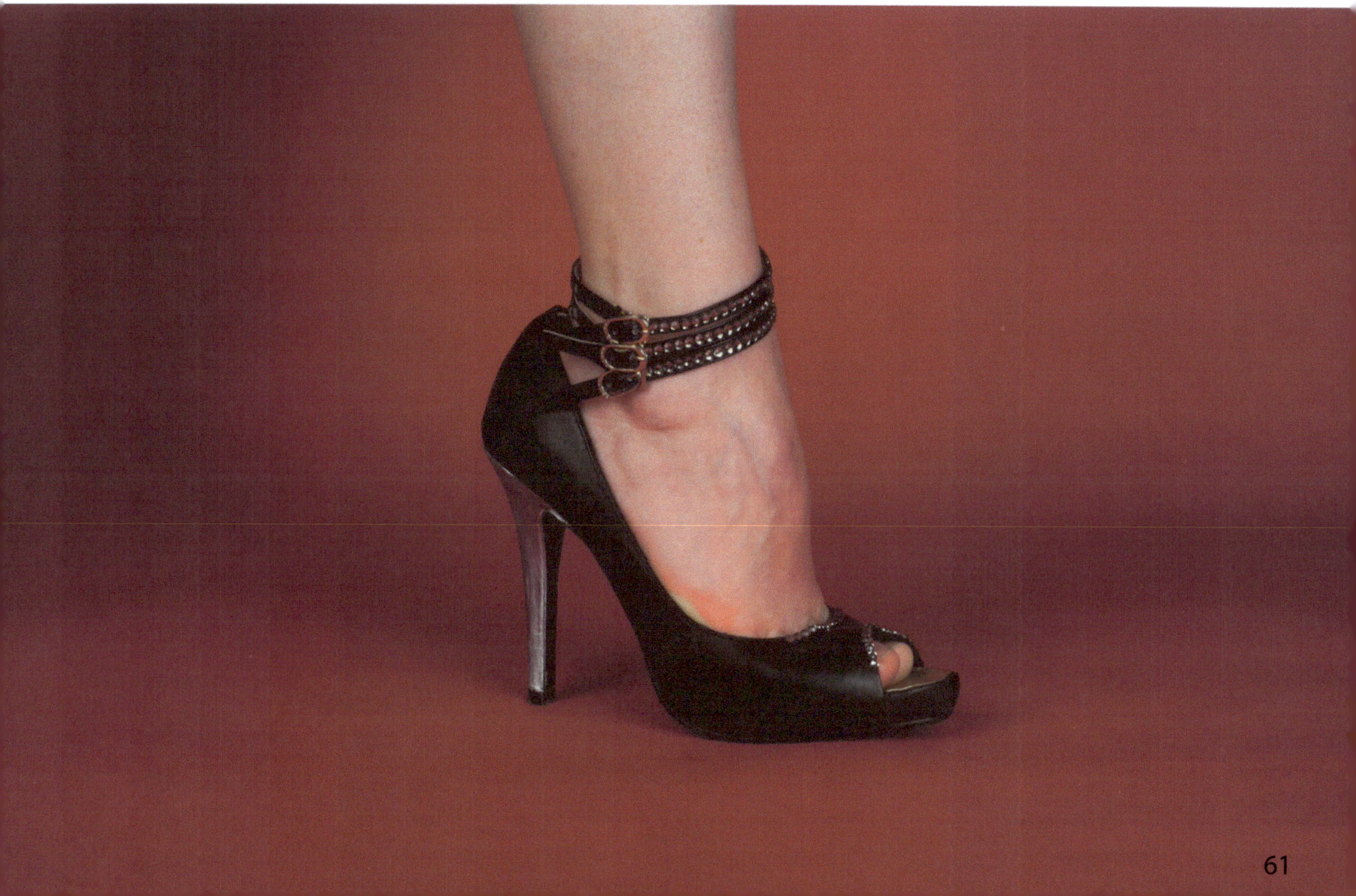

Yindong Ma

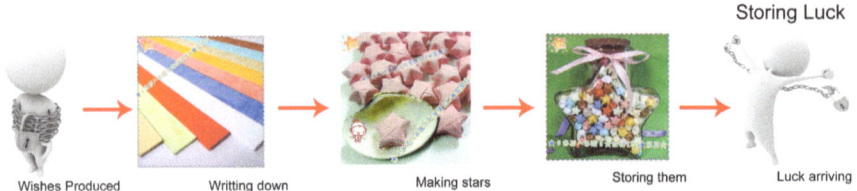

Wishes Produced → Writting down → Making stars → Storing them → Luck arriving

Storing Luck

First of all, I am a Chinese as Anna May Wang and the main theme of this assignment is "Lucky". So the inspiration of my design is from Chinese traditional way of "storing luck": Writing wishes down on bar-shape papers, Making them into lucky stars and store them. So I chose "intertwining" as my principal way to make my lucky shoes. By the way, about the colors I use on the shoes, Firstly, red, is well known the traditional color of Chinese. But also I chose yellow as my 2nd choice cause Anna May Wang was one of the most brightest stars and cause the original lucky shoe of her was a tiger shoe, So yellow is just the color of stars also the color on a tiger.

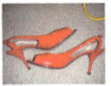 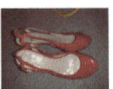

The original shoes

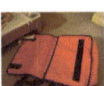 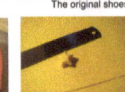

2nd hand bag   Yellow paper

Materials

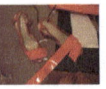 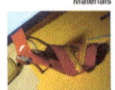

Processes

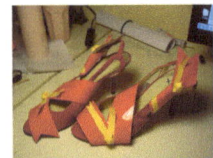 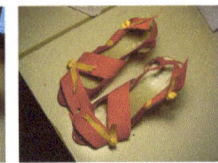

Anna May Wang's Lucky Shoe

Yindong Ma
309988

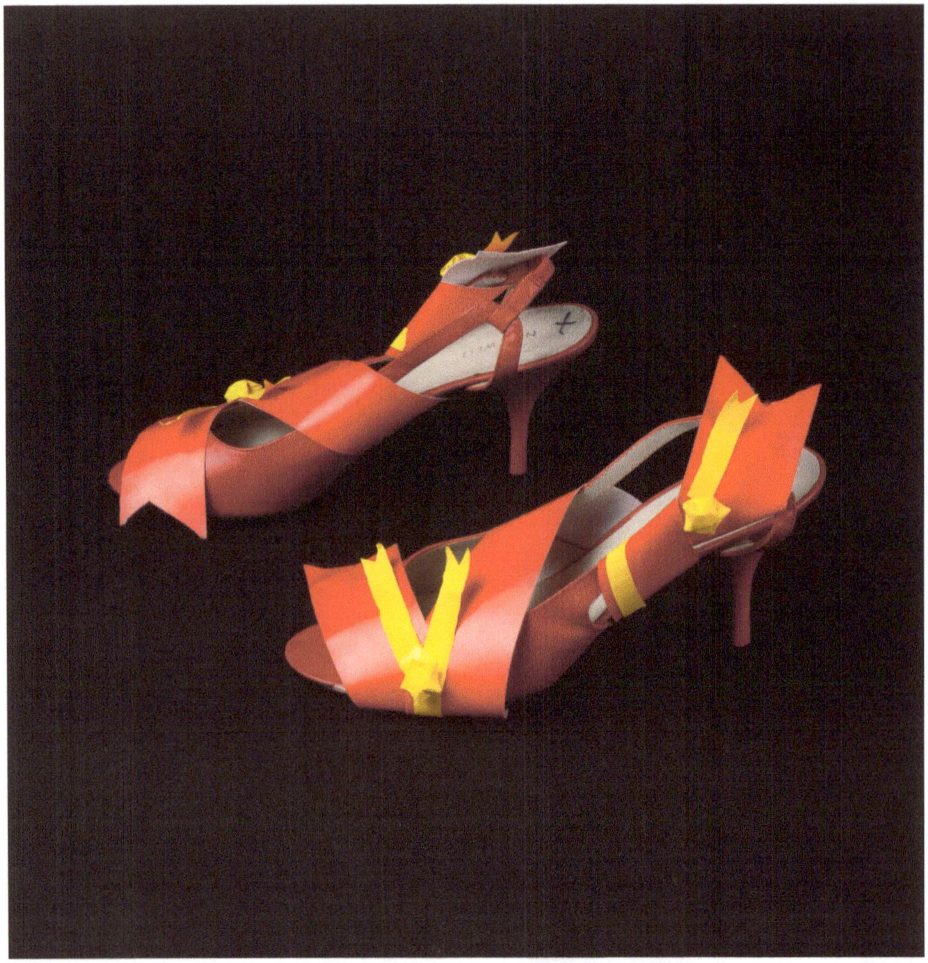

SAILING OVER THE DANCE FLOOR
ANNA MAY WONG'S TRAVEL BOOTS

SARAH MACISAAC 239 172 POPULAR ARCHITECTURE AND DESIGN

Sarah MacIsaac

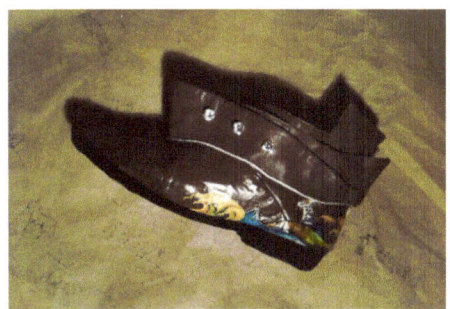

These grey knee-high boots have been transformed into an elegant grey boat with diamond portholes that is reminiscent of the glamorous era of international travel and the adventures that Anna May embarked upon. The boat travels on a high-sea of stylised and colourful waves, the Japanese prints that had so influenced Western Art at the beginning of the 20th Century. This is in contrast with Anna May's career in the USA where her difference was limiting her roles and she was not given a chance to innovate or influence.

When she travelled anywhere she maintained a strong link to her Chinese heritage, so although she sailed to far away lands, the boot has been re-soled with a map of China, as it was in 1939 when she bought a pair of shoes in a Melbourne department store.

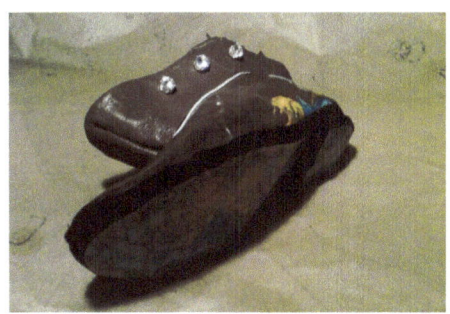

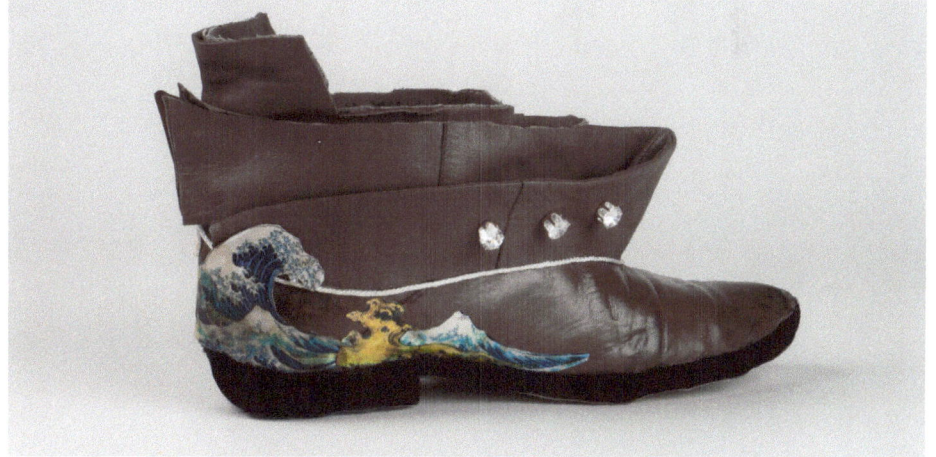

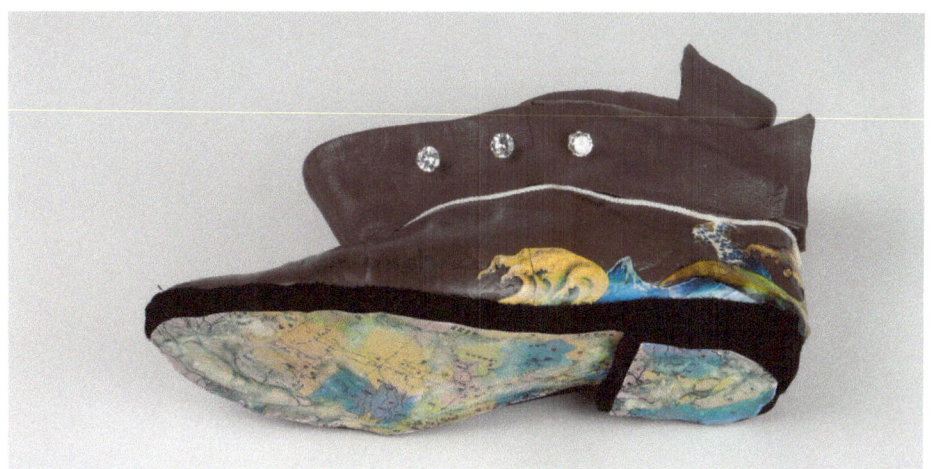

Paul Mak

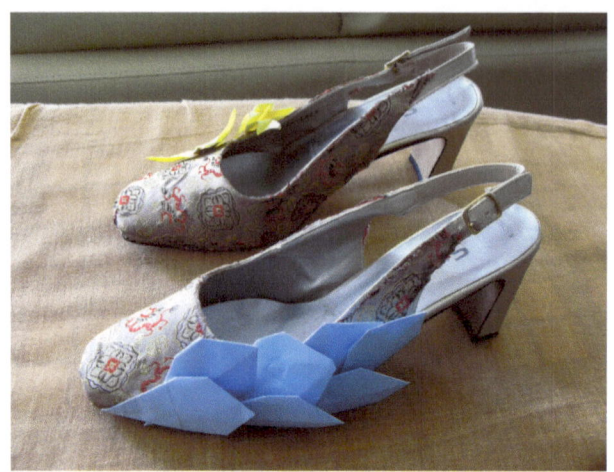

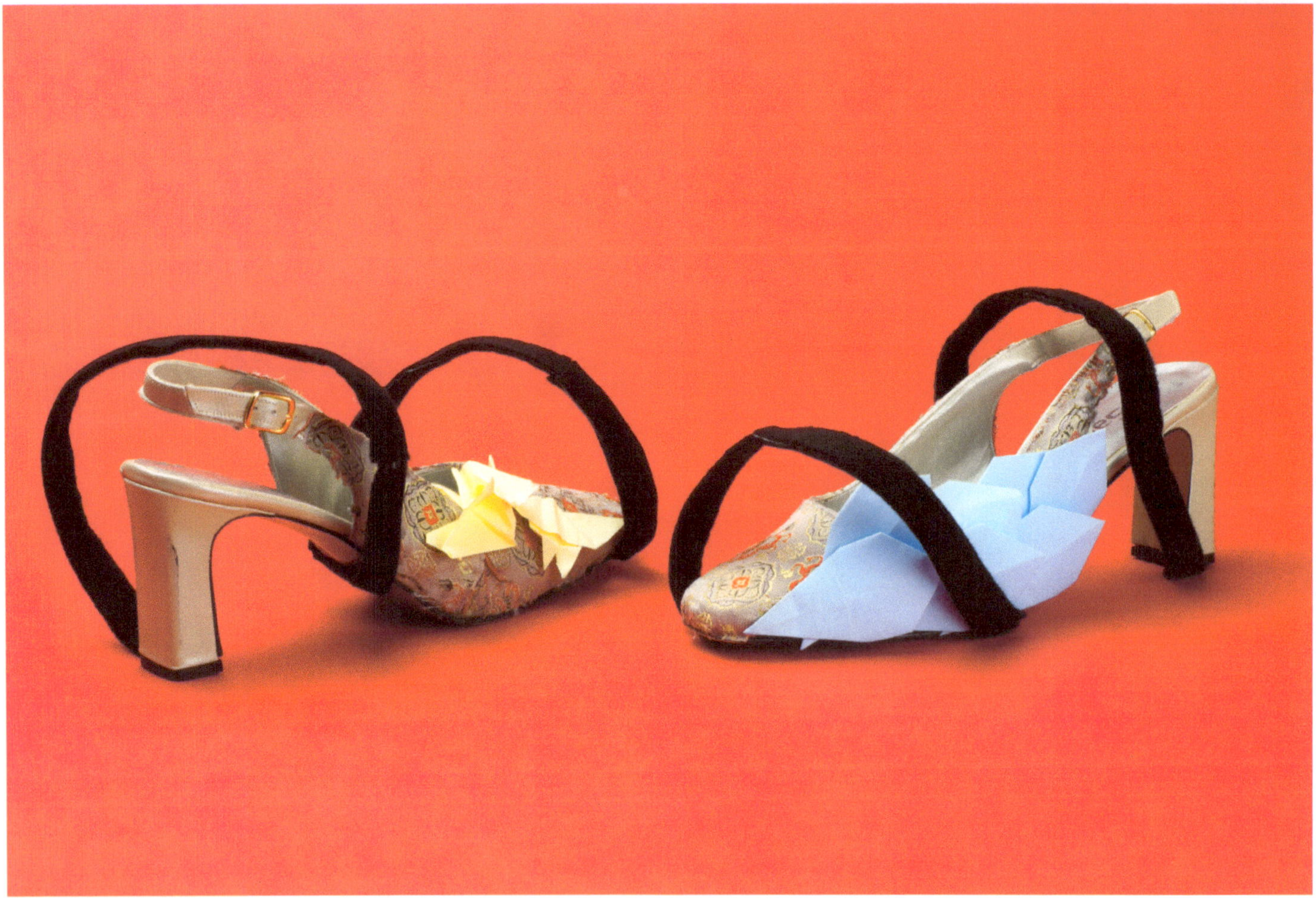

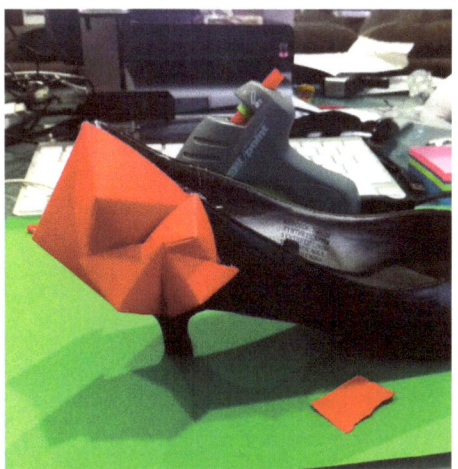
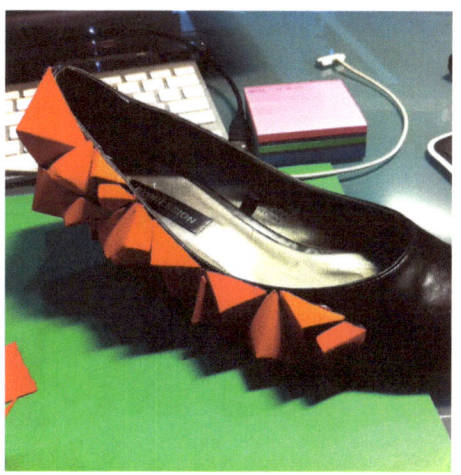

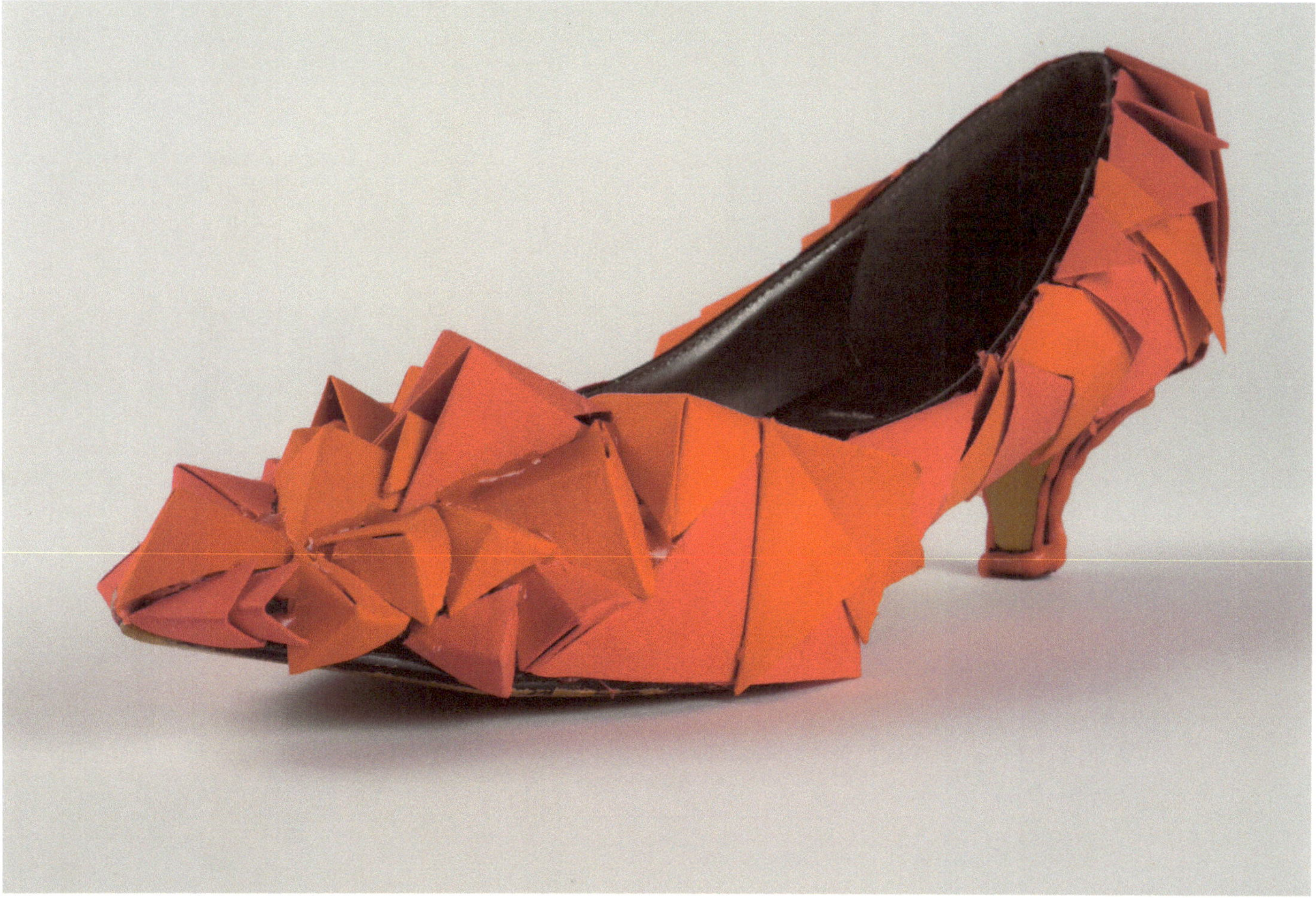

Daniela Melzer

Anna May Wong, January 3, 1905 - February 2, 1961, was an American actress, the first Chinese American movie star and the first Asian American to become an international star. Her long and varied career spanned both silent and sound film, television, stage, and radio. She began acting in films at an early age. During the silent film era, she acted in The Toll of the Sea (1922), one of the first movies made in color and Douglas Fairbanks' The Thief of Bagdad (1924). Wong became a fashion icon, and by 1924 had achieved international stardom. For decades after her death, Wong was remembered principally for the stereotypical "Dragon Lady" and "Butterfly" roles that she was often given. Her life and career were re-evaluated in the years around the centennial of her birth. Interest in her life story continues.

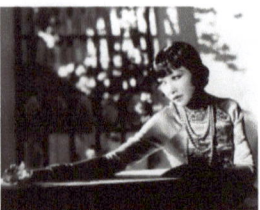

Lavender, lavandula spica, is a plant with narrow silver grey leaves and small flowers, which may be blue, violet or lilac. The name derived from the Latin 'lavare' to wash. Lavender is native to the mountains of the Mediterranean where it grows in sunny, stony habitats. The herb was a holy herb in the temple and the romans used it in their baths. Lavender produces slight calming, soothing, and sedative effects when its scent is inhaled. Essential oil of lavender has antiseptic and anti-inflammatory properties and has been used for medical purposes. It is very appreciate for its fragrance.

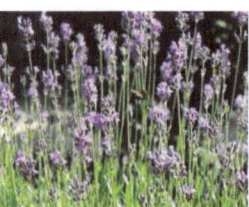

Lavender is my favourite in many ways. I have always loved the fragrance. I have had lavender in my closet all my life. For me the fragrance is home, safe and calming. The colour is nice and calming for the eye to look at. I have spent ours in the shops with lavender soap, perfumes and all sorts of things in Provence with my grandfather. For me that is times of happiness and luck. Anna May Wong has something sad and beautiful around her and a narrow appearance in some way and she makes me think of a lavender flower.

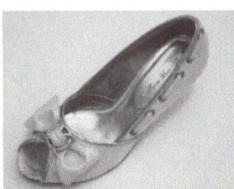

The original shoe from the Camberwell market for five dollars. High heels and an open toe.

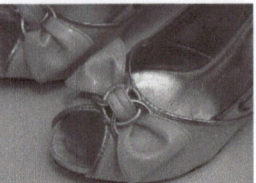

A beige plastic shoe with details in gold. A rosette attached with metal gold rings.

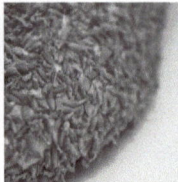

Dried lavender for the calming effect and the fantastic fragrance.

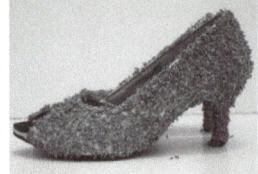

The lucky shoes for Anna May Wong with the lavender fragrance following her where ever she is.

Popular Architecture, Art and Design. Anna May Wong's Lucky shoes. Made by Daniela Melzer. 13 October 2010.

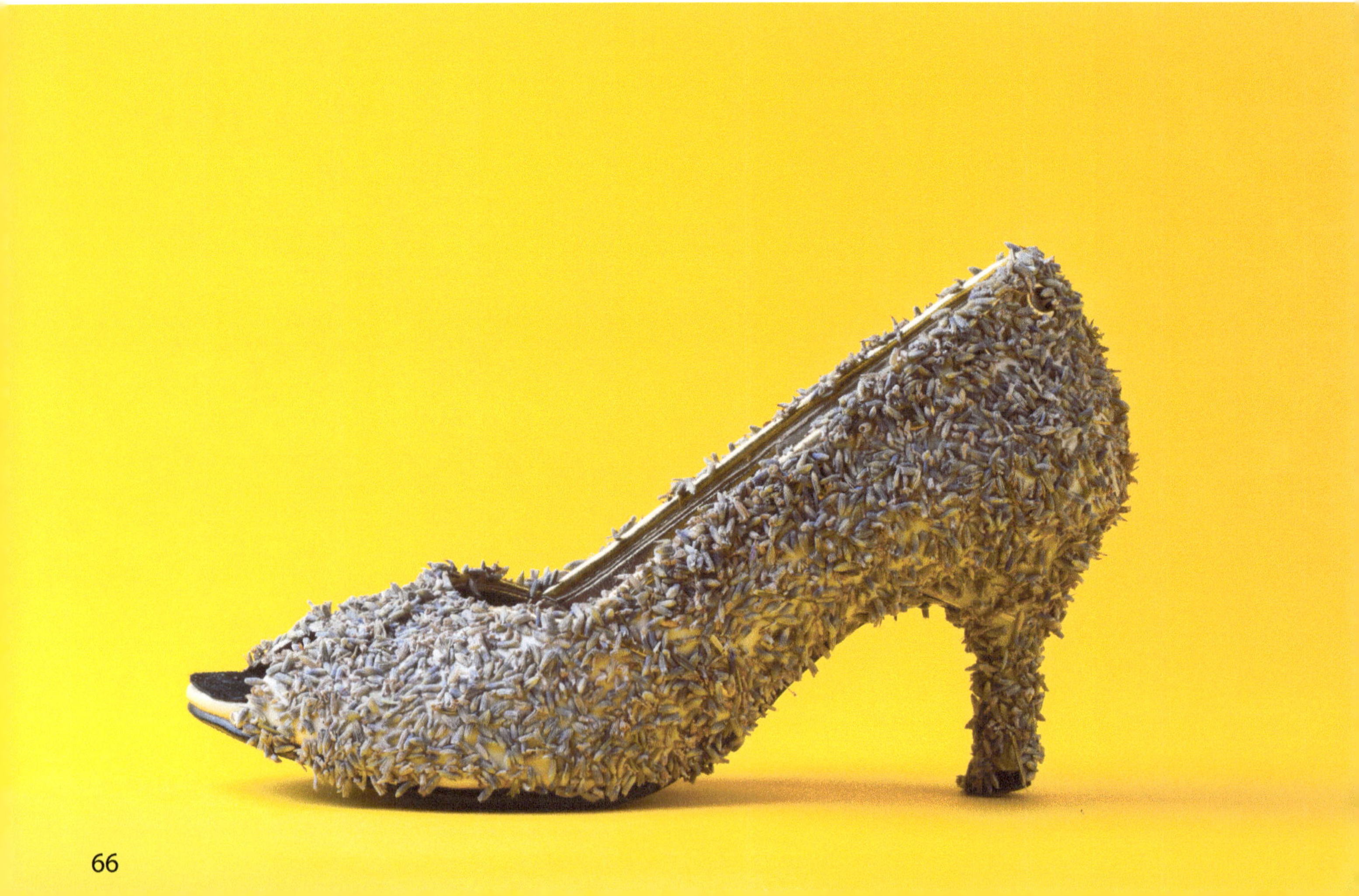

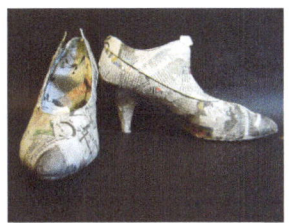
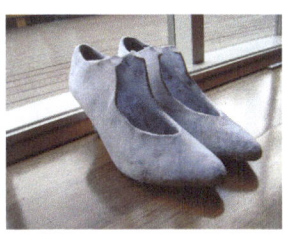
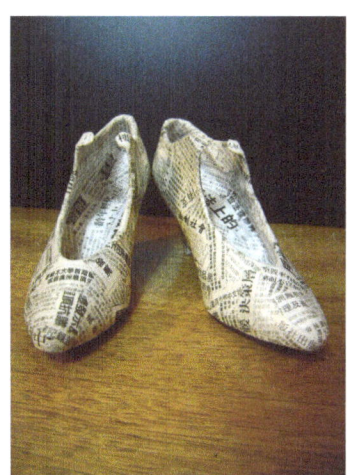

Katie Miller

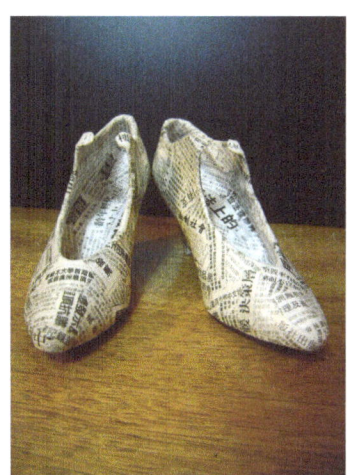

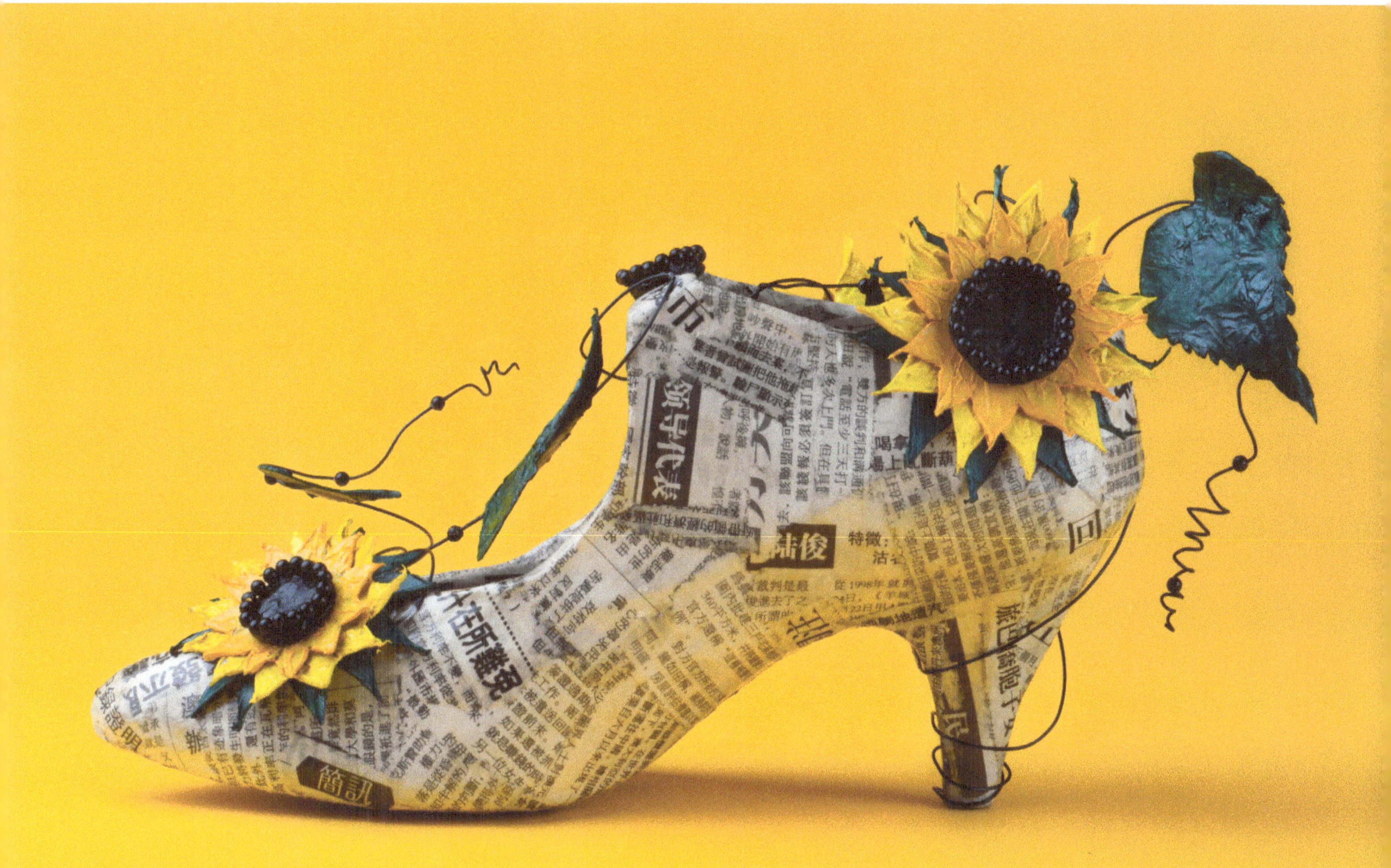

Lachlan Michael

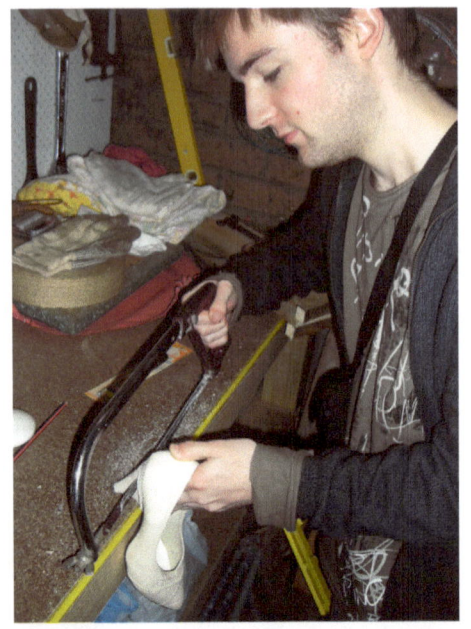
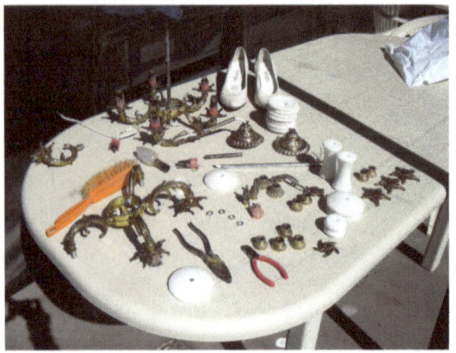
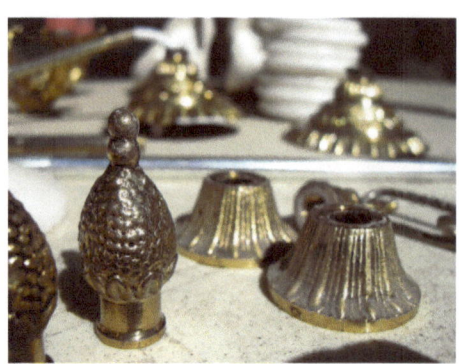
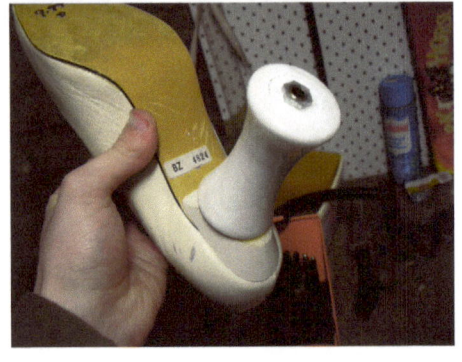
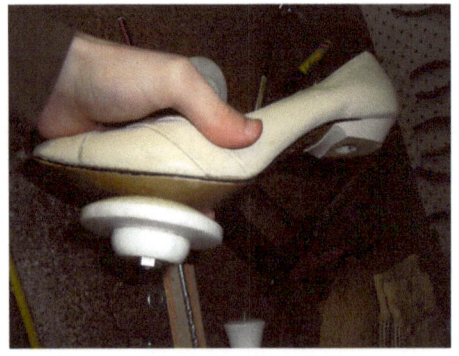
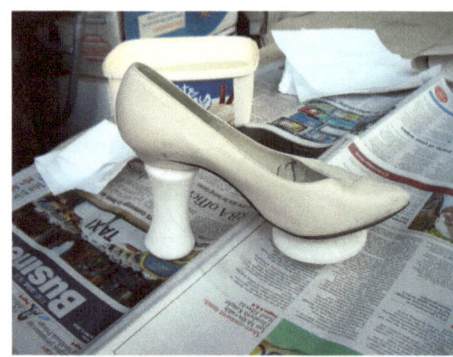
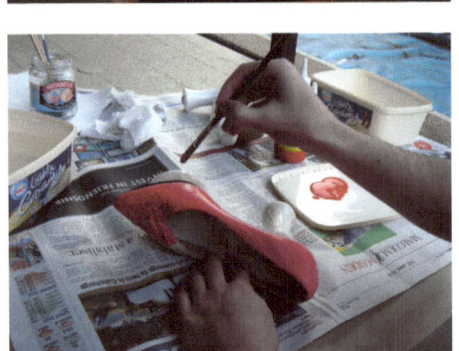
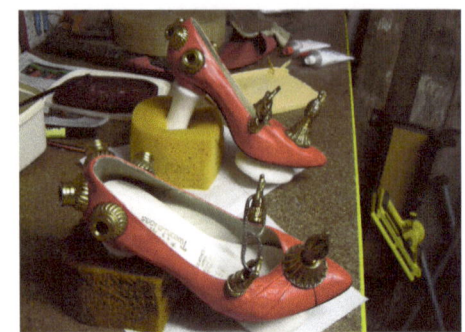
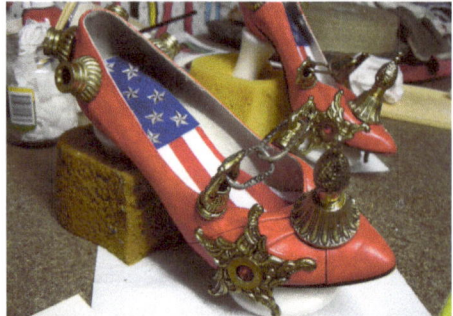

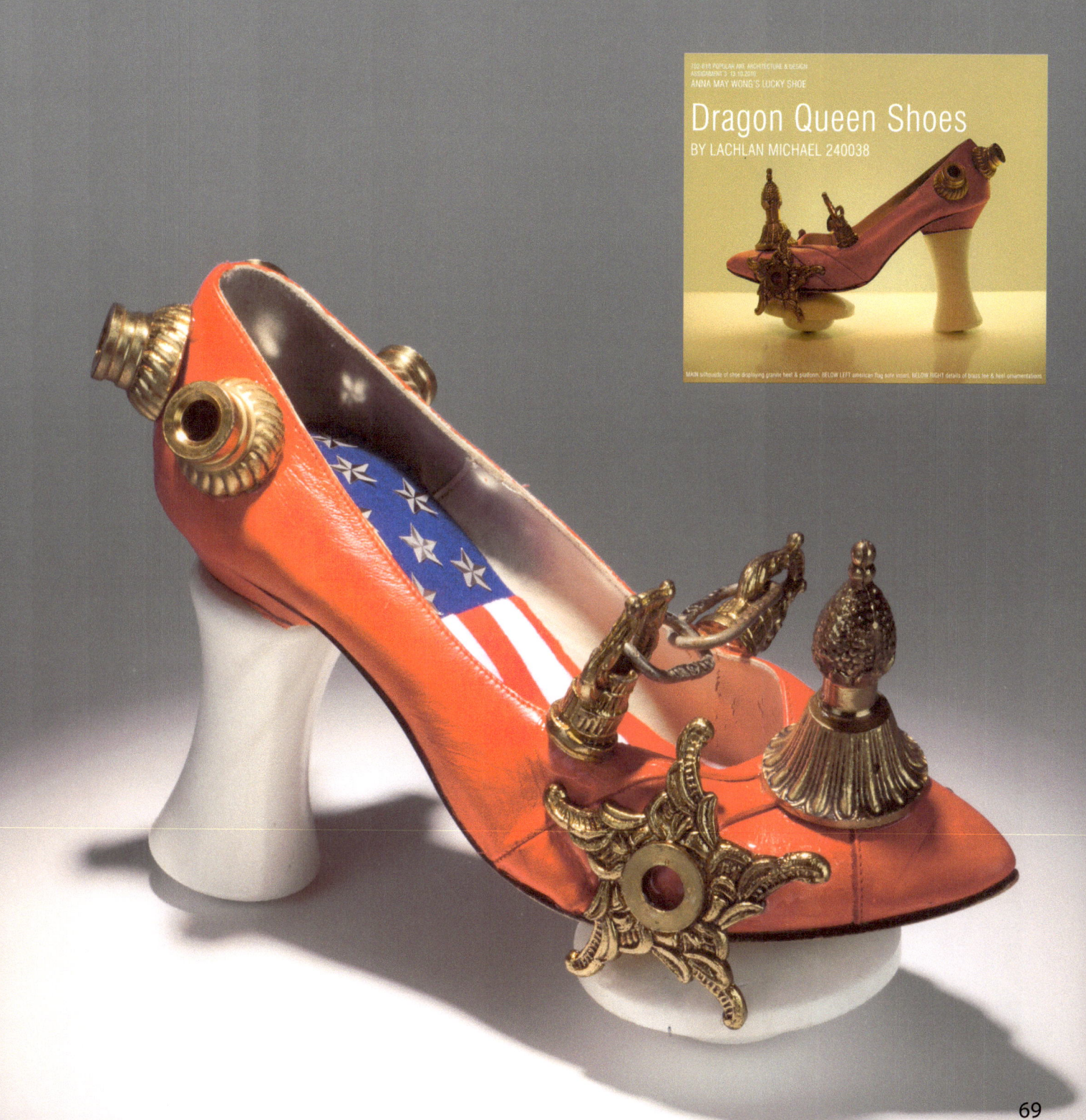

Dragon Queen Shoes
BY LACHLAN MICHAEL 240038

MAIN silhouette of shoe displaying granite heel & platform. BELOW LEFT american flag sole insert. BELOW RIGHT details of brass toe & heel ornamentations.

Sandra Mrowetz

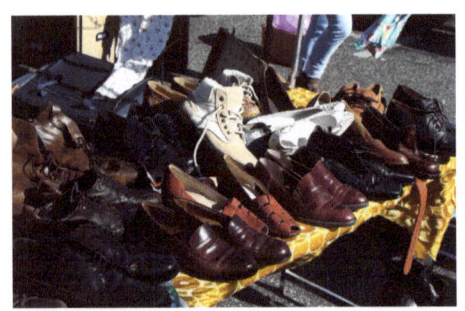

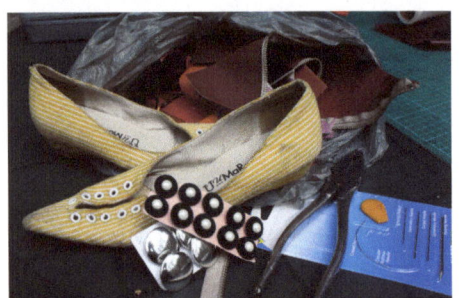

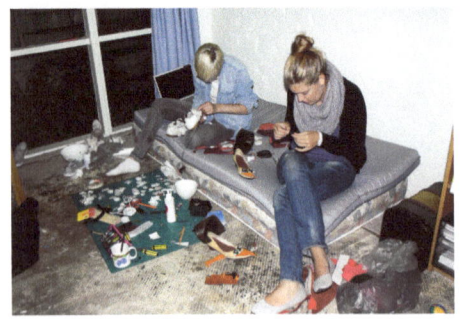

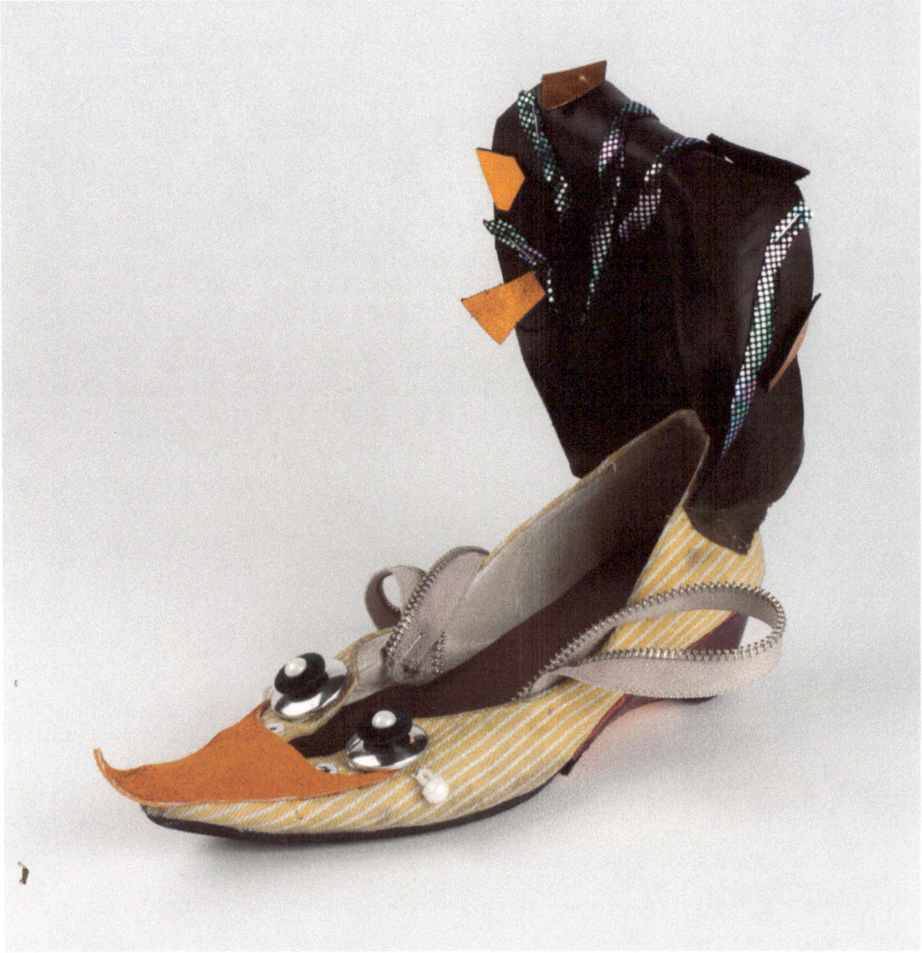

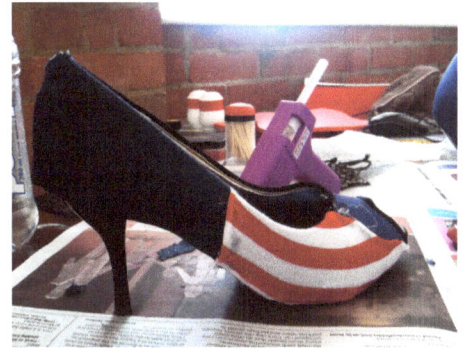

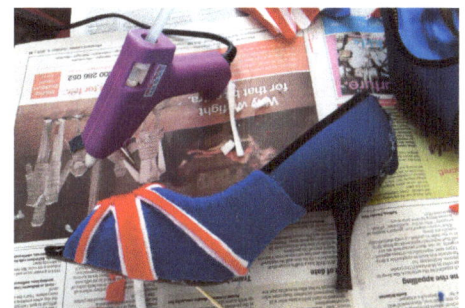

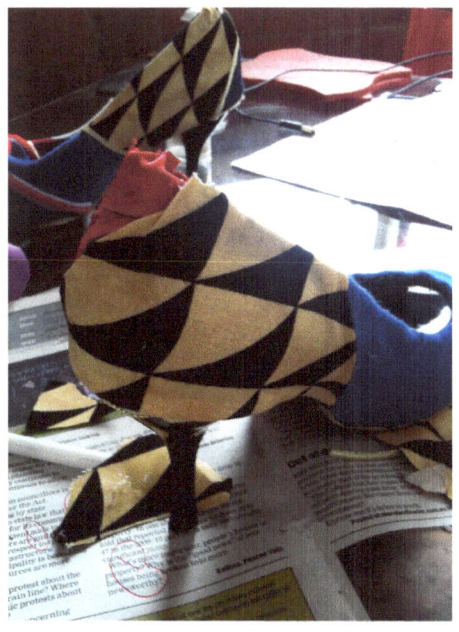

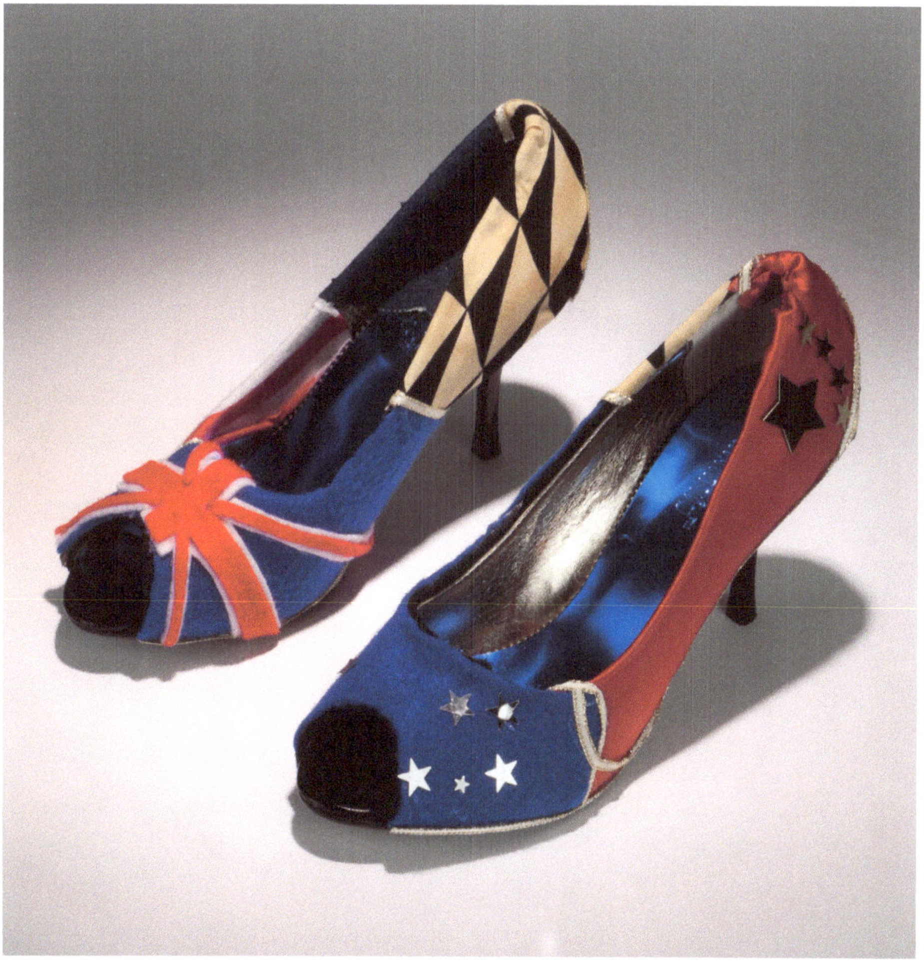

Kim Peeters

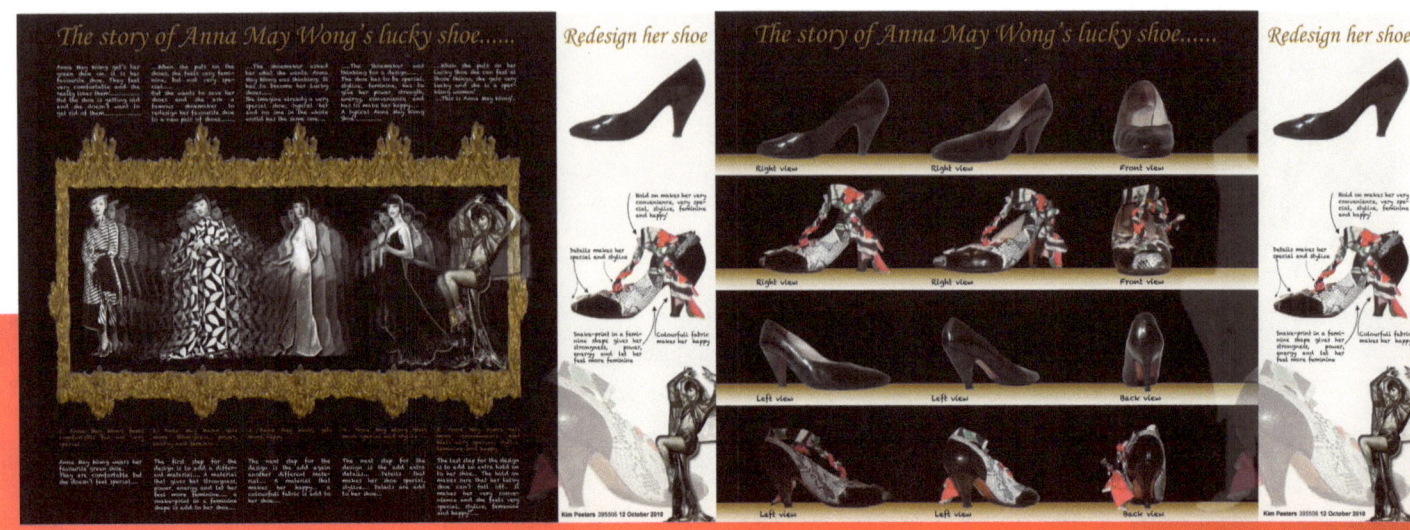

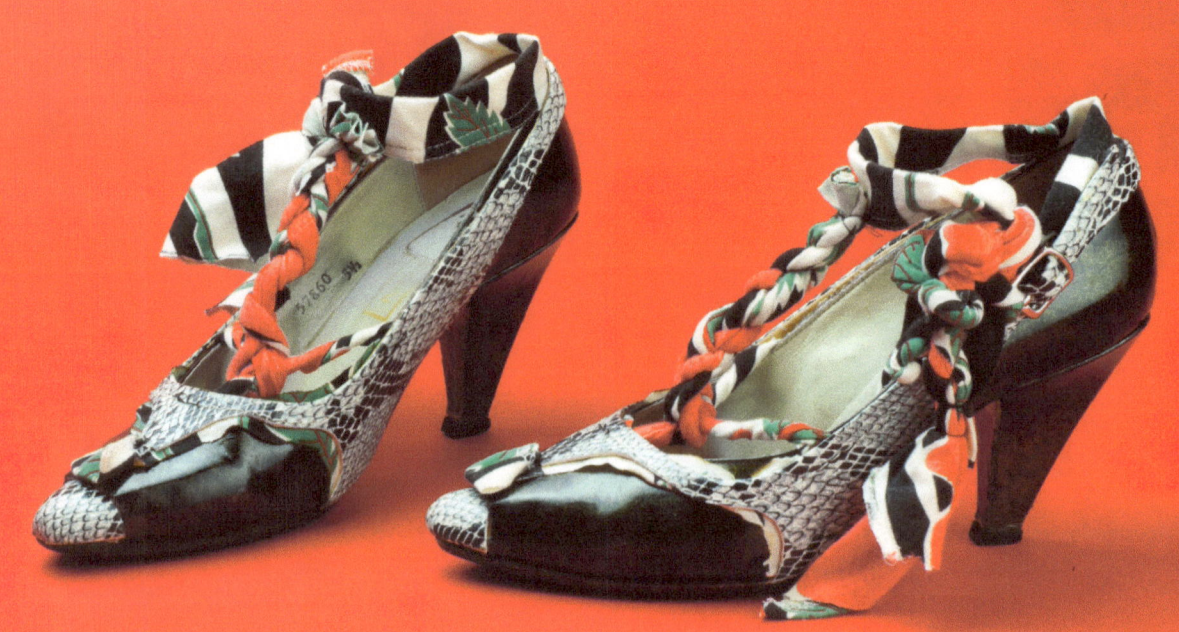

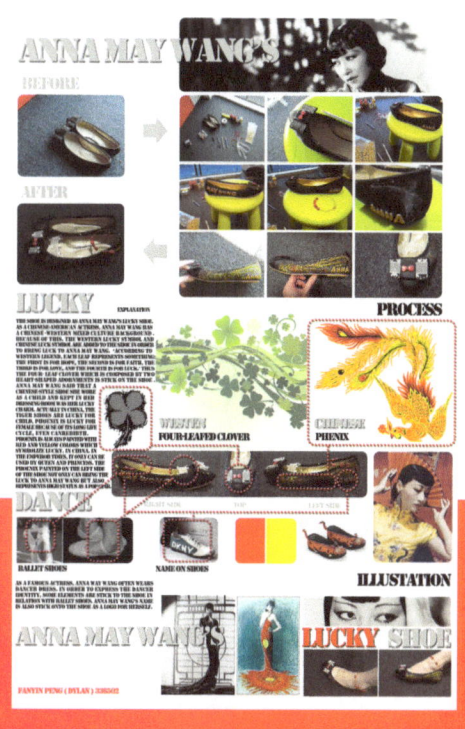

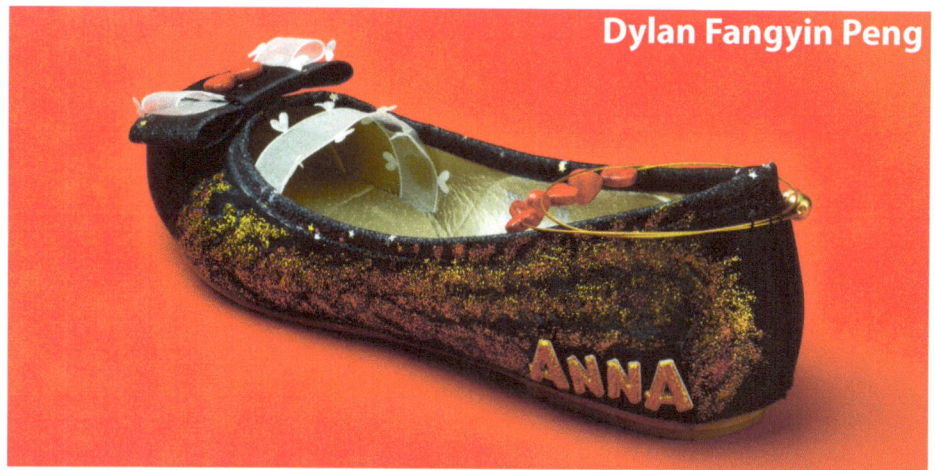

Dylan Fangyin Peng

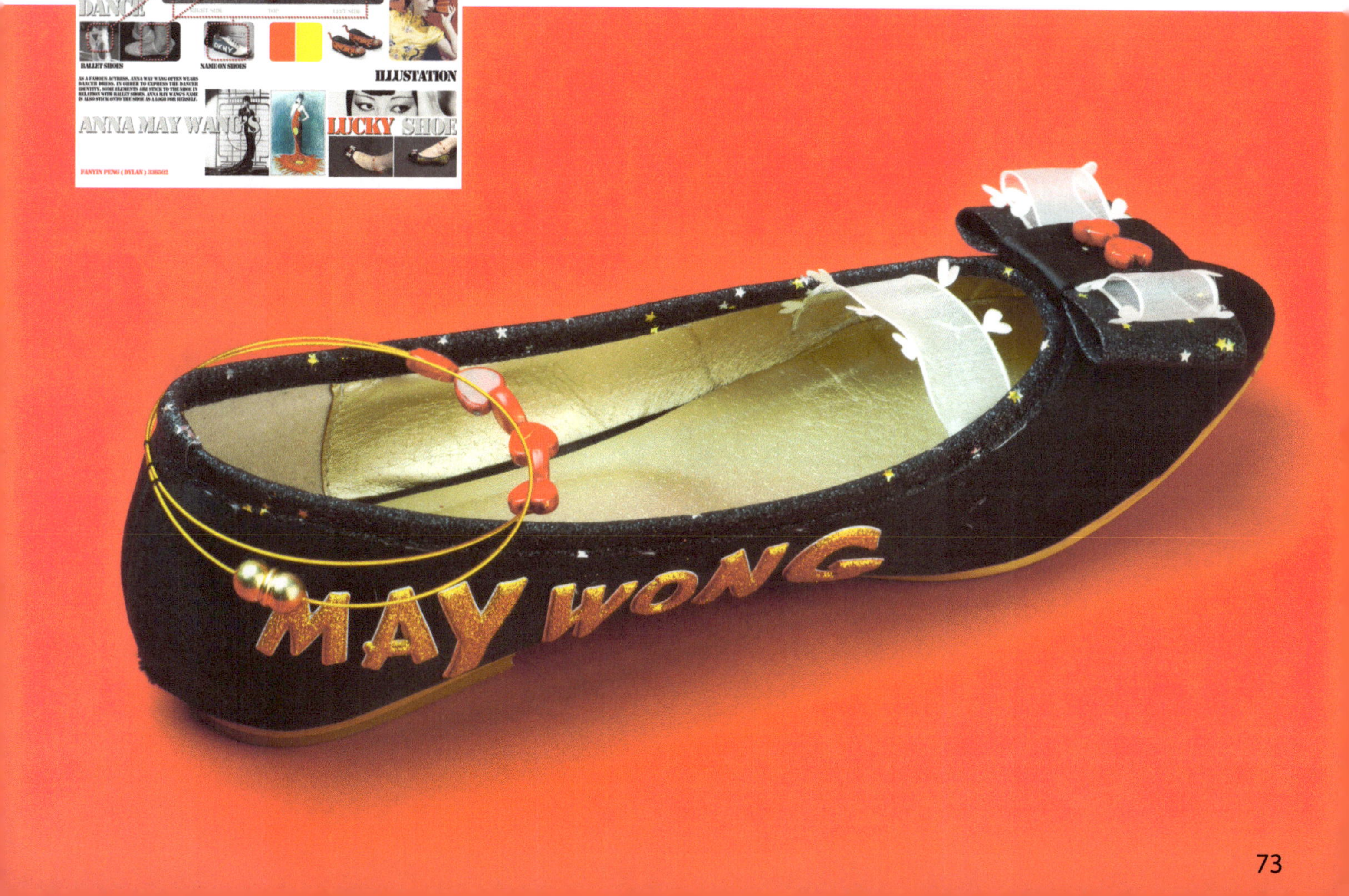

Callista Sie

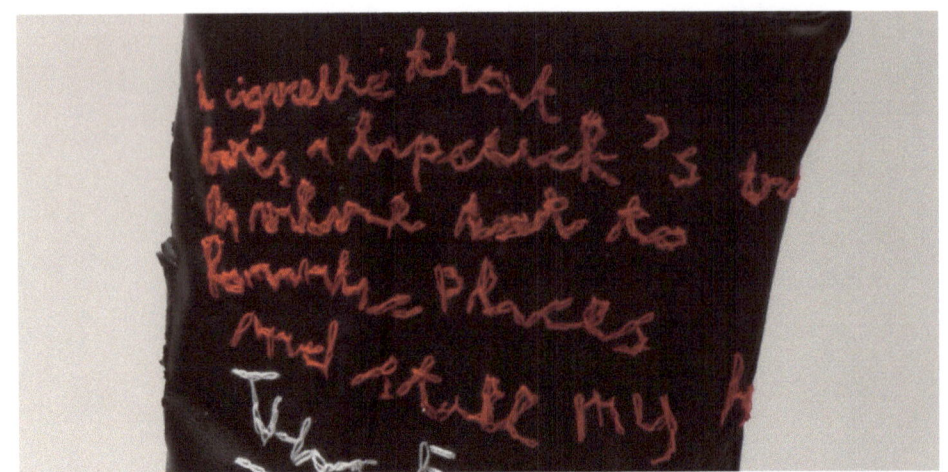

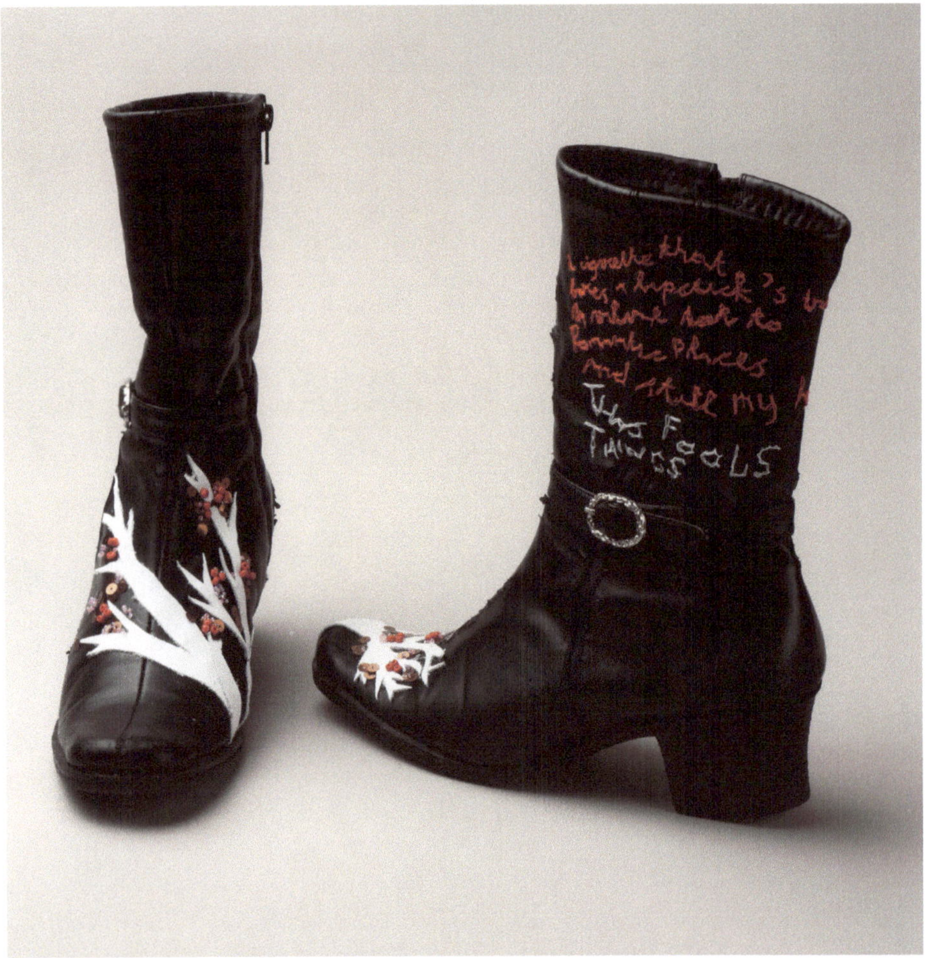

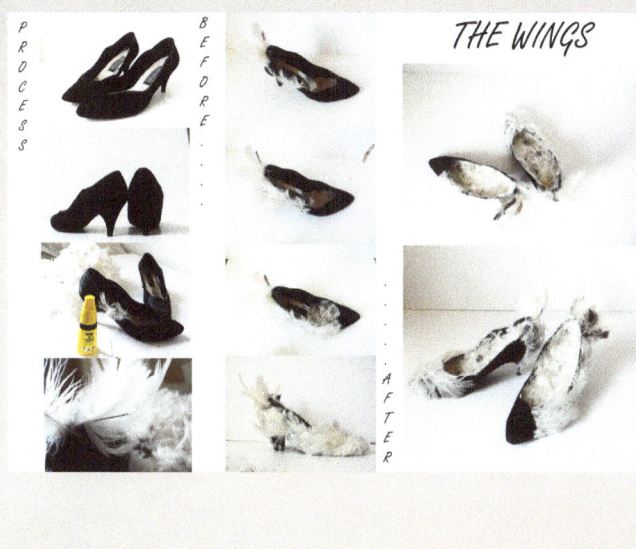

PROCESS

BEFORE....

....AFTER

THE WINGS

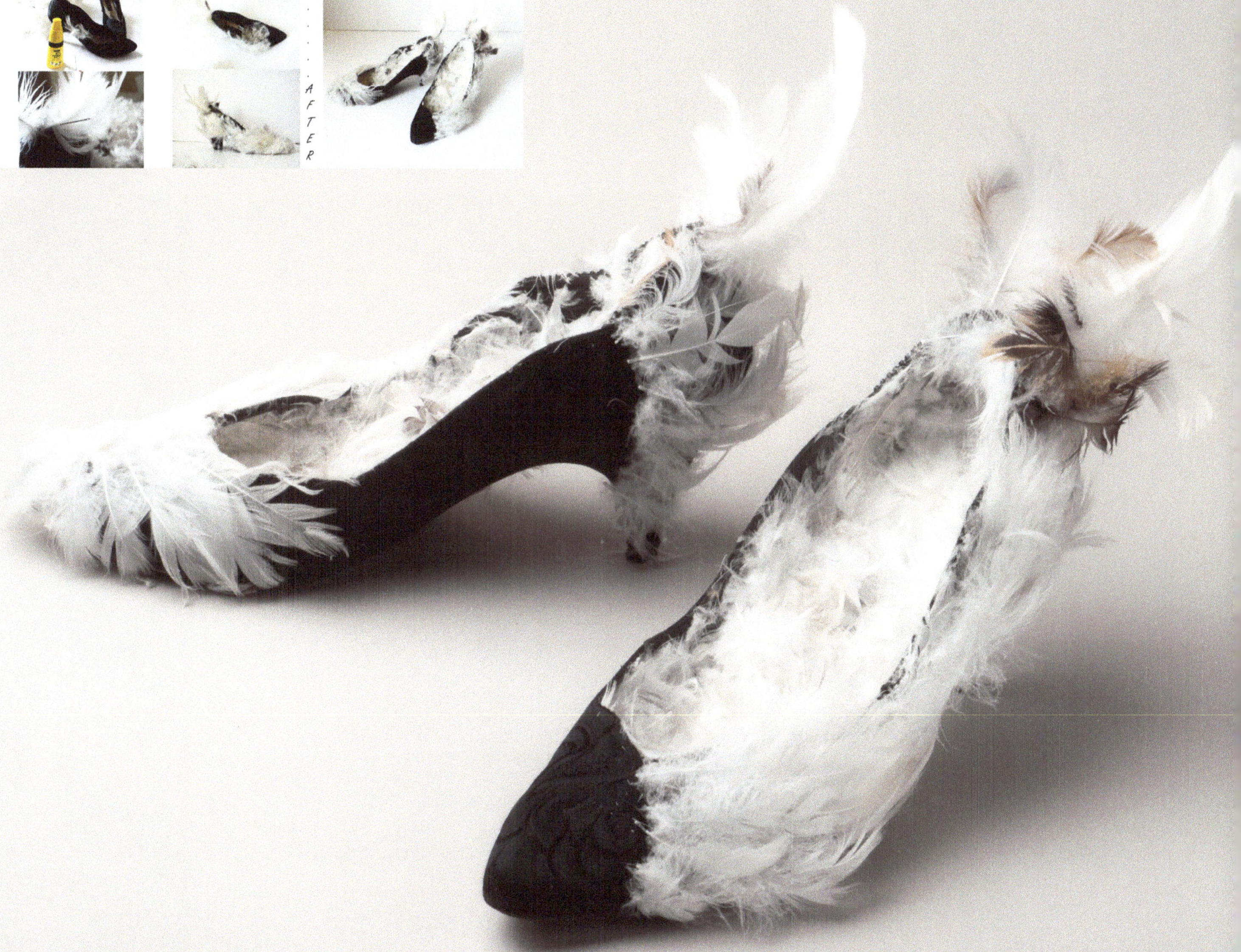

Amanda Pei-er Tan

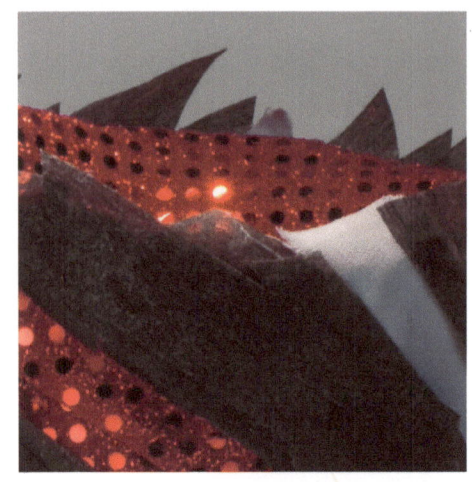

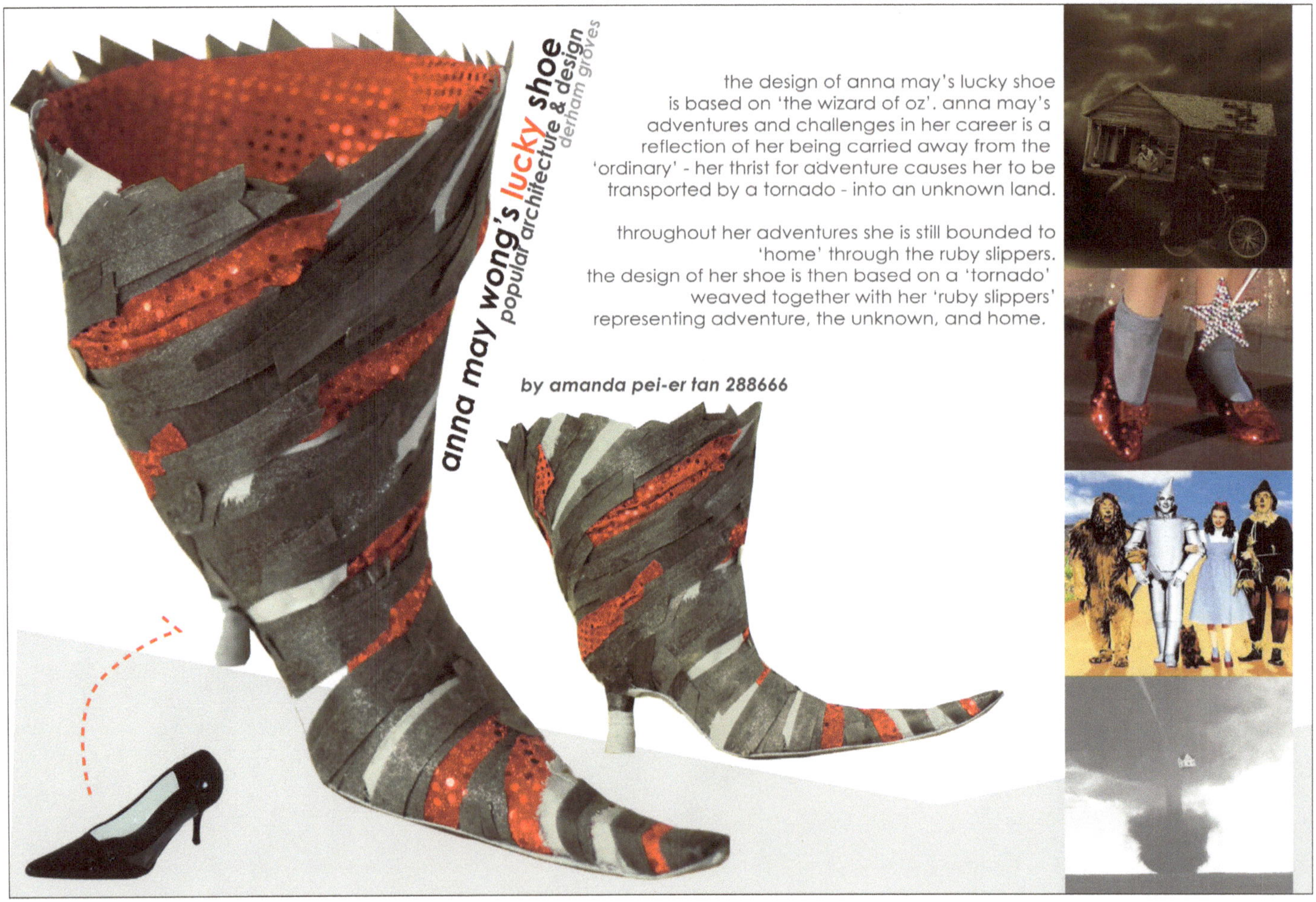

anna may wong's *lucky* **shoe**
popular architecture & design
denham groves

the design of anna may's lucky shoe
is based on 'the wizard of oz'. anna may's
adventures and challenges in her career is a
reflection of her being carried away from the
'ordinary' - her thrist for adventure causes her to be
transported by a tornado - into an unknown land.

throughout her adventures she is still bounded to
'home' through the ruby slippers.
the design of her shoe is then based on a 'tornado'
weaved together with her 'ruby slippers'
representing adventure, the unknown, and home.

by amanda pei-er tan 288666

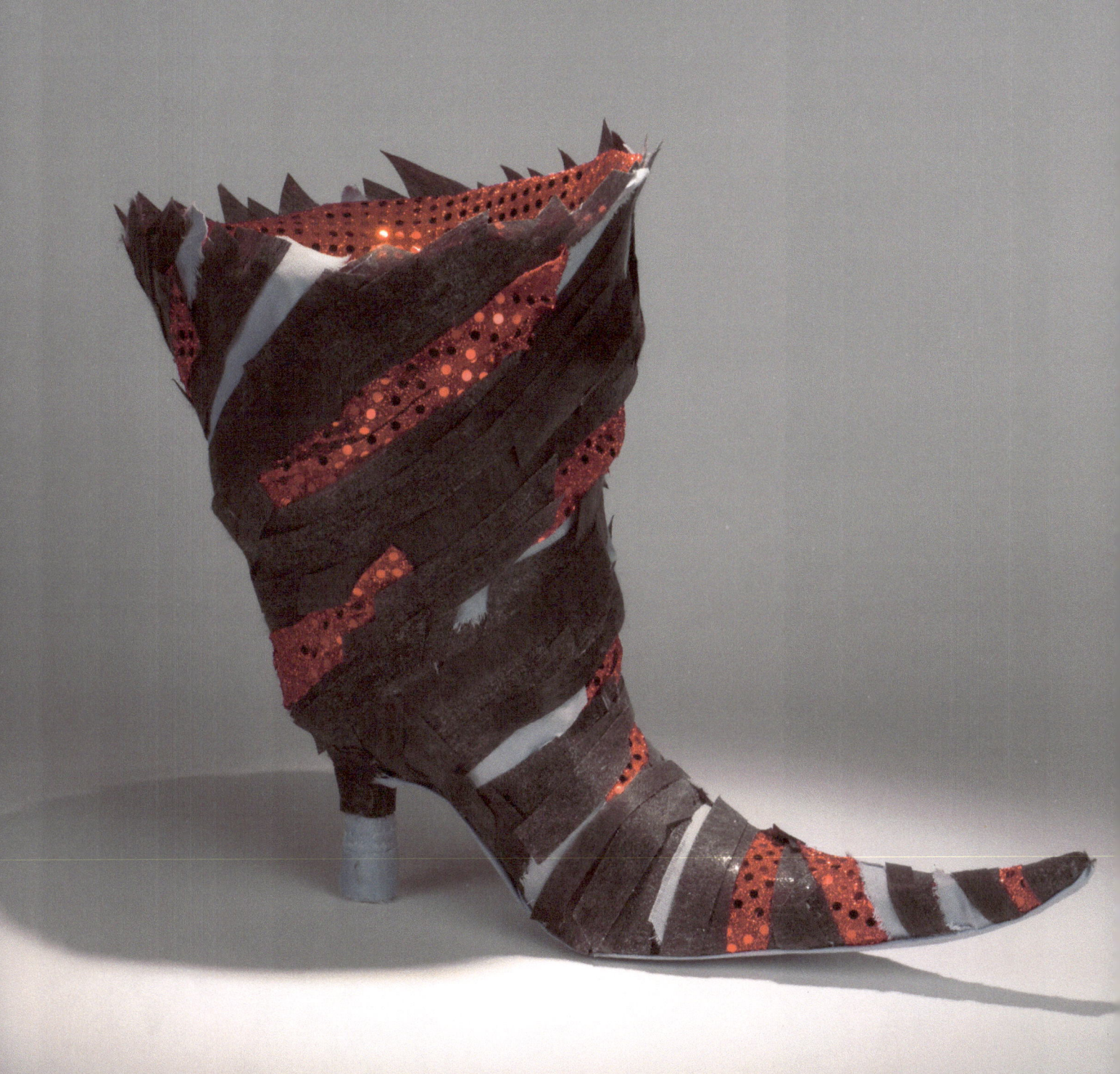

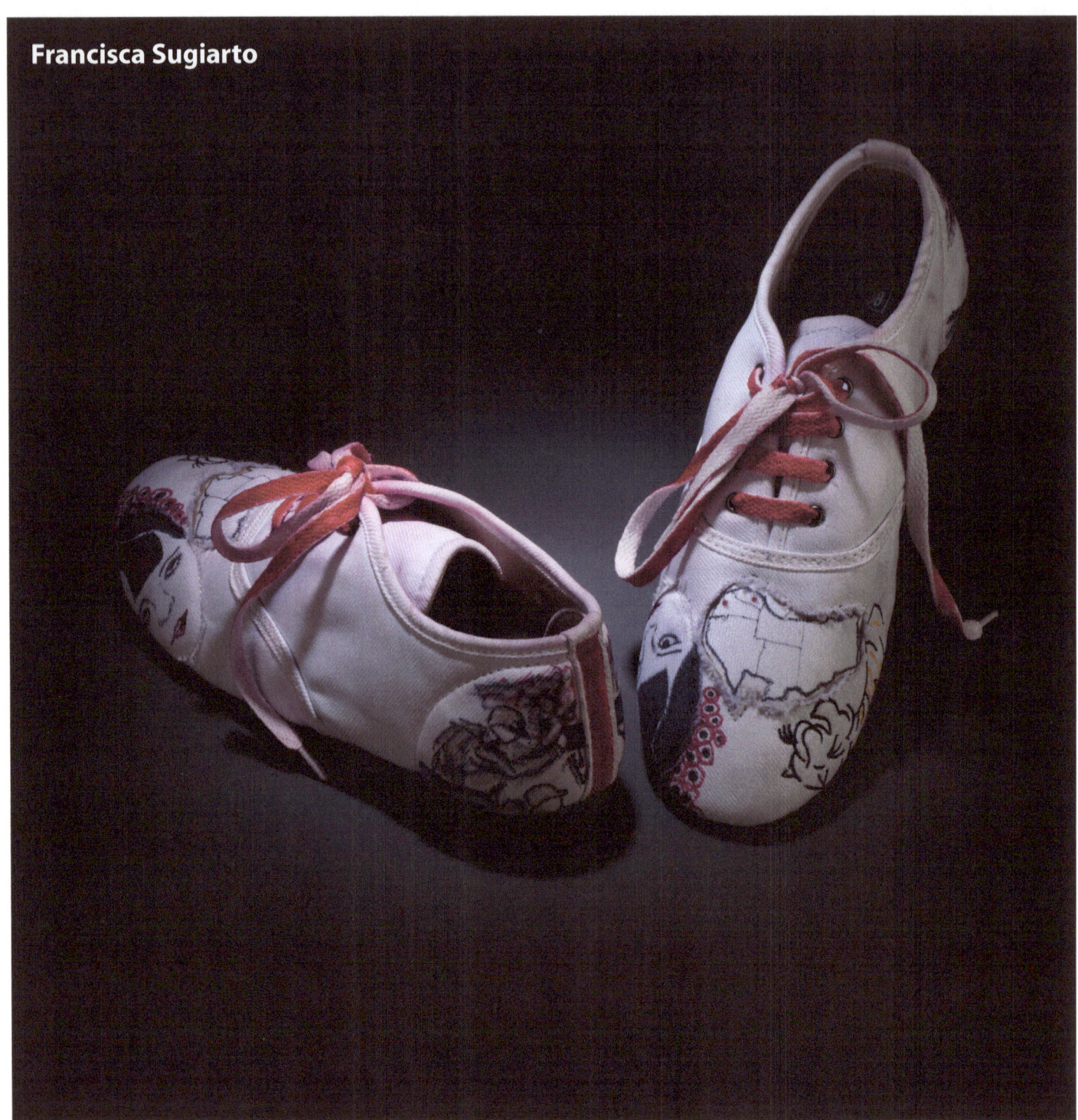

Francisca Sugiarto

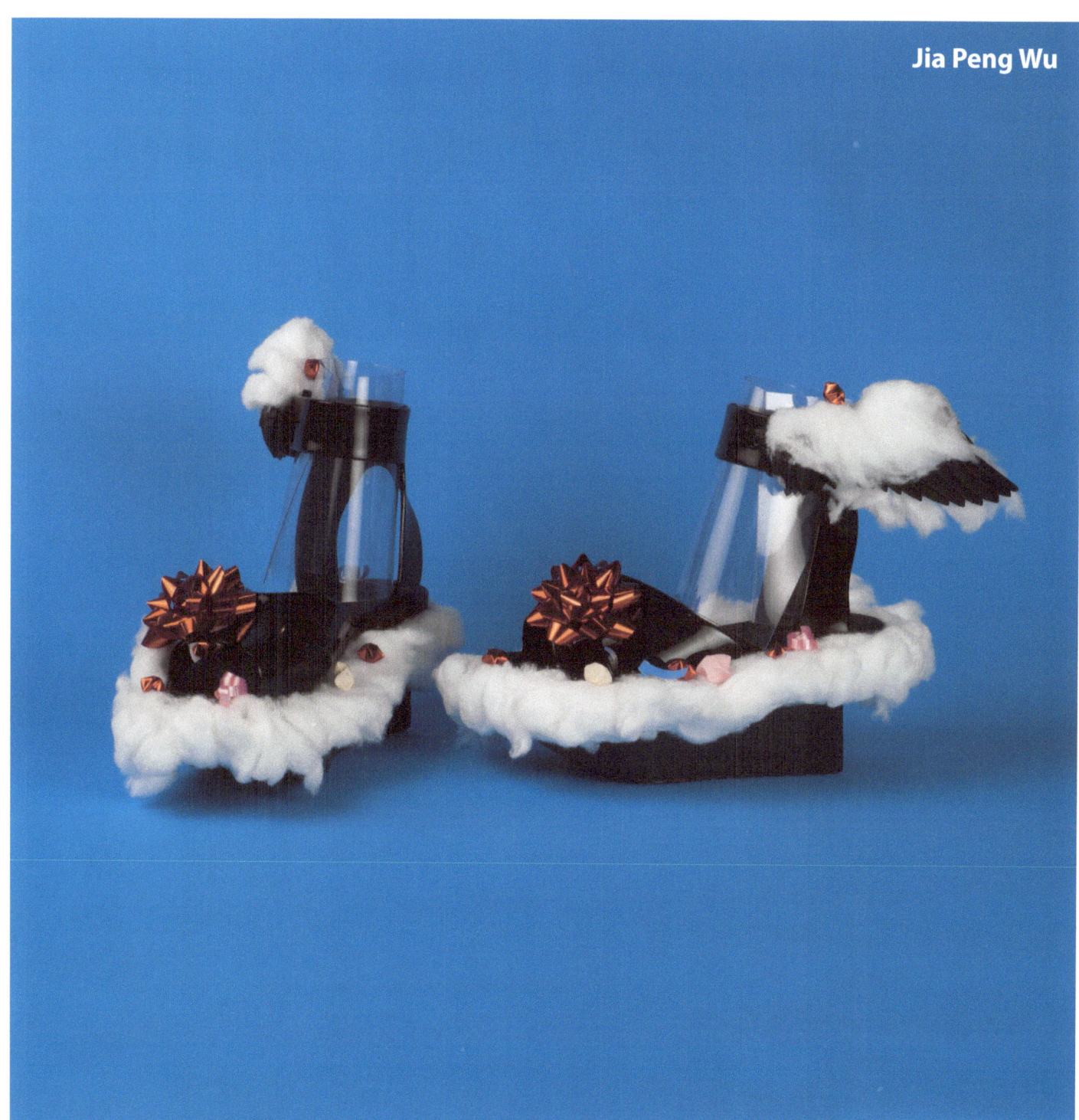

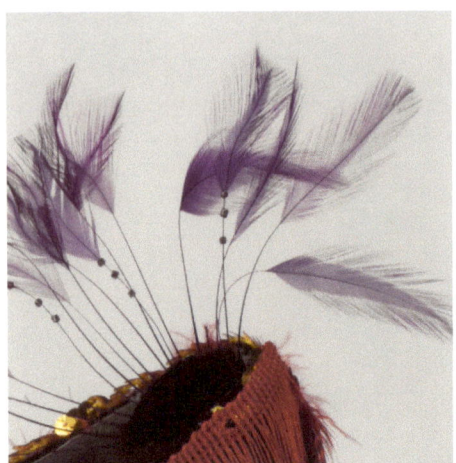
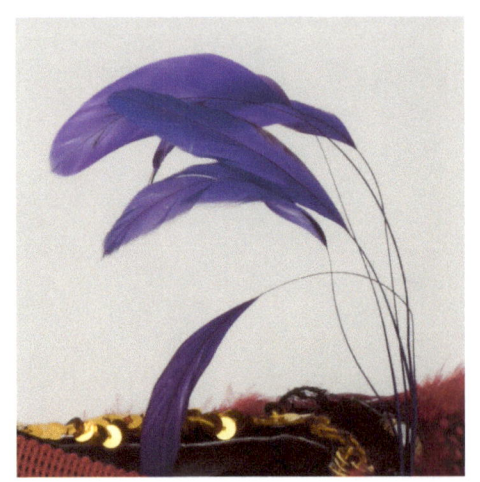

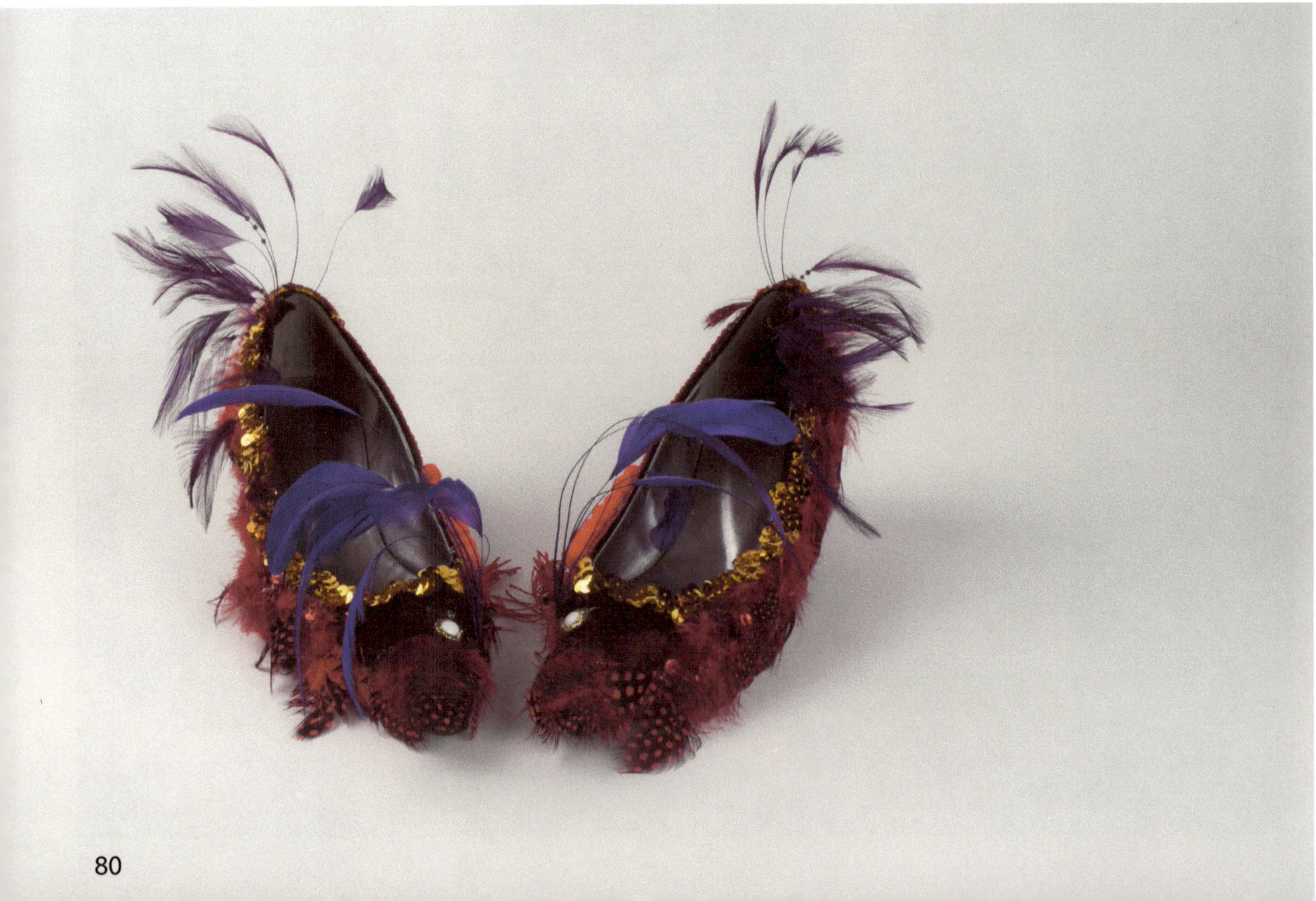

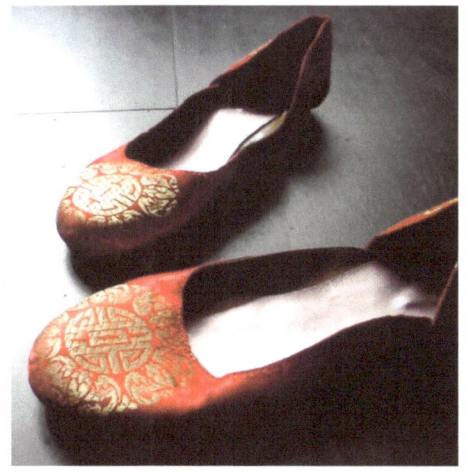

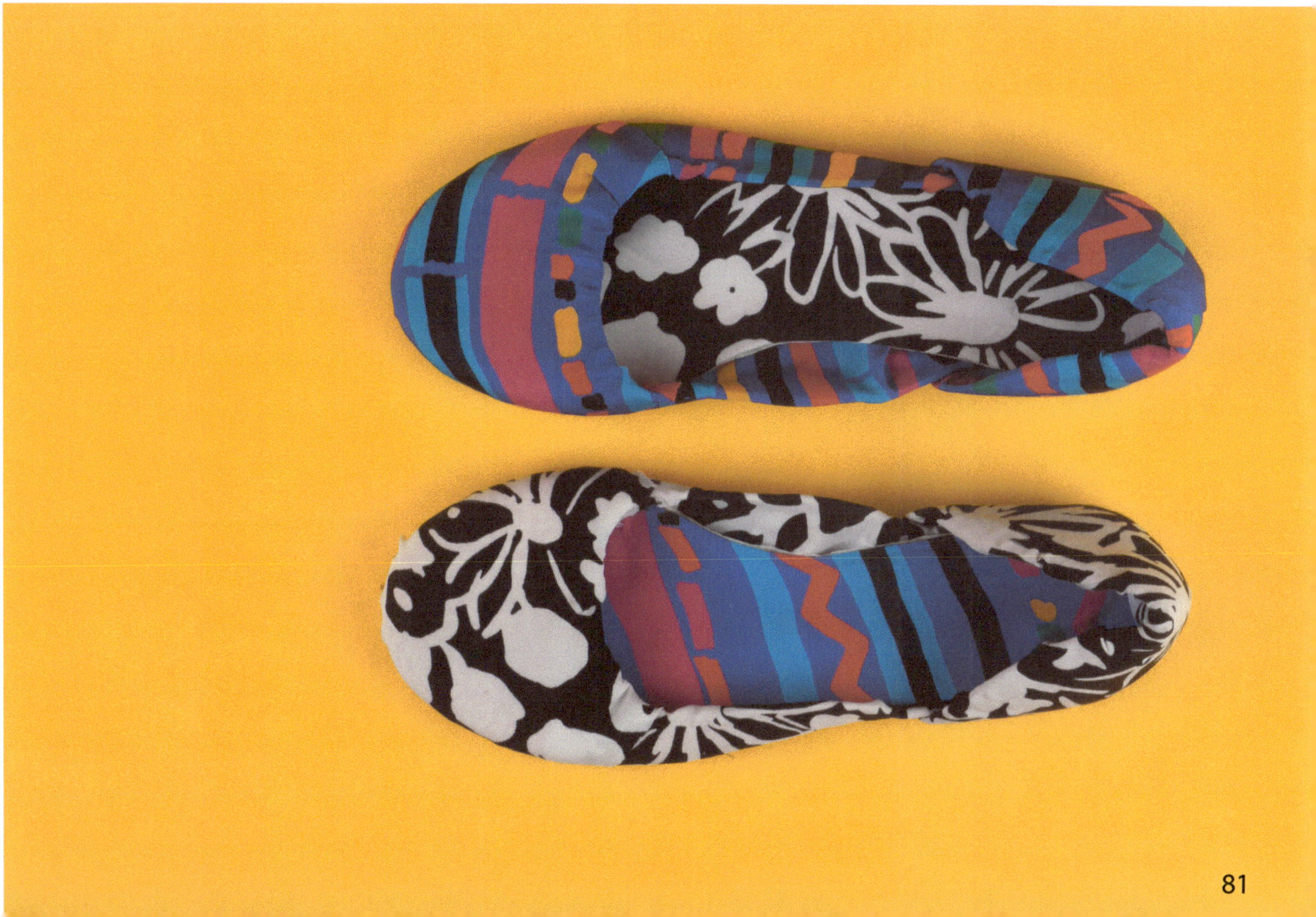

The Story Behind the shoe

Roos van Oss 395535

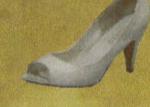

I attempted to design a shoe for Anna May Wong that gives a great deal of power from the inside. I began the design process with buying a second hand shoe which I thought captured the essence of a very feminine shoe. Elegant shape, high heal, simple form. I chose a white base, as the shoe can get more complex along the journey of dressing it.

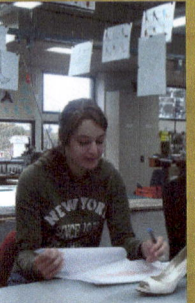
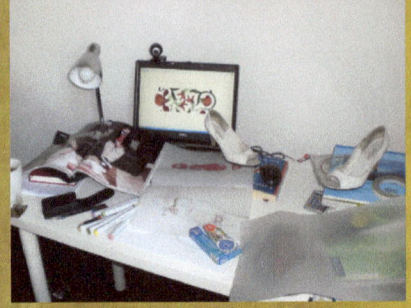
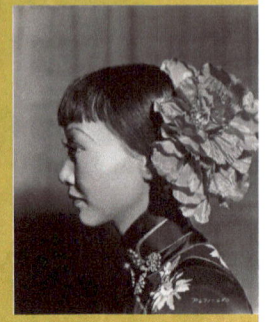

Armed with this shoe, I began sketching. I saw lots of opportunities to make to shoe more special.

As flowers have been important l n the Chinese I thought this was a good object to start working with. The lotus figures in a well -known adage -'even when the root is broken, the fibres do not break.' This has led to belief in the abiding quality of purity and divinity represented by the lotus. I used the lotus not only as decoration on top, but also the inside the shoe. This hidden pattern is only revealed a little bit near the toe. The textile comes from an old handbag, turned inside out.

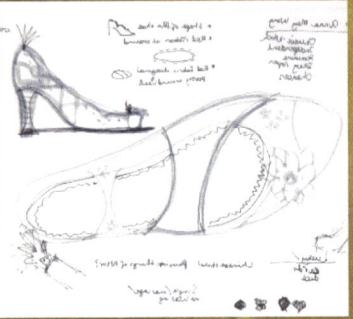
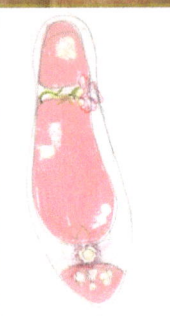
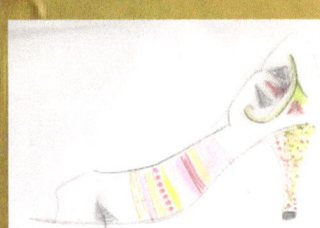

The small details, like the pearls on the edges, the inside out textile and the golden strap, make the shoe fit for Anna May Wong. She didn't have a 'normal' life. Complexity and change are keywords.

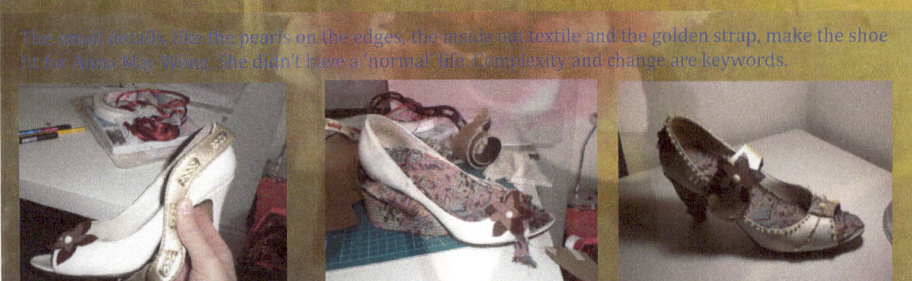

Francis Van Oss

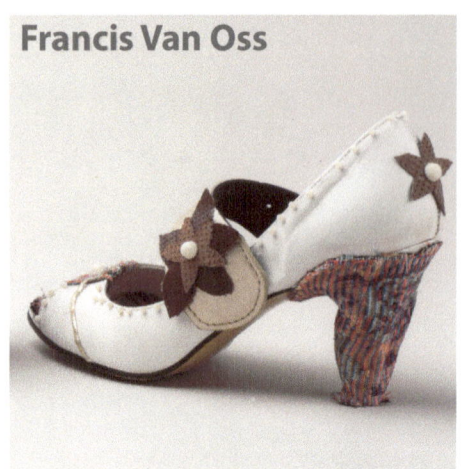
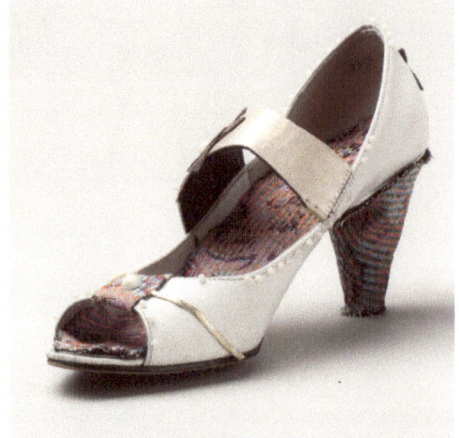
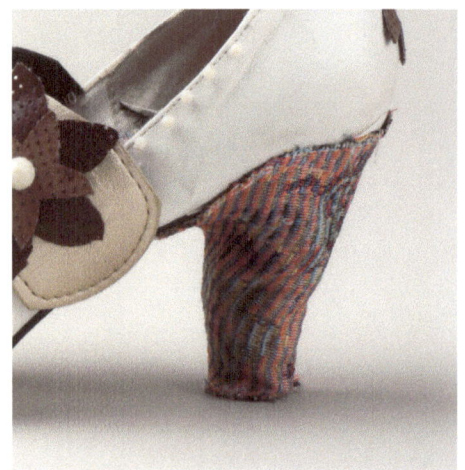

82

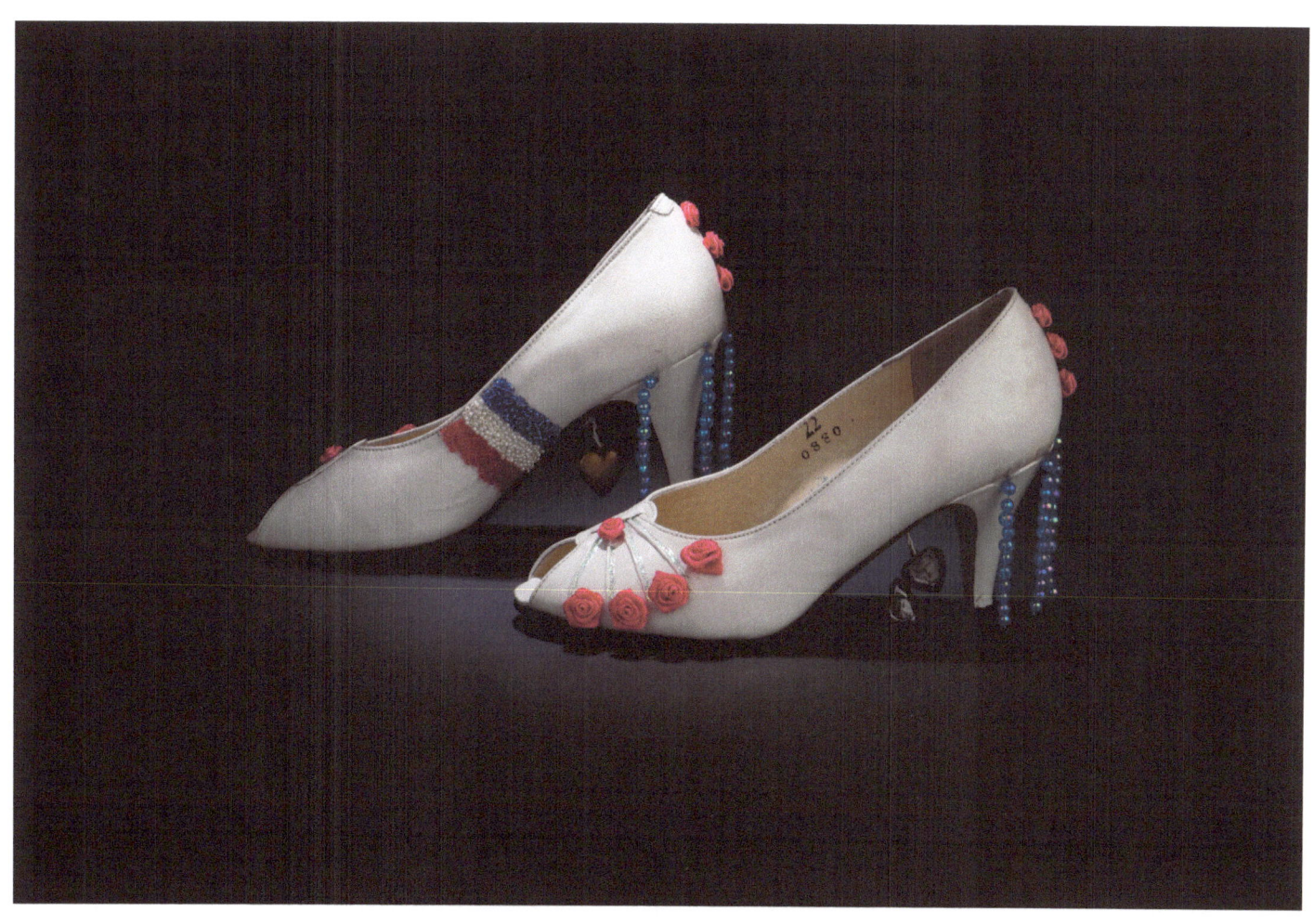

Alexandra Wall

Anna May Wong: a Chinese-American flower

Anna May strikes me as being akin to a flower of the orient: she is delicate, beautiful, strong and resilient. In designing a pair of shoes for her to wear, I drew inspiration from this idea and the recurring theme of flowers that seems to follow her. Her real name, Wong Liu Tsong, means "frosted yellow **willows**" in Chinese. She was born on **Flower** Street in Los Angeles. Her complexion has been described as "a **rose** blushing through old ivory." She has played many movie roles with flowers in her name: "Lotus Flower" in The Toll of the Sea, "A Flower of the Orient" in Old San Francisco, "Rose Li" in Drifting, and "Lotus Blossom" in Shame. She enjoyed wearing flowers in her hair and was often photographed with them (right).

Flowers have an honored position in Chinese culture, and they often appear in paintings and prints alongside birds perched on branches (below). I have replicated this in a fine gold floral print on the shoes; sitting underneath the foot to indicate that Anna May's Chinese heritage can be masked and hidden from view, but it is always with her. Pearls, crystals and ribbons embellish the shoes to appeal to her love of high fashion and elegance.

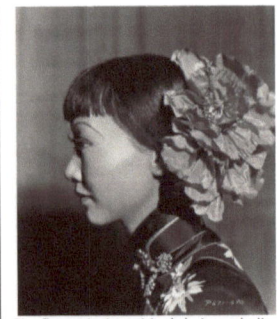

The flower in Anna May's hair symbolises prosperity, happiness and peace.

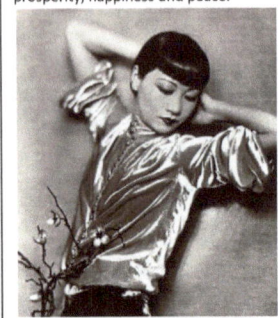

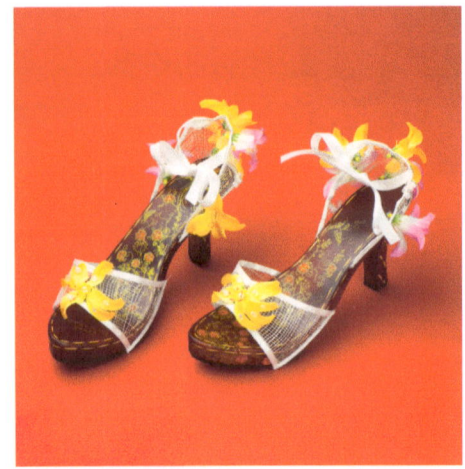

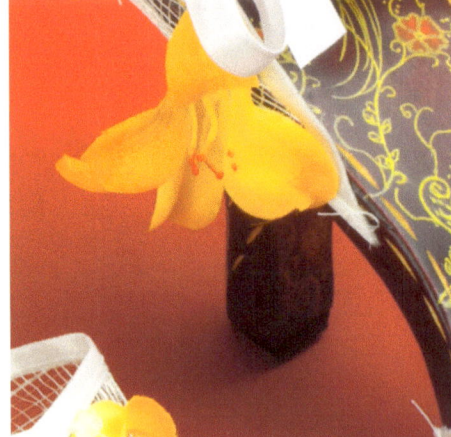

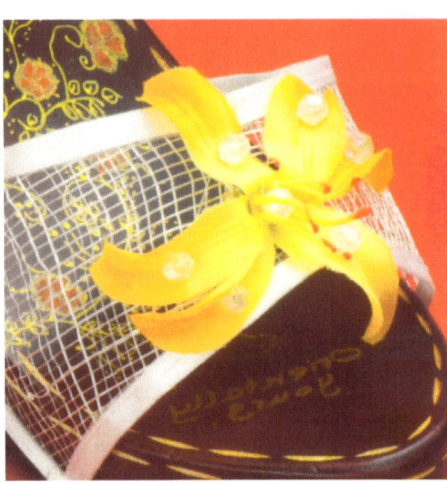

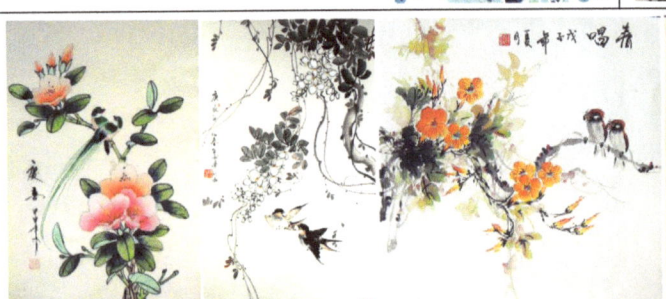

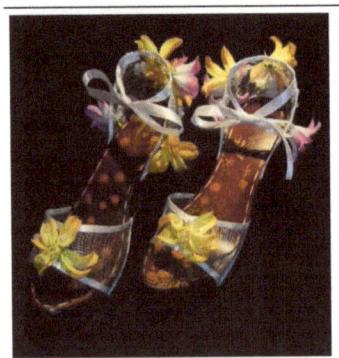

Shoes for Anna May Wong

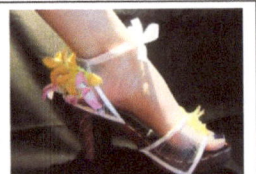

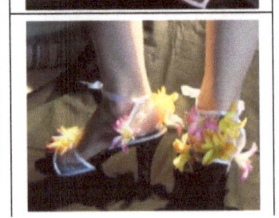

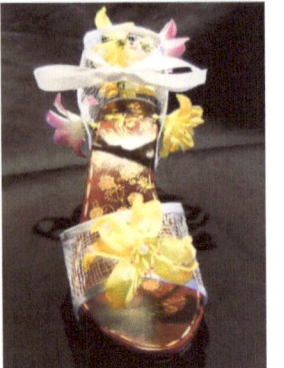

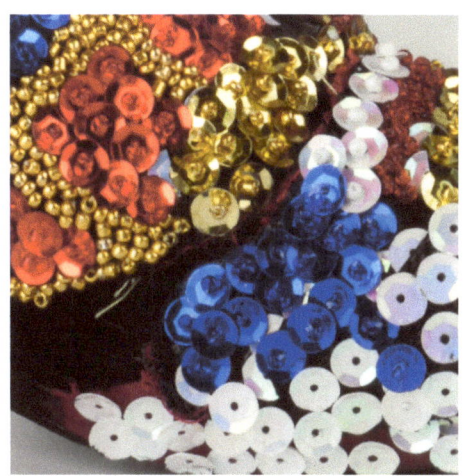 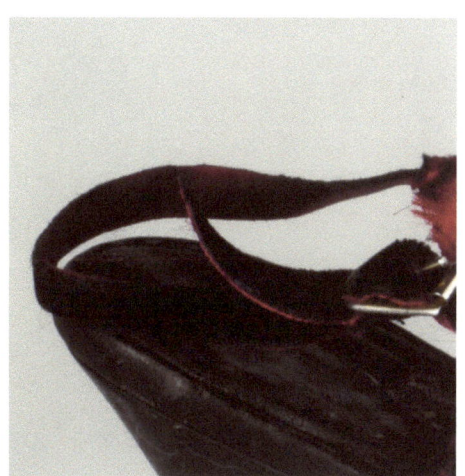

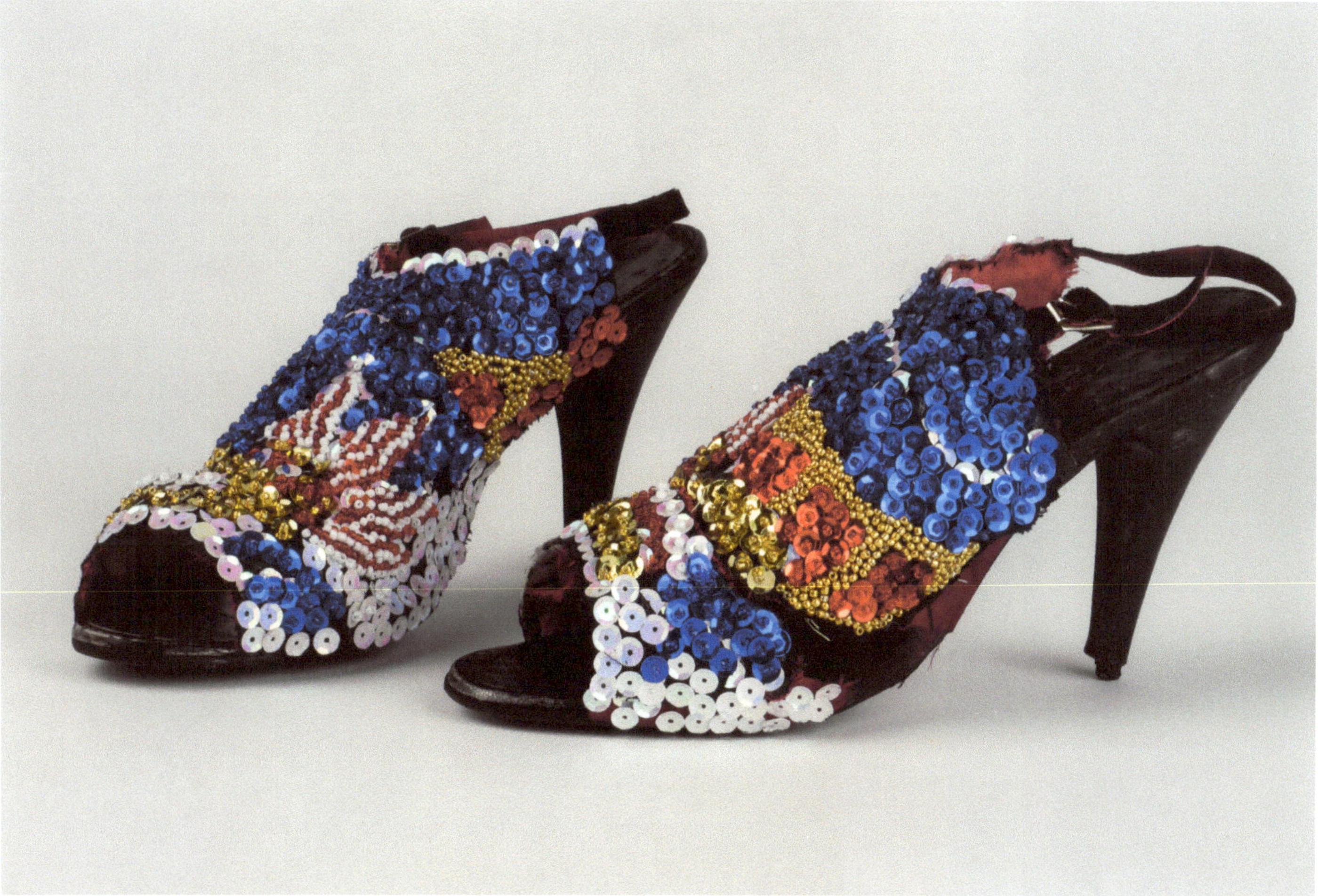

Enjie Wu

Anna May Wong (January 3, 1905 – February 2, 1961) was the first Chinese American movie star.
I considered four elements when designing shoes for her:
Flat shoes, Red color, butterfly, and bang.

There is a tradition in China that mom will make a pair of cotton flat shoes for her daughter before her marriage. And this tradition is believed to bring the young girl whole-life luckiness. So I chose flat shoes at the first step of design.

Red means lucky in China, people use red decorations during wedding, birthday, or other important occasions. In order to make a pair of lucky shoes specially for AMW, I chose red lace, red feather and red ribbon to decorate the shoes.

At the age of 17 she played her first leading role, in the movie The Toll of the Sea. The story was based loosely on Madama Butterfly. So I used red fake butterflies on the shoes to represent her start of "extraordinarily fine" acting life.

AMW was set as a typical Chinese Doll with straight hair bang and the scarlet lips. The ribbon bunches on the front of the shoes represent AMW's bang. And these feather and lace symbolize her first impression to the public—gaudery and heavy makeup.

DESIGNER:
ENJIE WU

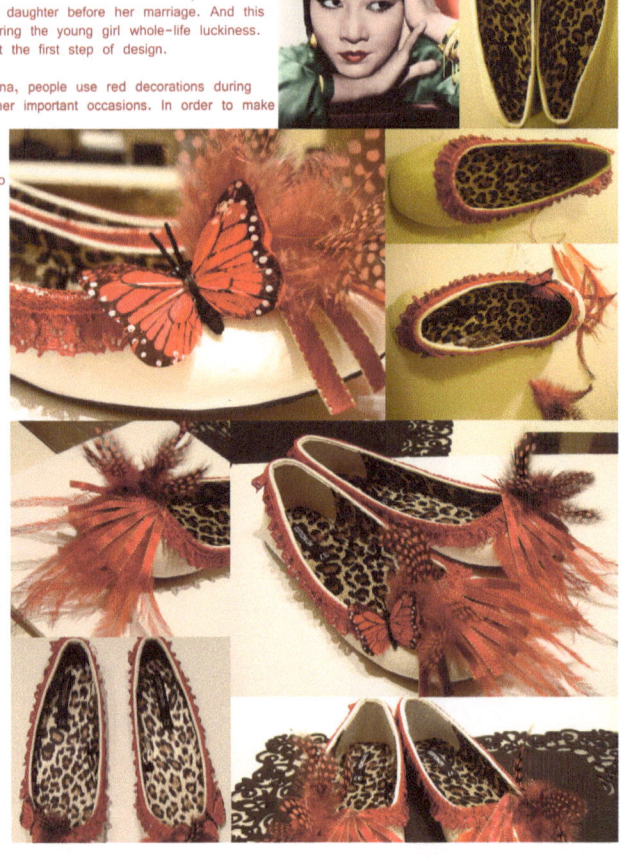

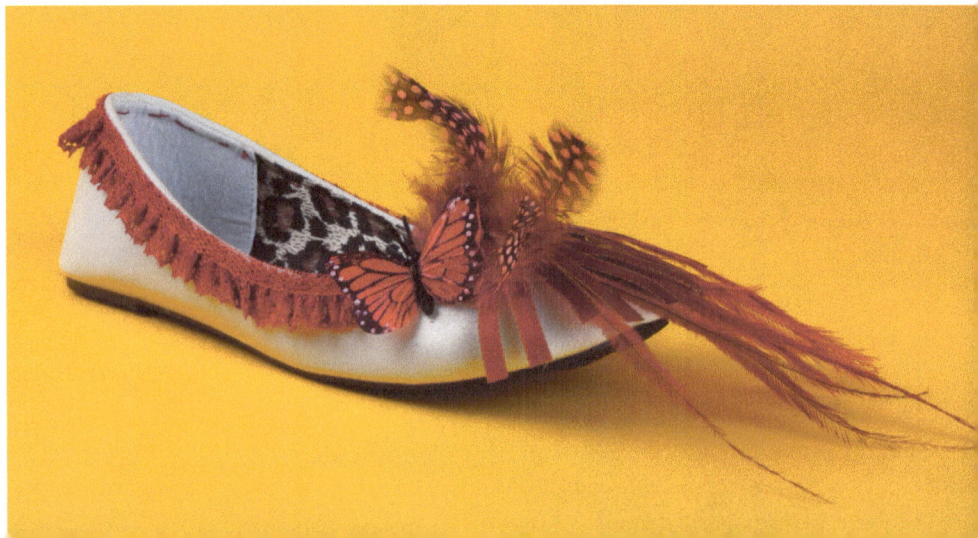

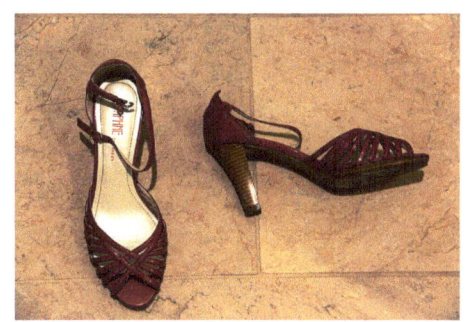

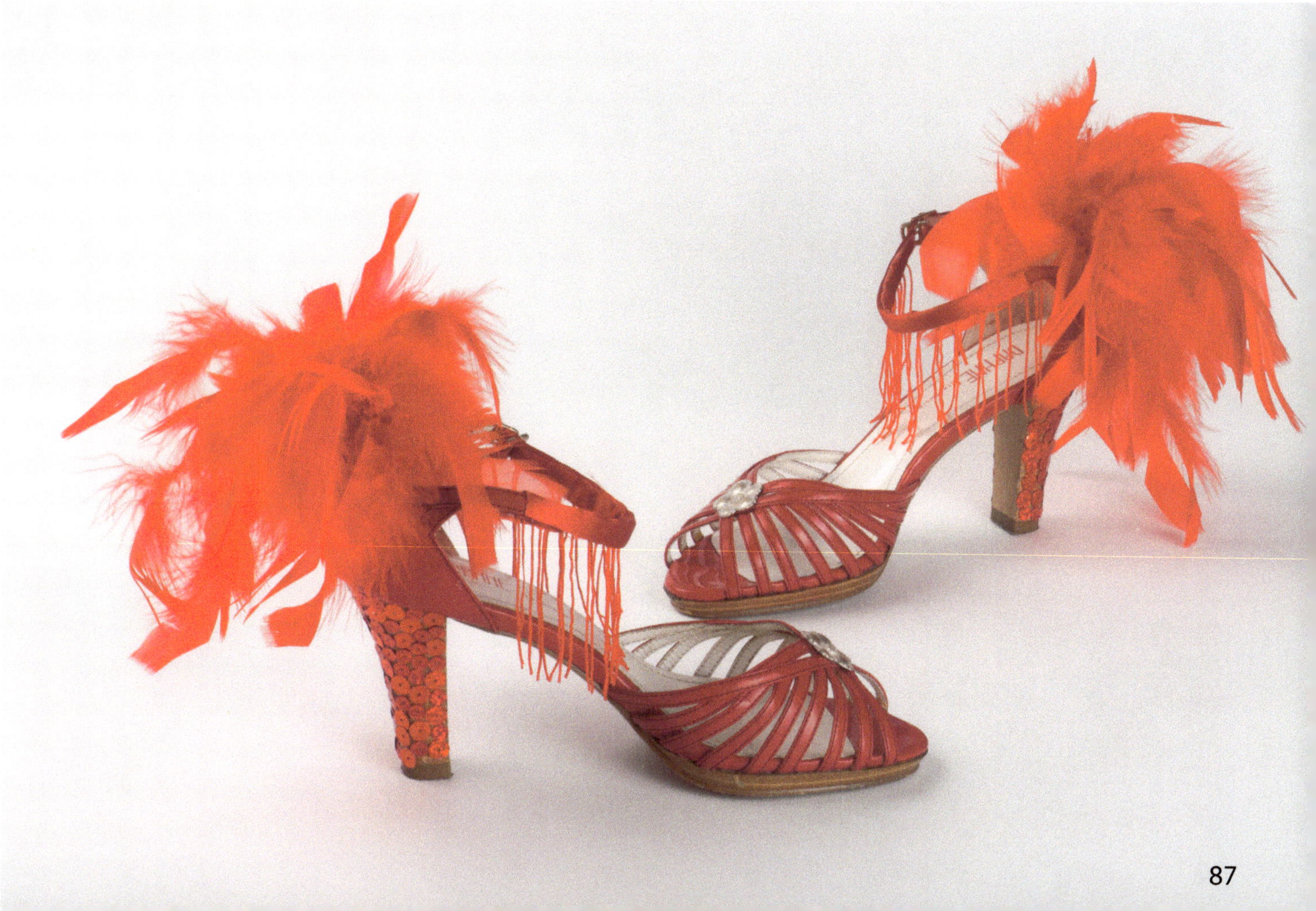

Si Xiong

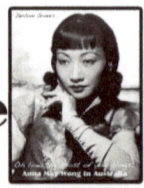

Anna May Wong's Needle shoes

Shoes must be worn on our own feet to see if they are suitable for oneself.

As a Chinese, I believe Anna May Wong is an American, because, apart from her oriental facial features, everything else is Western. She is the typical 'Banana Person', having an external "Yellow" skin and internal "White" heart. Even though she was highly regarded in America's film industry, hardly anyone in China knew about her.

However, the American's regarded her as Chinese, since she played many roles as an Asian figure, wearing traditional Chinese clothing. Yet, in her real life, she was completely westernised. Thus, this has shaped the intense contrast between her outer 'idolised' lifestyle and inner loneliness.

On one hand, because she was as a gifted person who also worked hard, this enabled her to be greatly successful in the film industry, even being nominated for an Oscar. On the other hand, she was subject to racial abuse. On the job, no matter how hard she worked, she was not accepted in mainstream western society. This was the social backdrop that that time, hence fashioned Anna May Wong's tragic life.

Shoes must be worn on our own feet to see if they are suitable for oneself.

The beautiful and colourful exterior is for others to see, what is most important is if the shoe is suitable for the feet inside.

Just like this pair of shoes, the glittering exterior has mesmerised everyone who has viewed it. However, what lies within is a reality that no one can see, but only felt by the person wearing it. There are numerous pins inserted into the shoe, stinging and tearing at the flesh, hurting the inner self. This is a true manifestation of Anna May Wong's life.

Popular Architecture and Design
Si Xiong 30/922

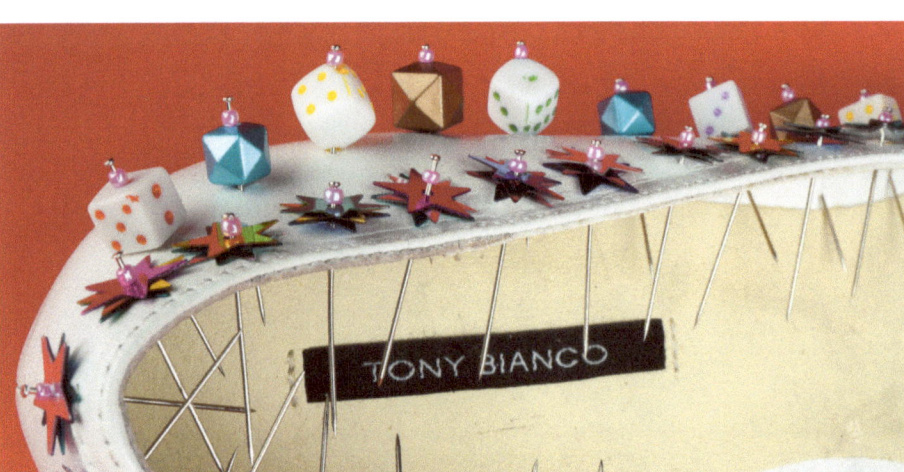

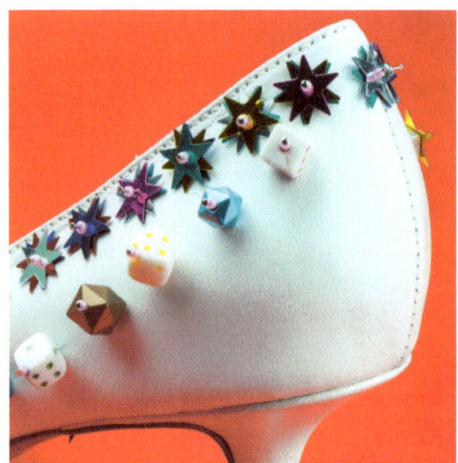

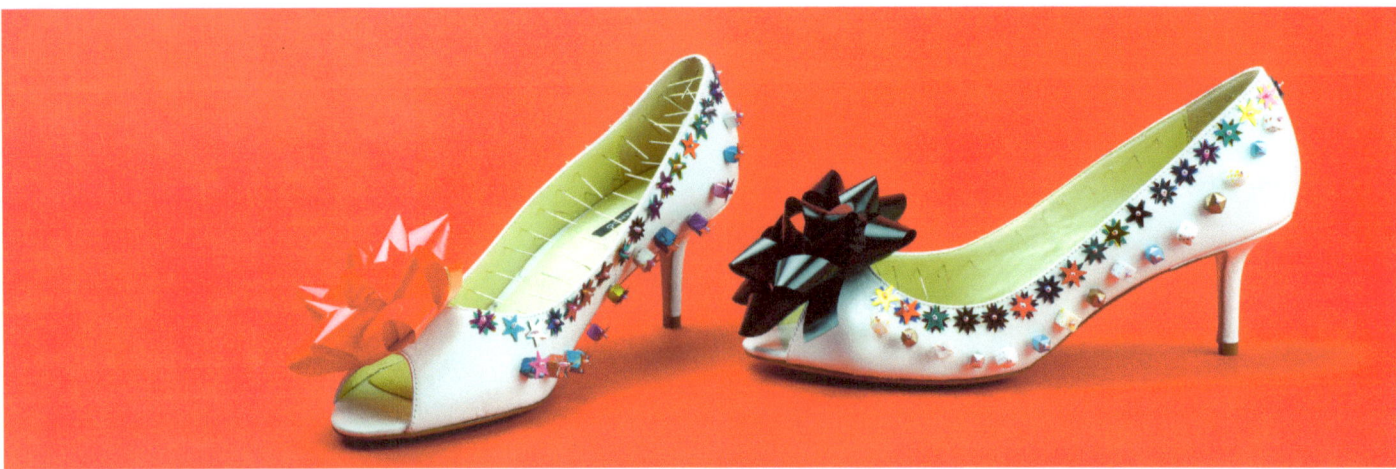

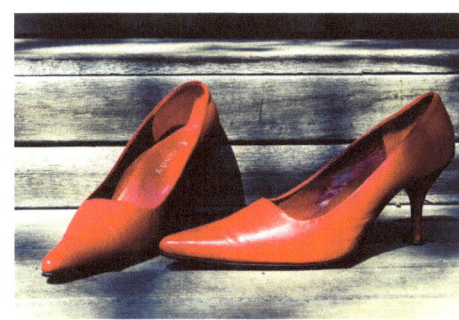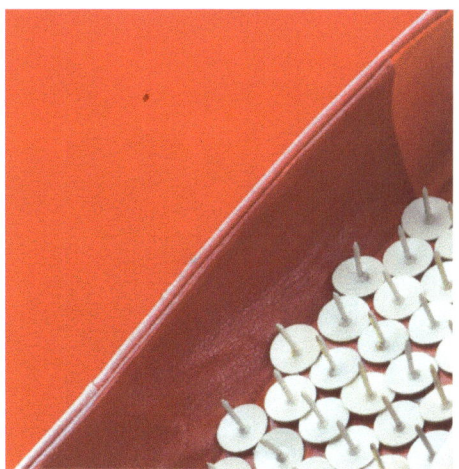

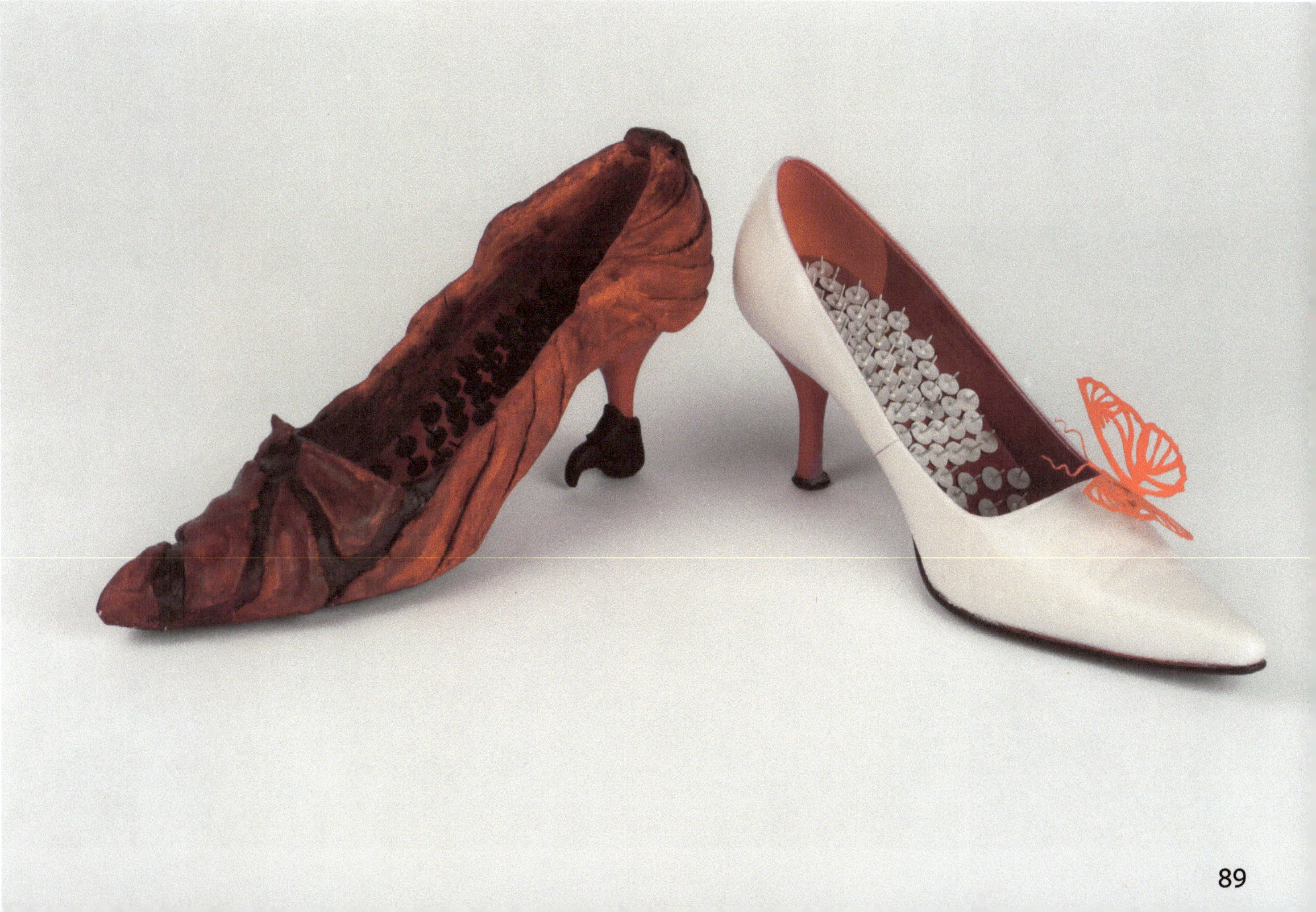

Nur Zafira Zainal Abidin

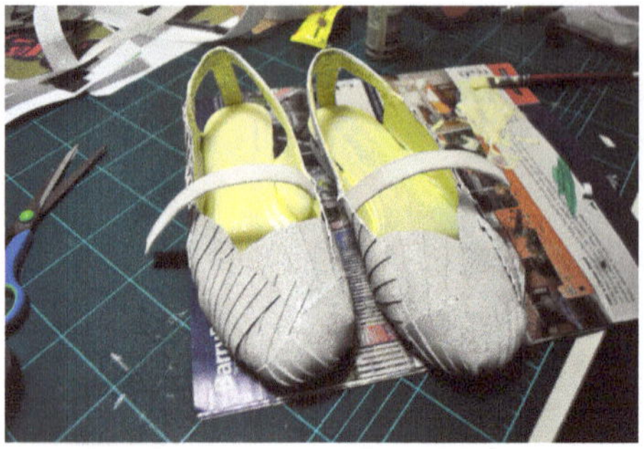

Paper Fan Mary Janes

The Mary Jane shoe was the shoe style of the 1920s and 30s. Although, in the 1930s shoes began to look heavier, but the toes was less pointed and more rounded. The Mary Jane shoe is chosen as it represents those time of when Anna May Wong was at her peak of becoming a wonderful actress. This shoe design is also inspired by the short movie by Metro-Goldwyn-Moyer called "Hollywood Party" in Technicolor, where Anna May Wong acting was presenting different type of Chinese gowns. She first came in with a brilliant Peking blue Chinese gown and also a Paper fan in her hand. She has always looked ravish in those shiny Chinese gowns. And so, from the pose she struts with the sprung open paper fan, came the idea of having the shoe with embossed pattern of a paper fan and a sexy look for the shoe. This shoe design will accentuate more when Anna May Wong wears her Chinese gowns to show off the best of her roots. Thus, the shoe is designed from the combination of the American style shoe, Mary Janes with the paper fan patterns of the Chinese. The colour chosen for the shoe is a shimmering Green to represent the Jade stone, as it is a special stone to the Chinese,

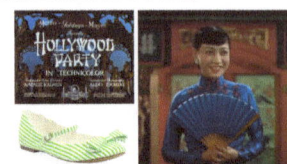

The Process :

Before   After

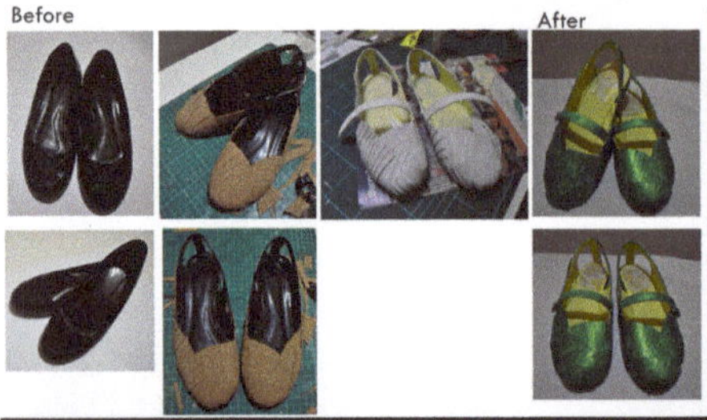

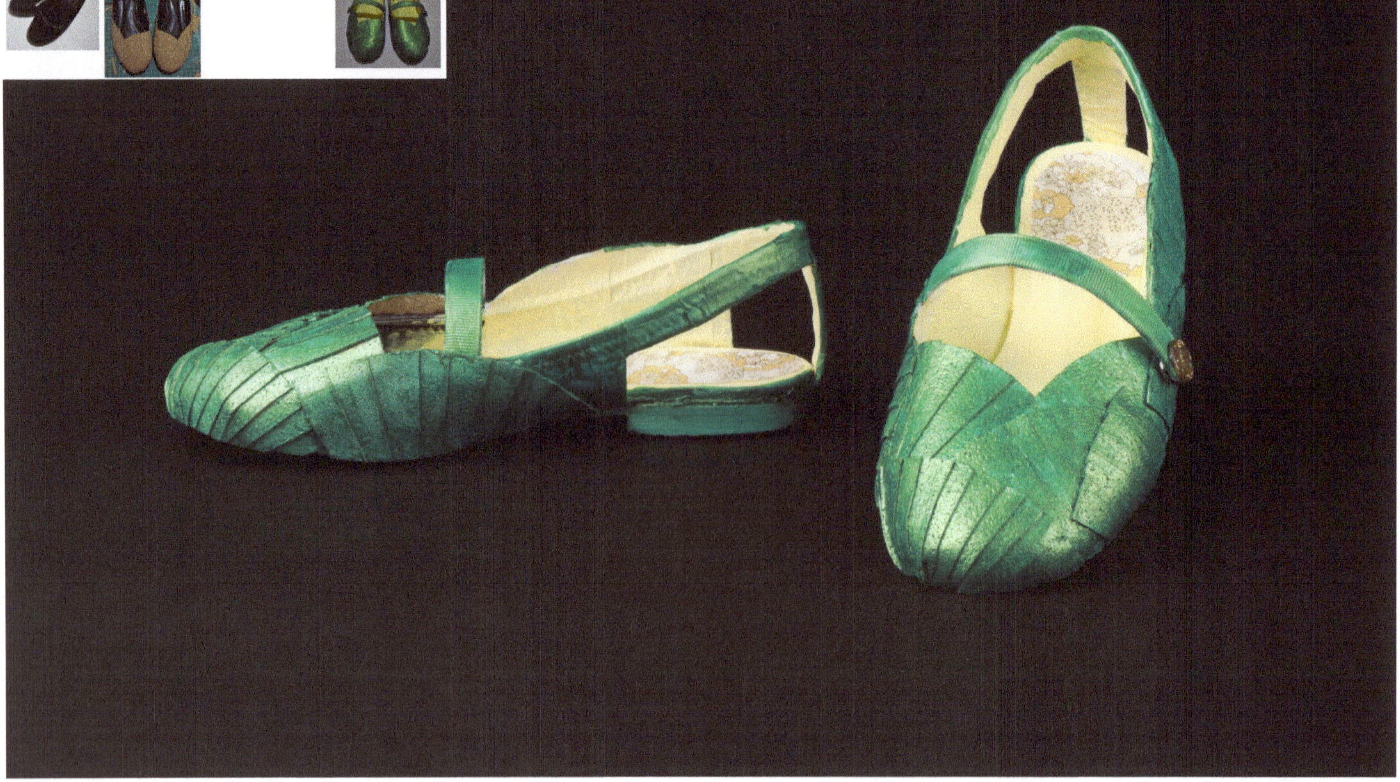

90

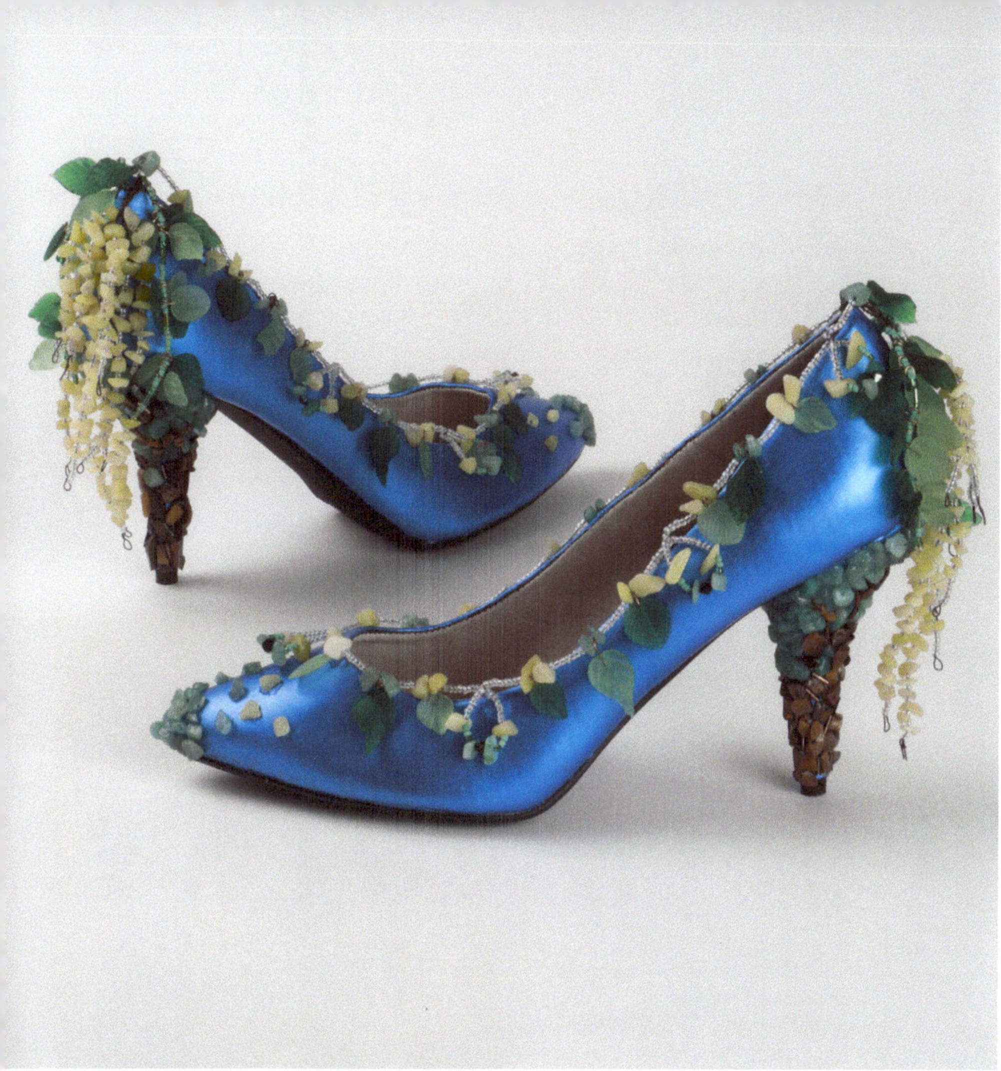

Audrey Zerafa

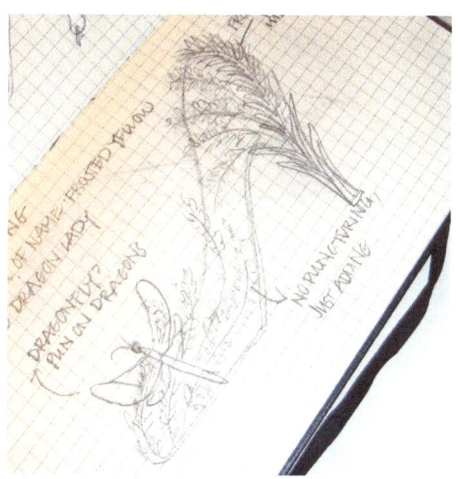

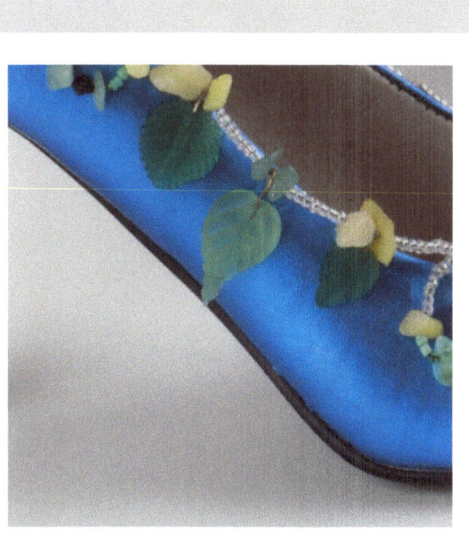

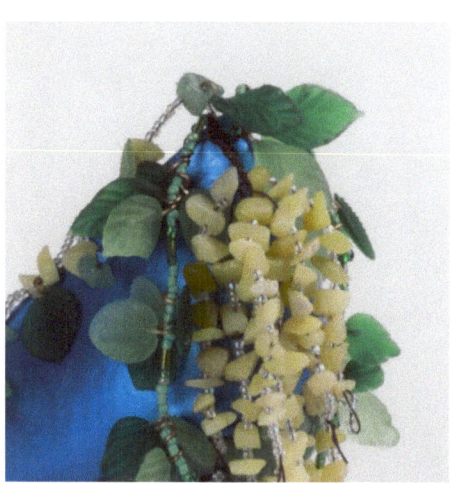

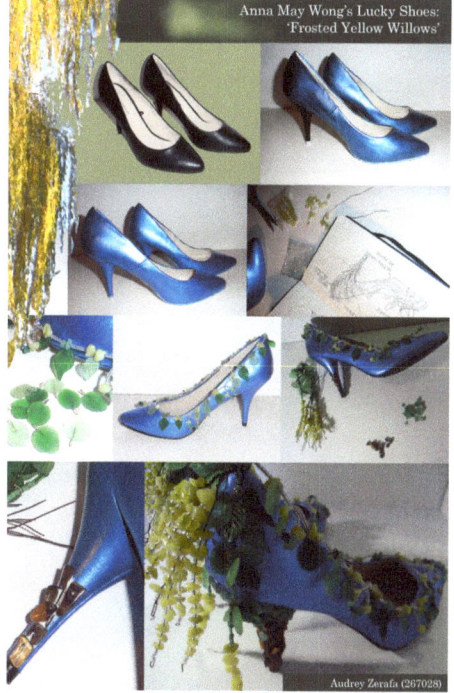

Anna May Wong's Lucky Shoes:
'Frosted Yellow Willows'

Audrey Zerafa (267028)

Bo Zhang

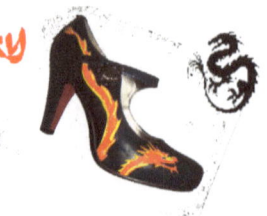

ANNA MAY WONG'S *Lucky*
Popular Architecture, Art and Design
Bo Zhang (352419)

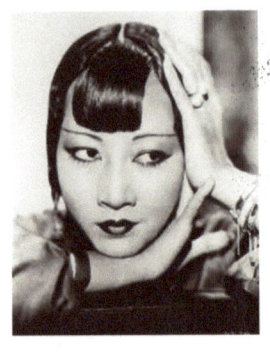

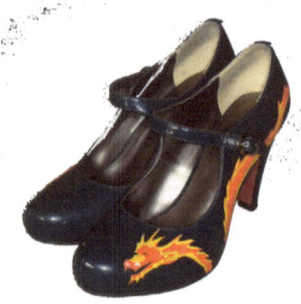

ANNA MAY WONG (JANUARY 3, 1905 – FEBRUARY 2, 1961) WAS AN AMERICAN ACTRESS, THE FIRST CHINESE AMERICAN MOVIE STAR, AND THE FIRST ASIAN AMERICAN TO BECOME AN INTERNATIONAL STAR. HER LONG AND VARIED CAREER SPANNED BOTH SILENT AND SOUND FILM, TELEVISION, STAGE, AND RADIO.

BORN NEAR THE CHINATOWN NEIGHBORHOOD OF LOS ANGELES TO SECOND-GENERATION CHINESE-AMERICAN PARENTS, WONG BECAME INFATUATED WITH THE MOVIES AND BEGAN ACTING IN FILMS AT AN EARLY AGE. DURING THE SILENT FILM ERA, SHE ACTED IN THE TOLL OF THE SEA (1922), ONE OF THE FIRST MOVIES MADE IN COLOR AND DOUGLAS FAIRBANKS' THE THIEF OF BAGDAD (1924). WONG BECAME A FASHION ICON, AND BY 1924 HAD ACHIEVED INTERNATIONAL STARDOM.

MY IDEA ABOUT THSI PAIR OF LUCKY SHOES CAME FROM THE REPRESENTATION OF CHINESE, DRAGON. SINCE ANNA MAY WONG IS A CHINESE ACTRESS, SHE IS ALSO BLESSED BY THIS CHINESE TRADITIONAL ELEMENT.

DRAGON, IS THE HIGHEST GROLRY SYMBOL OF CHINA, IN THE PAST TIME, ONLY IMPERIAL FAMILY MEMEBERS CAN WEAR CLOTH OR SHOES WITH DRAGON. SO WE CAN SEE HOW LUCKY IT MEANS TO CHINESE PEOPLE.

I USED TO THINK ABOUT PHOENIX AS WELL, SINCE IT REPRESENT FEMALE AS IMPORTANT AS DRAGON TO MALE. BUT,THEN I CHANGE MY IDEA BECAUSE I GOT INSPIRATION FROM ONE OF HER FILM POSTER WHICH HAS A DRAGON ON IT. SO IT IS MORE CORRELATIVE WITH ANNA MAY WONG.

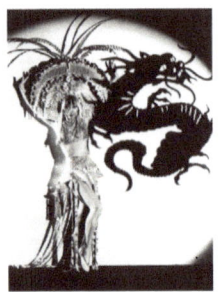

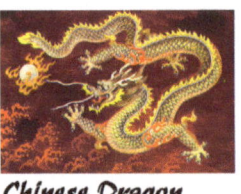

Chinese Dragon and Wong's film poster

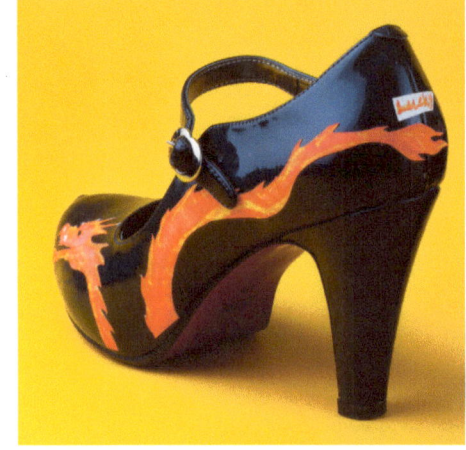

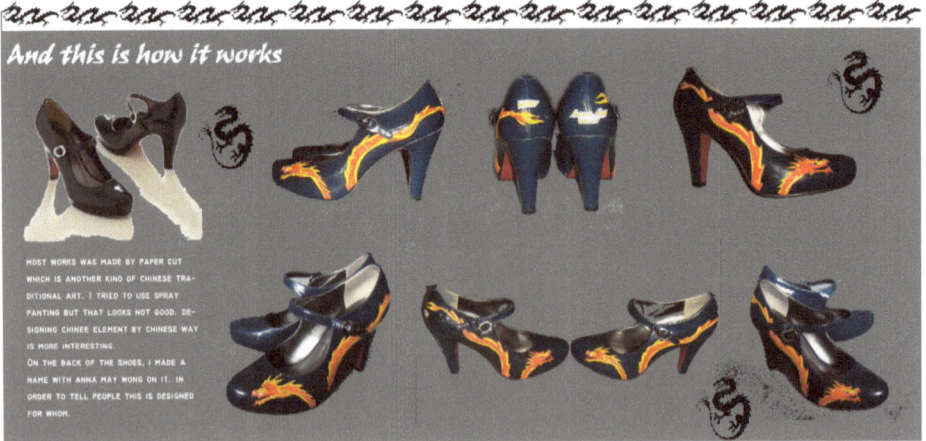

And this is how it works

MOST WORKS WAS MADE BY PAPER CUT WHICH IS ANOTHER KIND OF CHINESE TRADITIONAL ART. I TRIED TO USE SPRAY PANTING BUT THAT LOOKS NOT GOOD. DESIGNING CHINEE ELEMENT BY CHINESE WAY IS MORE INTERESTING.

ON THE BACK OF THE SHOES, I MADE A NAME WITH ANNA MAY WONG ON IT. IN ORDER TO TELL PEOPLE THIS IS DESIGNED FOR WHOM.

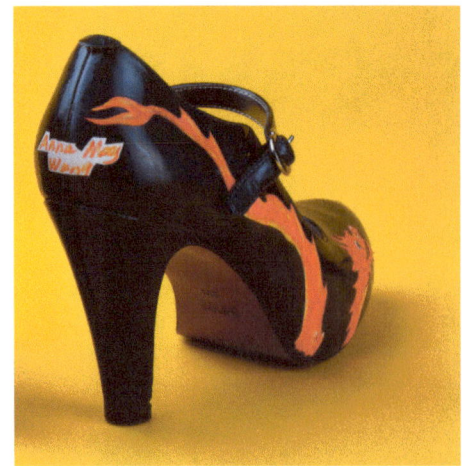

ANNA MAY WONG'S LUCKY SHOE

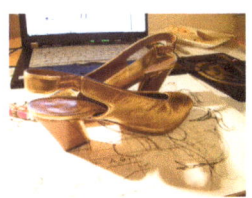

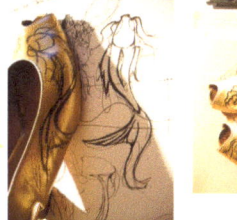

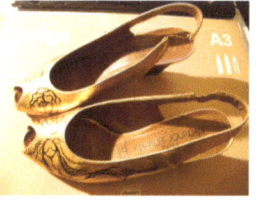

ORIGINAL SHOES

This lucky shoes design is based on my personal understanding of Anna May Wong's life style. Although Anna May Wong is a chinese, she has been influenced a lot by american's culture, therefore from my perspective her new Lucky shoes should be a pair of elegant, noble,graceful semi-china style western shoes.

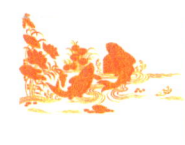

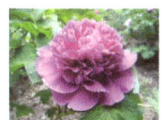

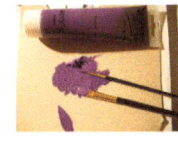

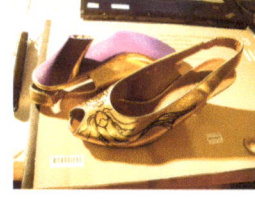

4 main idea for lucky shoes.
1.Carp - It is a symbol of good luck, happiness in china.
2.Peony - It represents the meaning of elegant, noble, and wealthy in china.
3.Purple - It is a decent and elice color in all over the world.
4.embroidered shoes - This is one kind of typical chinese traditional shoes, and the image's style on my shoe imitates the style of embroidered shoes.

and the reasons why i picked this shoe as the basic of lucky shoe are because the golden color, and the sort of this shape of shoe is called fish head shoes. Both of them are qualified to be the lucky shoe in my mind. (Elegant & happiness)

Finished by Yue Zhao 353255

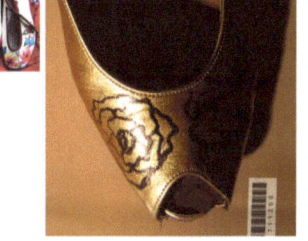

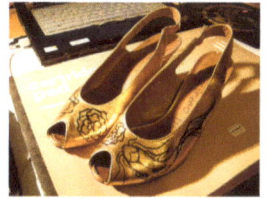

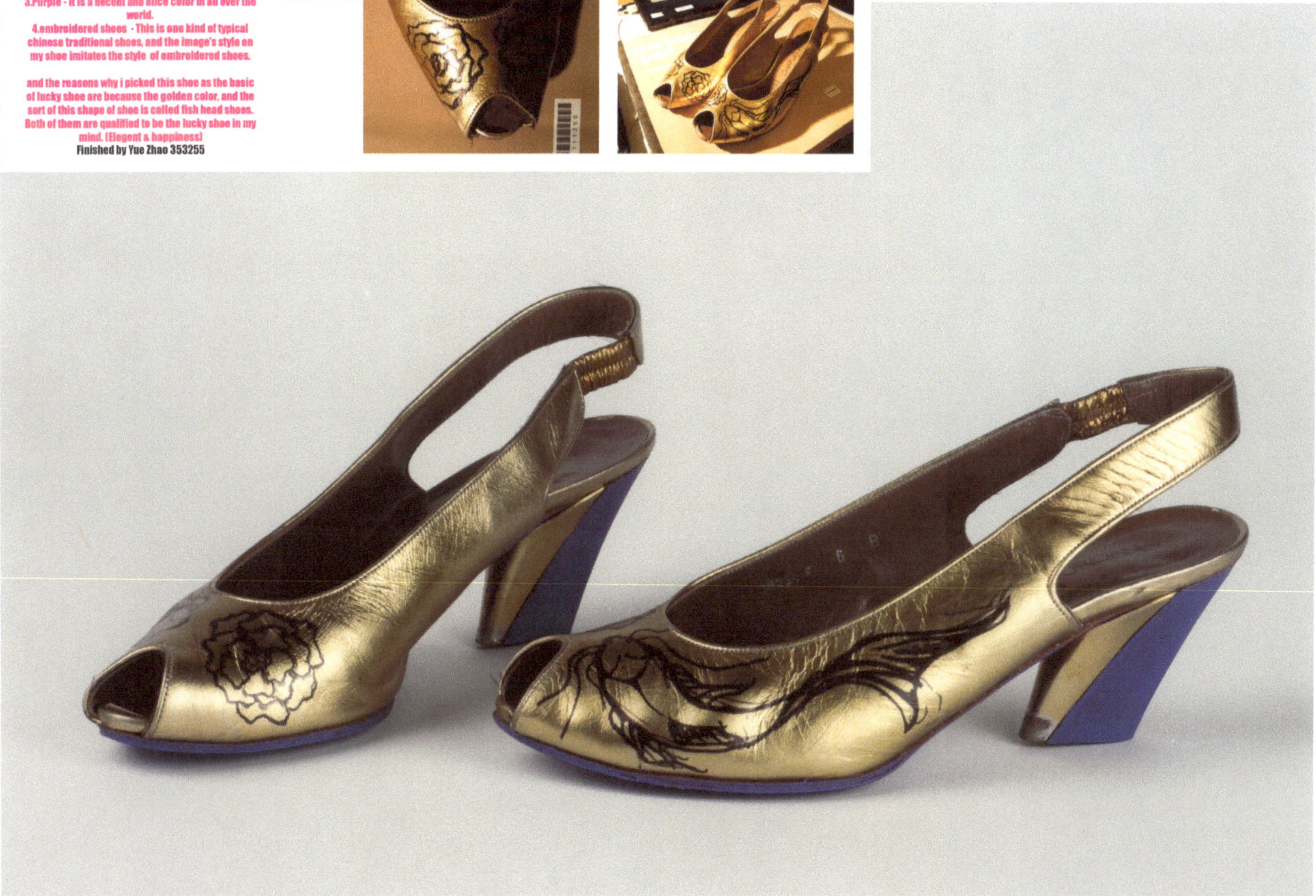

Jia Yuan Yang

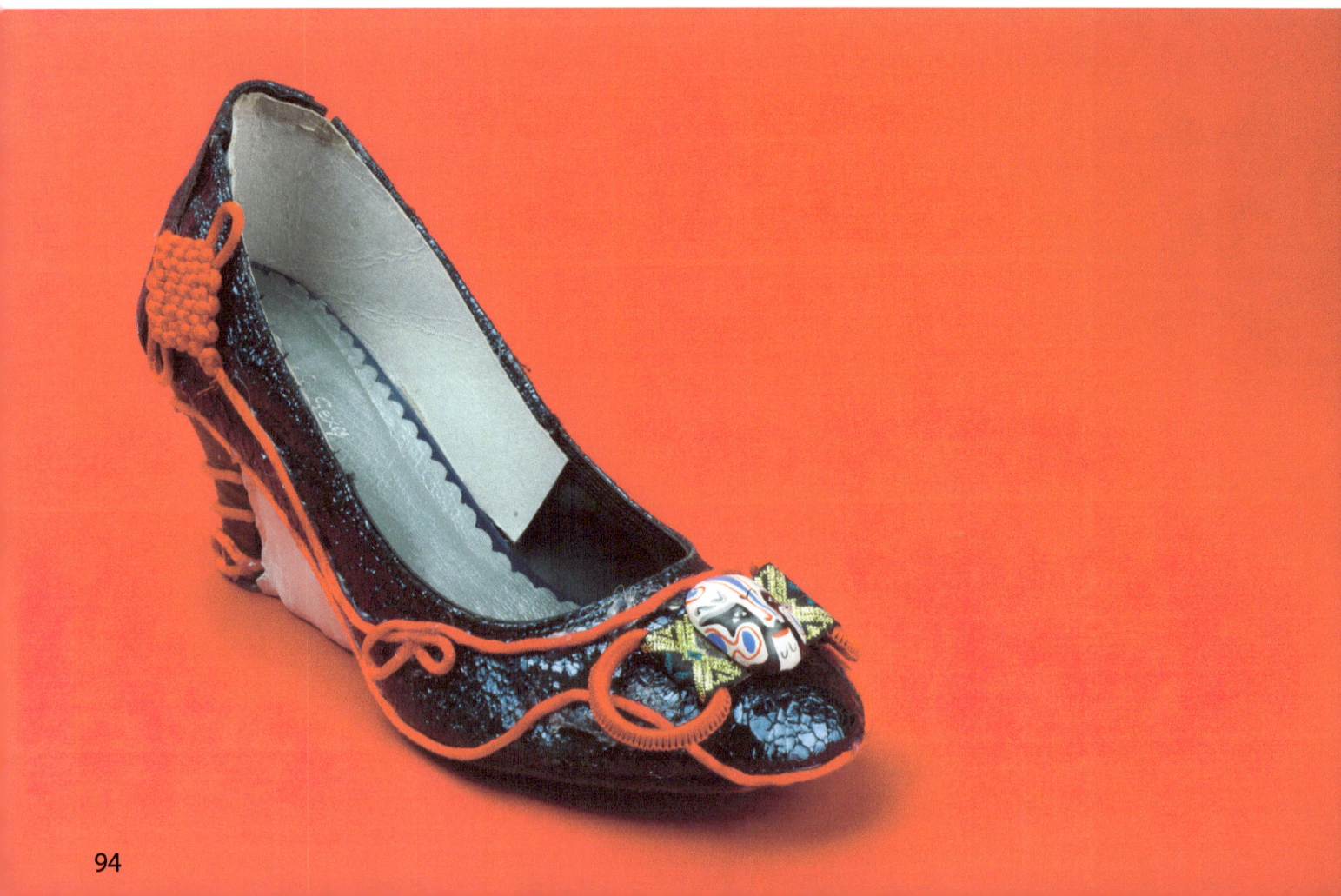

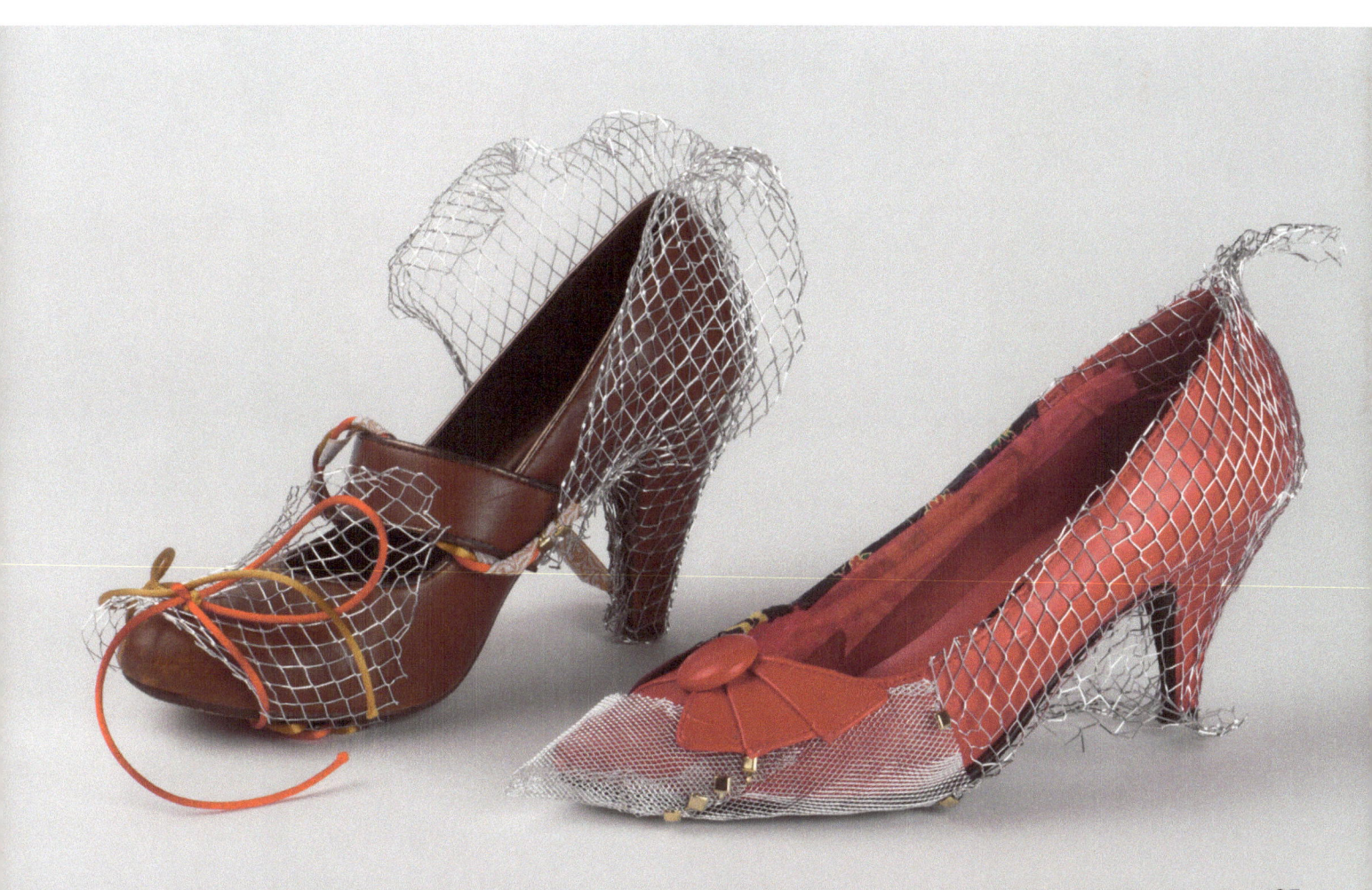

Linna Zheng

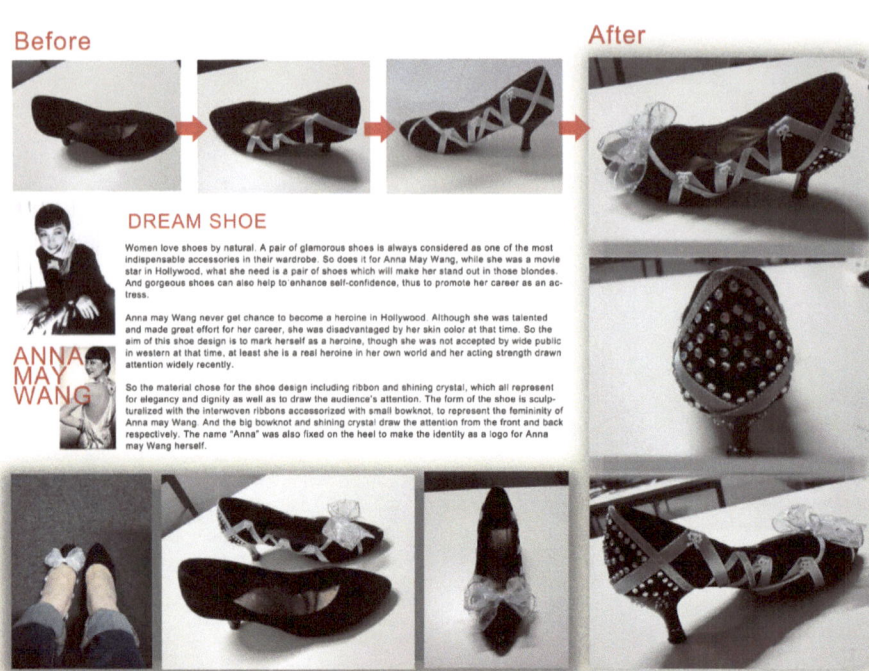

Before → **After**

DREAM SHOE

ANNA MAY WANG

Women love shoes by natural. A pair of glamorous shoes is always considered as one of the most indispensable accessories in their wardrobe. So does it for Anna May Wang, while she was a movie star in Hollywood, what she need is a pair of shoes which will make her stand out in those blondes. And gorgeous shoes can also help to enhance self-confidence, thus to promote her career as an actress.

Anna may Wang never get chance to become a heroine in Hollywood. Although she was talented and made great effort for her career, she was disadvantaged by her skin color at that time. So the aim of this shoe design is to mark herself as a heroine, though she was not accepted by wide public in western at that time, at least she is a real heroine in her own world and her acting strength drawn attention widely recently.

So the material chose for the shoe design including ribbon and shining crystal, which all represent for elegancy and dignity as well as to draw the audience's attention. The form of the shoe is sculpturalized with the interwoven ribbons accessorized with small booknot, to represent the femininity of Anna may Wang. And the big bowknot and shining crystal draw the attention from the front and back respectively. The name "Anna" was also fixed on the heel to make the identity as a logo for Anna may Wang herself.

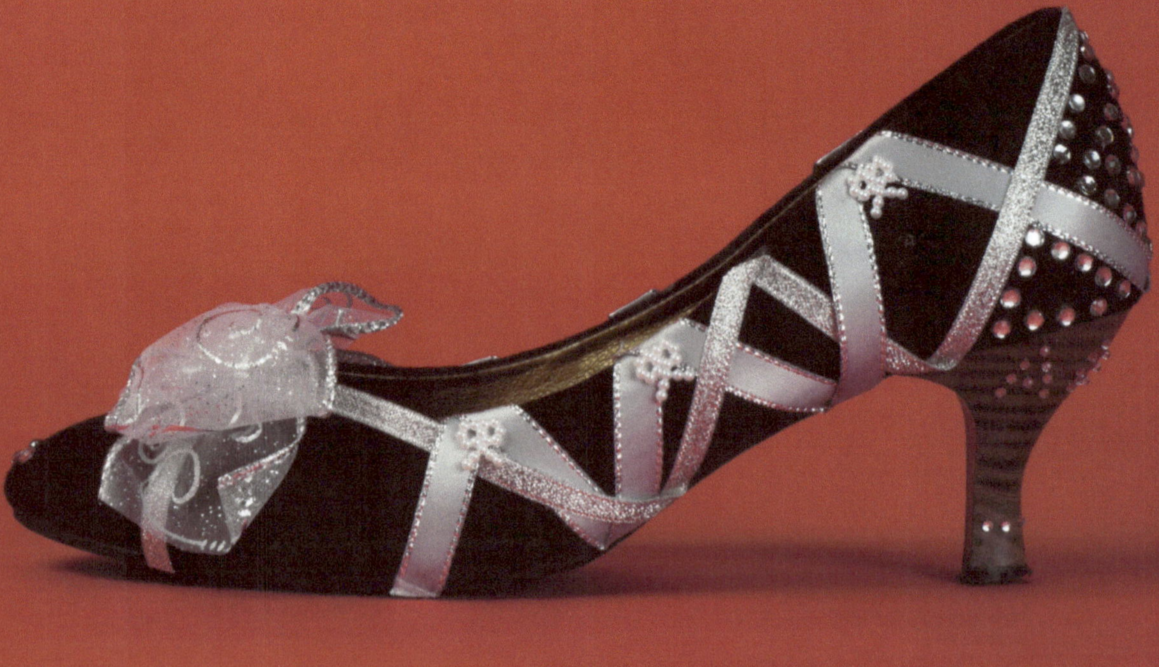

Endnotes

[1] This is a line from the song, "These Foolish Things" (1936), which was written by Eric Maschwitz for Anna May Wong (more about this later).

[2] See Graham Russell Gao Hodges. *Anna May Wong: From Laundryman's Daughter to Hollywood Legend:* 198. Maryland: Palgrave Macmillan, 2004. Anthony B. Chan. *Perpetually Cool: The Many Lives of Anna May Wong (1905-1961):* 80. Lanham, Maryland: Scarecrow Press Inc., 2003. Philip Leibfried and Chei Mi Lane. *Anna May Wong: A Complete Guide to Her Film, Stage, Radio and Television Work:* 156. Jefferson, North Carolina: McFarland & Company, Inc., 2004.

[3] "World Famous Chinese Actress." *The Age* (Melbourne, Victoria), the 3rd of June 1939: 16.

[4] "The Feminine Angle." *The Canberra Times* (Canberra, Australian Capital Territory), the 17th of May 1939: 3.

[5] See Leibfried and Lane: 77-78.

[6] "News of the World." *Northern Territory Times* (Darwin, Northern Territory), the 17th of January 1930: 2.

[7] Lon Jones. "Anna May Wong to Visit Australia. Chinese Star Will Arrive in Few Weeks." *The Sydney Morning Herald* (Sydney, New South Wales), the 1st of May 1939: 8.

[8] "Anna May Wong. Impatient of Being 'Typed.'" *The Age,* the 6th of June 1939: 8.

[9] F.K.M. "Going Back-Stage to Meet the Star! The *Table Talk* Interviewer Sees a Talkie—and Then Meets the Leading Actress! An Interview with Attractive Anna May Wong, the Famous Film Star Now at the Tivoli." *Table Talk* (Melbourne), the 15th of June 1939: 5.

[10] W.J. Passingham. "Influences of Screen on Lives of Women. 'Hundreds of Colberts and Shearers.' Changes in the East." *The Sydney Morning Herald, Women's Supplement,* the 7th of July 1936: 8.

[11] See "Frank Neil's Death. Accident Finding." *The Argus* (Melbourne), the 9th of January 1940: 5. Frank Van Straten. *Tivoli:* 109. Melbourne: Thomas C. Lothian Pty. Ltd., 2003.

[12] Nancye Bridges and Frank Crook. *Curtain Call:* 67. North Ryde: Cassell Australia Ltd., 1980.

[13] "Centenary Vaudeville. Many Overseas Artists Engaged." *The Argus,* the 28th of July 1934: 22. See "Revue for Australia. Mr. Frank Neil's Plans. Three Companies Engaged." *The Argus,* the 5th of September 1934: 6.

[14] "Personal." *The Sydney Morning Herald,* the 30th of August 1934: 9.

[15] F.K.M.

[16] Jones.

[17] True enough, however Wong seems to have forgotten about the Chinese-Australian actress, Rose Quong (1879-1972), who she appeared with in the play, *The Circle of Chalk* (1929). See "The World of Women. Rose Quong's Success." *The Argus,* the 18th of January 1939: 7. "Quong, Rose Maud (1879-1972)." *Australian Dictionary of Biography Online Edition:* <http://adbonline.anu.edu.au/biogs/AS10404b.htm>.

[18] Jones.

[19] "Hollywood's Oriental Star Here Next Week." *The Herald* (Melbourne), the 3rd of June 1939: 42.

[20] Chan: 131.

[21] Hodges: 198.

[22] On page 148 of his biography, Anthony B. Chan claimed that Wong donated much of her Australian earnings to the China War Relief Fund, but he did not give any references to substantiate it. However, I doubt its validity, because in the very extensive Australian newspaper coverage of the film star's trip, her intention to do this was never mentioned (more about this later).

[23] "Philosophy is a Heritage. Importance of Relaxing." *The Sydney Morning Herald,* the 18th of July 1939: 4.

[24] See Karen J. Leong. *The China Mystique. Pearl S. Buck, Anna May Wong, and the Transformation of American Orientalism:* 57-105. Berkeley: University of California Press, 2005: 57-105.

[25] Hodges: 198.

[26] Unfortunately, I did not have access to any Honolulu newspapers to either confirm or refute what I strongly suspect.

[27] Hodges: 198.

[28] Jones.

[29] The full names of the Tivoli artists were written on the "Personal Statement and Declaration" migration forms of the following: Lorenzo Andreini; Frank Andrini; Alfredo R. Garcia; Jack Vinton Lane; Howard Alan Wilson; Joaquin Aguilar Garay; William Frank Evers; and Merrill La Fontaine. (The National Archives of Australia, Canberra.) The

descriptions of the artists are from *Highlights From Hollywood*: unpaged. Melbourne: The Tivoli Circuit, 1939. (Note: There is an early printing of the Melbourne theater program in the State Library of Victoria, Melbourne, and a later printing of it in the Performing Arts Museum, Melbourne.)

[30] This information is recorded on the artists' "Personal Statement and Declaration" forms.

[31] "Luncheon. R.M.S. *Aorangi*. Cabin Class. 14th May 1939." (Derham Groves' collection.)

[32] "Dinner. R.M.S. *Aorangi*. Cabin Class. 14th May 1939." (Derham Groves' collection.)

[33] "Returning by the *Aorangi*." *The Sydney Morning Herald*, the 23rd of May 1939: 4.

[34] "Heir to the DJs Dynasty was Proud to be 'In Trade.'" <http://www.brisbanetimes.com.au/national/obituaries/heir-to-the-djs-dynasty-was-proud-to-be-in-trade-20100713-109de.html>.

[35] Bridges and Crook: 83.

[36] Letter to C.J.A. Moses from Charles Brandreth, the 9th of May 1939. (The National Archives of Australia.)

[37] C.J.A. Moses. "Memorandum to the Federal Program Controller, the Controller of Celebrity Concerts, the Federal Controller of Music, the Federal Controller of Productions," the 11th of May 1939. (The National Archives of Australia.)

[38] In *Shanghai Express*, Anna May Wong played a high-class Chinese prostitute named Hue Fei. The other members of the cast included Marlene Dietrich, Clive Brook and Warner Oland. In 1932, the film won the Academy Award for Best Cinematography and received Academy Award nominations for Best Production and Best Director. See Leibfried and Lane: 95-100.

[39] See "Negress Film Star. Nina Mae McKinney." *The Argus*, the 7th of September 1937: 10.

[40] E. Chapple. "The General Manager. Anna May Wong," the 18th of May 1939. (The National Archives of Australia.)

[41] Letter to Charles Brandreth from C.J.A. Moses, the 20th of May 1939. (The National Archives of Australia.)

[42] See "Today's Radio Programs." *The Advertiser* (Adelaide, South Australia), the 12th of July 1939: 16.

[43] See "Today's Radio Programs." *Examiner* (Launceston, Tasmania), the 12th of July 1939: 9.

[44] See *Highlights From Hollywood*.

[45] See "Chickenpox in *Aorangi*." *The Courier-Mail* (Brisbane, Queensland), the 30th of May 1939: 3.

[46] See "*Aorangi* Running Late." *The Sydney Morning Herald*, the 30th of May 1939: 16.

[47] See "News in Films." *The Courier-Mail*, the 10th of June 1939: 9.

[48] See "Broadcasting. A Touring Studio. Many Records. Under and Above Sydney." *The Sydney Morning Herald*, the 21st of June 1939: 7.

[49] "Hollywood 'Saner' Now. Anna May Wong in Sydney." *The Courier-Mail*, 5th June 1939:3. The identical story also appeared in *The Argus*, the 5th of June 1939: 2, *The West Australian* (Perth), the 5th of June 1939: 10 and *The Advertiser*, the 5th of June 1939: 28.

[50] "Chinese Film Star Arrives." *The Courier-Mail*, the 7th of June 1939: 3. Also see "Miss Anna May Wong." *The Townsville Daily Bulletin* (Townsville, Queensland), the 13th of June 1939: 8.

[51] "Gardening and Cooking. Chinese Star's Hobbies." *The Sydney Morning Herald*, the 5th of June 1939: 4.

[52] Ibid.

[53] Ibid.

[54] Ibid.

[55] See "George Zaharias." *Wikipedia*: <http://en.wikipedia.org/wiki/George_Zaharias>.

[56] See "Babe Didrikson. Outstanding Sports Woman. Visitor to Sydney. Tremendous Driver at Golf." *The Sydney Morning Herald*, the 5th of June 1939: 15.

[57] "Coming by the *Aorangi*." *The Sydney Morning Herald*, the 30th of May 1939: 16.

[58] "Twenty Tidy Little Choristers." *The Sydney Morning Herald*, the 5th of June 1939: 4.

[59] See "News in Films".

[60] *The Sydney Morning Herald*, the 3rd of June 1939: 2.

[61] See "Anna May Wong. Film Star Arrives in Sydney." *The Canberra Times*, the 5th of June 1939: 1.

[62] See "From Day to Day. Arrangements Cancelled." *The Sydney Morning Herald*, the 1st of June 1939: 20.

[63] "China's Friendship. Young Lady Diplomat. On Refugee Organization." *The Cairns Post* (Cairns, Queensland), the 26th of June 1939: 9.

[64] "Theater Notes. Shaw Tilts at Dictators. Big Stage Freeze." *The Argus*, the 2nd of June 1939: 12.

[65] See *The Age*, the 6th of June 1939: 15.

[66] "In Person. Anna May Wong. The Famous Stage and Screen Star." *The Age*, the 3rd of June 1939: 36.

[67] See Te Pana (Nelson Burns). "Chinese Star Silent on Hollywood." *The Argus*, the 6th of June 1939: 4.

[68] See "In Person. Anna May Wong. The Famous Stage and Screen Star."

[69] See "Chinese Film Star Arrives." *The Argus*, the 6th of June 1939: 5.

[70] See *The Sun News-Pictorial* (Melbourne), the 6th of June 1939: 29.

[71] Te Pana. "Chinese Star Silent on Hollywood."

[72] "Music and Drama. Anna May Wong—Lotte Lehmann's Recitals—'I Married an Angel.'" *The Sydney Morning Herald,* the 11th of March 1939: 20.

[73] Jones.

[74] "World-Famed Chinese Actress."

[75] See Leibfried and Lane: 161.

[76] Jonathan Swift. "Here, There and Everywhere." *The Sun News-Pictorial,* the 13th of June 1939: 7.

[77] Email from Robert McBride, a nephew of Merrill La Fontaine, to Derham Groves, the 17th of July 2008.

[78] Hodges: 140.

[79] Ibid.

[80] Ibid.

[81] "Bright Show at Tivoli. Anna May Wong." *The Argus,* the 13th of June 1939: 12.

[82] "Anna May Wong." *Table Talk,* the 15th of June 1939: 3.

[83] Bridges and Crook: 55.

[84] An advertisement in the *Highlights From Hollywood* stated: "The Beautiful Floral Tributes handed out to the Tivoli Artists on every opening night of New Companies are from Miss R. Floyd, Florist, No. 2, 'C,' Eastern Market." (The copy in the State Library of Victoria.)

[85] Mayfair. "Heard Here and There." *The Sydney Morning Herald,* the 27th of July 1939: 20. The same item also appeared in "Gossip." *The Townsville Daily Bulletin,* the 3rd of August 1939: 8.

[86] "Bright Show at Tivoli. Anna May Wong."

[87] Ibid.

[88] See Jack Lane. *A Gallery of Stars: The Story of the Hollywood Brown Derby's Wall of Fame.* Baltimore: Luminary Press, 2005.

[89] "Bright Show at Tivoli. Anna May Wong."

[90] I strongly suspect that Betty Burgess and Sonny Lamont traveled to Australia onboard the *Aorangi* with the other American performers in *Highlights From Hollywood,* however I cannot find their "Personal Statement and Declaration" forms. I know that George Zaharias definitely traveled to Australia onboard the *Aorangi,* but I cannot find his form either, which suggests that some records are missing or unavailable. I have a newspaper photograph of Burgess and Zaharias that was taken shortly after their wedding on Tuesday the 5th of January 1960, which has the following written on the back of it: "Las Vegas, Nev. George Zaharias, 50, former husband [of] the late world famous athlete Babe Didrikson, who died last year of cancer, and Better Burgess, 42, [of] Los Angeles, former film actress, were married [on the] 1/5 at the Desert Inn in Las Vegas, where they are spending their honeymoon. Zaharias, a former wrestler now in the real estate business, and his wife have known each other for 21 years." Given that Burgess and Zaharias first met each other in 1939 (i.e. 1960 minus 21 years equals 1939), rightly or wrongly, I am assuming this happened onboard the *Aorangi* while they were both sailing to Australia.

[91] See "Private Views. By *The Australian Women's Weekly* Film Reviewer. *The Story of Irene and Vernon Castle.*" *The Australian Women's Weekly,* the 12th of August 1939: 60. "The Story of Irene and Vernon Castle (1939)." *IMDb:* <http://www.imdb.com/title/tt0031983/>.

[92] "The Adventures of the Masked Phantom (1939)." *IMDb:* <http://www.imdb.com/title/tt0031023/>.

[93] "Bright Show at Tivoli. Anna May Wong."

[94] See "Theater Notes. Fine Actress Coming. Pauline Lord's Tour." *The Argus,* the 10th of June 1939: 5. However, Bugs Wilson's performance is not credited in: "The Big Broadcast of 1938 (1938)." *IMDb:* <http://www.imdb.com/title/tt0029912/>.

[95] See *Highlights From Hollywood.* Geoffrey Hutton. "Theater Notes. Playgoers Like to Barrack. Comedienne's Debut." *The Argus,* 27th of May 1939: 17. "Hollywood Highlights." *The Age,* the 10th of June 1939: 10. "Anna May Wong. A Propagandist Sketch." *The Sydney Morning Herald,* the 21st of July 1939: 13.

[96] See "Snow White and the Seven Dwarfs (1937)." *IMDb:* <http://www.imdb.com/title/tt0029583/>.

[97] "Voice of Snow White." *The Argus,* the 11th of October 1938: 4.

[98] See "Theater Notes. Fine Actress Coming. Pauline Lord's Tour."

[99] "Anna May Wong. A Propagandist Sketch."

[100] *Highlights From Hollywood.*

[101] "Bright Show at Tivoli. Anna May Wong."

[102] See J.B. Kaufman. *South of the Border with Disney: Walt Disney and the Good Neighbor Program, 1941-1948:* 219. New York: Disney Editions, 2009. *The Three Caballeros* (1944). *IMDb:* <http://www.imdb.com/title/tt0038166/>.

[103] "Bright Show at Tivoli. Anna May Wong."

[104] See Gregg Miner, "'Notable' Historical Players of Harp Guitars and Related Instruments." *Encyclopaedia of Harp Guitar Players of the Past:* <http://www.harpguitars.net/players/encyclopedia_of_hg_players.htm>.

[105] See the "Personal Statement and Declaration" forms of Frank Andrini and Lorenzo Andreini.

[106] See Greg Miner.

107 See *Highlights From Hollywood*. The 16 members of the Tivoli Ballet were Jean Beinke; Lorna Belden; Alma Chippendale; Pat Corrigan; Phyl Dolphin; Rosie Fitzgerald; Phyl Hall; Sylvia Harvey; Gwennie Mackintosh; Elsma Matthews; Irene McGregor; Claire Miller; Rita Mitchell; Rosie Simpson; Lorna Waters; and Sunday Wenman.

108 "Bright Show at Tivoli. Anna May Wong."

109 *Highlights From Hollywood.*

110 "Bright Show at Tivoli. Anna May Wong."

111 See Jennifer. "Passing Show. Chit Chat." *The Western Mail* (Perth), the 2nd of March 1939: 33.

112 *Highlights From Hollywood.*

113 "Bright Show at Tivoli. Anna May Wong."

114 See "The Tivoli." *The Sydney Morning Herald*, the 19th of October 1936: 6.

115 "Bright Show at Tivoli. Anna May Wong."

116 Ibid.

117 "Anna May Wong." *The Argus*, the 1st of July 1939: 2.

118 See "Tientsin Incident." *Wikipedia:* <http://en.wikipedia.org/wiki/Tientsin_Incident>.

119 *Highlights From Hollywood.* (The copy in the Performing Arts Museum.)

120 Jack Meander. "Movement in the City." *The Sydney Morning Herald*, the 21st of July 1939: 4.

121 "Philosophy is a Heritage. Importance of Relaxing." Also see "Talking to Anna May Wong." *The Western Mail*, the 16th of February 1939: 28.

122 Fred Parsons. *A Man Called Mo:* 64. Melbourne: William Heinemann Australia Pty. Ltd., 1973.

123 See "Tivoli—'Hollywood Highlights.'" *The Sydney Morning Herald*, the 22nd of July 1939: 9.

124 "Anna May Wong." *The Sydney Morning Herald*, the 15th of July 1939: 9.

125 "Anna May Wong. A Propagandist Sketch."

126 Hodges: 149.

127 Richard Corliss. "Anna May Wong Did it Right." *Time*, the 29th of January 2005: <http://www.time.com/time/columnist/corliss/article/0,9565,1022536-2,00.html>.

128 "Anna May Wong. A Propagandist Sketch."

129 "Amusements." *The Sydney Morning Herald*, the 17th of August 1939: 2.

130 Jack Meander. "Eyes and Ears in Town." *The Sydney Morning Herald*, the 16th of August 1939: 7.

131 Te Pana. "Te Pana's Film Parade. Screen Idols who Suffer for Art." *The Courier-Mail*, the 9th of November 1939: 16.

132 See "Amusements."

133 See Te Pana. "George Robey at Tivoli. Fellow of Great Jest." *The Argus*, the 18th of July 1939: 4.

134 See Leibfried and Lane: 80-83.

135 Fred Archer. *The Treasure House:* 47. Melbourne: Self-published, no date.

136 Bugs Wilson gave the Arcade Hotel (a.k.a. the Royal Arcade Hotel) as his temporary Melbourne address on his "Personal Statement and Declaration" form.

137 *Highlights From Hollywood.* (The copy in the State Library of Victoria.)

138 "S.O.S. Children's Hospital Calling… *Gala Theatrical Entertainment*. Princess Theater. Tuesday, the June 6th of 1939." (Bruce McBrien's collection.)

139 "Gala Show at Princess." *The Argus*, the 7th of June 1939: 15.

140 "Babies' Ward. Closing Avoided." *The Argus*, the 1st of June 1939: 12.

141 "Gala Show at Princess."

142 "S.O.S. Children's Hospital Calling… *Gala Theatrical Entertainment*. Princess Theater.

143 "Gala Show at Princess."

144 "International Club. Aims Explained." *The Argus*, the 6th of April 1935: 12.

145 "1,000 at International Club's Ball." *The Argus*, the 8th of June 1939: 17.

146 Ibid.

147 "Miss Anna May Wong Welcomed." *The Age*, the 12th of June 1939: 3.

148 Ibid.

149 See Leibfried and Lane: 122-126.

150 *The Age*, the 15th of June 1939: 15. The caption read: "Miss Anna May Wong, the celebrated Chinese film star, receiving a large bouquet from a page boy, when she attended the film in which she stars at the Capitol Theater."

151 *The Argus*, the 15th of June 1939: 5. The caption read: "Busy days for Miss Anna May Wong, screen actress, shown leaving the Capitol Theater yesterday, where she is making personal appearances before a film in which she is starred is screened. Miss Wong also appears twice daily at the Tivoli Theater."

152 "Watched Operation to get Atmosphere." *The Courier-Mail*, the 3rd of August 1939: 19.

153 F.K.M.

154 Ibid.

155 Shirley Jennifer Lim. *A Feeling of Belonging. Asian American Women's Public Culture, 1930-1960:* 47. New York: New York University Press, 2006.

156 *"King of Chinatown." The Sydney Morning Herald*, the 31st of July 1939: 5.

157 Raymond Lew-Boar interviewed by Sophie Couchman from the Museum of Chinese Australian History, Melbourne, no date: unpaged.

158 Email from Raymond Lew-Boar to Derham Groves, the 28th of September 2009.

159 "The Best Meal I Ever Had…" *The Australian Women's Weekly*, the 5th of August 1939: 20.

160 See "Miss Anna May Wong Writes About Her Remington Portable." *The Sun News-Pictorial*, the 15th of June 1939: 10. An identical advertisement also appeared in *The Sun News-Pictorial*, the 30th of June 1939: 16.

161 Ibid.

162 Letter from Anna May Wong to Fania and Carl Van Vechten, the 11th of September 1939. (The Beinecke Rare Book and Manuscript Library, Yale University, New Haven.)

163 Ibid.

164 Meander. "Eyes and Ears in Town."

165 See *The Argus*, the 17th of June 1939: 18. The caption read: "Miss Anna May Wong, now appearing at the Tivoli Theater, photographed while shopping at Foy's Fashion Corner."

166 Te Pana. "A Film Critic's Diary. Some British Subjects." *The Argus*, 28 June 1939: 15.

167 See "The Movie Ball. Glimpses of Hollywood." *The Advertiser*, the 12th of July 1929: 19. "Entertainments. Movie Crazy Ball." *The Mercury* (Hobart, Tasmania), the 16th of December 1932: 6. "C.W.A. Ball. Opening of A.L. and S. Ltd. New Premises." *The Cairns Post*, the 9th of September 1933: 9. "Fancy Dress Movie Ball." *The Northern Standard* (Darwin), the 9th of October 1934: 5. "Menzies. Movie Ball." *The Western Argus* (Kalgoorlie, Western Australia), the 22nd of October 1935: 7. " The Reelers' Ball. Breezy Non-Stop Show at the Embassy." *The Sunday Times* (Perth), the 29th of August 1937: 27.

168 See Cerberus. "The Dog World. Canine Government." *The Courier-Mail*, the 15th of December 1934: 19. "Dogs on Parade. Pomeranian and Irish Setter Champions." *The Courier-Mail*, the 31st of August 1936: 19. "Dog Show Awards. Sunshine Club." *The Argus*, the 19th of April 1938: 13.

169 Jones.

170 "Social and Personal." *Healesville and Yarra Glen Guardian* (Healesville, Victoria), the 24th of June 1939: 2.

171 See "Personal." *The Argus*, the 19th of June 1939: 8.

172 *The Age*, the 19th of June 1939: 15.

173 Jack Meander. "Wit of Miss Wong." *The Sydney Morning Herald*, the 18th of July 1939: 4.

174 "Prima Donna Charms Her Audience." *The Argus*, the 23rd of June 1939: 15.

175 "University Luncheon Parties." *The Argus*, the 24th of June 1939: 7.

176 "Flowers for Artist." *The Argus*, the 30th of June 1939: 15.

177 See "Coming Events." *The Argus*, the 11th of July 1939: 2.

178 "Social Notes, Personal." *The Argus*, the 27th of June 1939: 7.

179 See "Social and Personal." *The Argus*, the 1st of July 1939: 16.

180 "Brilliant Ball at Palais. Golden Gate Fiesta." *The Argus*, the 1st of July 1939: 15.

181 "Back From Melbourne." *The Mercury*, Women's Realm: Supplement to "The Mercury": the 5th of July 1939: 6.

182 See Leibfried and Lane: 161-162.

183 F.K.M.

184 Meander. "Wit of Miss Wong."

185 See *The Mercury*, the 21st of July 1939: 6. The caption read: "When Anna May Wong, Chinese film star, returned to Sydney this week, she was presented with a bouquet of red roses by Mrs. Mane on behalf of the New South Wales China Women's Relief Fund Committee." The identical photograph and caption also appeared in *The Advertiser*, the 22nd of July 1939: 27.

186 See *The Sydney Morning Herald*, the 18th of July 1939: 14. The caption read: "The Chinese film star, Anna May Wong, arrived in Sydney from Melbourne yesterday and was welcomed by members of the Chinese community. She is shown acknowledging the greetings of the crowd."

187 "Philosophy is a Heritage. Importance of Relaxing."

188 Ibid.

189 "Social and Personal. Party for Anna May Wong." *The Sydney Morning Herald*, the 19th of July 1939: 7.

190 "Anna May Wong." *The Home*, August 1939: 50-51.

191 See "Tivoli Theater." *The Sydney Morning Herald*, the 1st of July 1939: 10.

192 "Bright and Fast. New Tivoli Show." *The Argus*, the 2nd of May 1939: 3.

193 "'Broadway Hotshots.' New Tivoli Show." *The Sydney Morning Herald*, the 16th of June 1939: 13.

194 "Other Entertainments. Tivoli Theater." *The Argus*, the 8th of May 1939: 4.

195 "'Broadway Hotshots.' New Tivoli Show."

196 Ibid.

197 "Amused King. Former U.S. Senator." *The Argus*, the 25th of April 1939: 7.

198 "Bright and Fast. New Tivoli Show."

199 Geoffrey Hutton. "Theater Notes. Ideas From Vienna." *The Argus*, the 28th of April 1939: 3.

200 "Music and Drama. A Boom in Concerts—Schnabel and Boys' Choir." *The Sydney Morning Herald*, the 10th of June 1939: 12.

201 Meander. "Movement in the City."

202 "Talking to Anna May Wong."

203 Ibid.

204 See "Stage and Screen Personalities." *The Sydney Morning Herald, Women's Supplement,* the 7th of December 1937: 11.

205 Jonathan Swift.

206 Hodges: 11.

207 Mayfair. "Heard Here and There." *The Sydney Morning Herald,* the 20th of July 1939: 20.

208 Jack Meander. "Among Those Present." *The Sydney Morning Herald,* the 24th of July 1939: 4.

209 "Well-Known People Enjoying Themselves in Snow and City." *The Sydney Morning Herald,* the 27th of July 1939: 17.

210 See Meander. "Movement in the City."

211 Meander. "Wit of Miss Wong."

212 See Kerwin Maegraith. *The Autobiography of Kerwin Maegraith.* Australia: Spaark Books, 2010.

213 Kerwin Maegraith. "Hollywood is a Gamble—Says Anna May Wong. Brother Kim Wants to be Film Actor." *The Sydney Morning Herald, Women's Supplement,* the 24th of July 1939: 4.

214 Ibid.

215 Ibid.

216 Email from Hannah Hall to Derham Groves, the 30th of July 2008.

217 "From Day to Day in Sydney. Film Star Entertained." *The Sydney Morning Herald,* the 27th of July 1939: 18.

218 Ibid.

219 "From Day to Day in Sydney. Anna May Wong Ball." *The Sydney Morning Herald,* the 28th of July 1939: 4.

220 "Consul-General Entertained. Played in '*Macbeth.*'" *The Sydney Morning Herald,* the 28th of July 1939: 4.

221 Ibid.

222 Ibid.

223 See "Parties Yesterday at University and International Club." *The Sydney Morning Herald,* the 28th of July 1939: 4. The caption read: "Mrs. Maurice Gulson, the Consul-General for Poland, Mr. L. De Noskowski, Miss Anna May Wong, who presented him with a buttonhole, and Mrs. De Noskowski at the cocktail party given by the International Society yesterday afternoon in honor of the Consul-General and his wife and Miss Wong."

224 "Hollywood Merry-Go-Round. Fortune Made From '*Snow White.*' 1914 Film was Best Money Maker." *The Barrier Miner* (Broken Hill, New South Wales), the 3rd of August 1939: 7.

225 If Anna May Wong did in fact plan to donate much of her Australian earnings to the China War Relief Fund, as Anthony B. Chan suggested in his biography of the actress, then perhaps she prudently changed her mind after she was sacked by Paramount Pictures Inc.?

226 "Social and Personal. Welcome Home Party." *The Sydney Morning Herald,* the 5th of August 1939: 11.

227 See "Kelly, Thomas Herbert (1875-1948)." *Australian Dictionary of Biography Online Edition:* <http://adbonline.anu.edu.au/biogs/A090560b.htm>.

228 "Welcome Home Party." *The Sydney Morning Herald,* the 9th of August 1939: 7.

229 "*The Silence of Dean Maitland* (1934)." *IMDb:* <http://www.imdb.com/title/tt0026995/>.

230 "Chinese Film Star at Ball." *The Sydney Morning Herald,* the 9th of August 1939: 6.

231 "The World's Most Beautiful Chinese Girl." *Look,* the 1st of March 1938: 36-37.

232 Jesse Collings. "There is No Virtue in a Shiny Nose." *The Sydney Morning Herald,* the 14th of August 1939: 4.

233 "Folk and Traditional Song Lyrics: Home Sweet Home." <http://www.traditionalmusic.co.uk/folk-song lyrics/Home_Sweet_Home.htm>.

234 Meander. "Eyes and Ears in Town."

235 "Chinese Clothes in Parade." *The Sydney Morning Herald,* the 31st of March 1950: 9.

236 Meander. "Eyes and Ears in Town."

237 "From Verity's Notebook…Interesting Travellers." *The Courier-Mail,* the 4th of October 1939: 16.

238 Hodges: 198.

239 Letter from Anna May Wong to Fania Marinoff and Carl Van Vechten, the 11th of September 1939. (The Beinecke Rare Book and Manuscript Library, Yale University, New Haven.)

240 "Vienna Boys' Choir." *GNT History:* <http://www.abc.net.au/gnt/history/Transcripts/s1071232.htm>.

241 G. Aigremont. *Foot and Shoe Symbolism and Eroticism.* Leipzig: Verlags-Aktien-Gesellschaft, 1909. Quoted in William A. Rossi. *The Sex Life of the Foot and Shoe:* 13-14. New York: E.P. Dutton & Co., Inc., 1976.

242 E.T. Renbourn. "The Foot and Shoe in Body and Mind." Quoted in William A. Rossi: 3-4.

243 Mother Goose. "There was an Old Woman Who Lived in a Shoe." *Poetry Foundation:* <http://www.poetryfoundation.org/poem/176344>.

244 Uncle Joey. "Haines Shoe House—The Shoe House of the Wizard." *Off the Beaten Path:* <http://www.shoehouse.us/>.

245 "I.N.G. Headquarters, Amsterdam. Meyer & Van Schooten Architecten 2002." *Ga-*

linsky. *People Enjoying Buildings Worldwide:* <http://www.galinsky.com/buildings/ing/>.

[246] See *Lacoste:* <http://www.lacoste.com/zahahadid/>.

[247] David Sokol. "Architects Tread in New Territory: Shoe Design." *Architectural Record:* <http://archrecord.construction.com/news/daily/archives/091012architects_shoes.asp>.

[248] See Leibfried and Lane: 19-20.

[249] See Leibfried and Lane: 20-23.

[250] See Leibfried and Lane: 25-26.

[251] See Leibfried and Lane: 35-39.

[252] See Leibfried and Lane: 48-51.

[253] "Gardening and Cooking. Chinese Star's Hobbies."

[254] See "Westminster Flower Show." *The West Australian,* the 6th of August 1937: 23.

[255] Philip Leibfried. "Anna May Wong. First Asian American Star!" *USAsians.net for All People, for All Worlds:* <http://us_asians.tripod.com/features-am-wong.html>.

[256] Alexandra Wall. Unpublished written statement that accompanied her pair of shoes, 2010.

[257] Susan Johnston and Lindsay Nation. *Australia 1939:* 42-43. Kensington, New South Wales: New South Wales University Press, 2003.

[258] See "Gala Show at Princess."

[259] Rossi: 30-41.

[260] Rossi: 45.

[261] See "Eric Maschwitz." *Wikipedia:* <http://en.wikipedia.org/wiki/Eric_Maschwitz>.

[262] "These Foolish Things Lyrics." *LyricsFreak:* <http://www.lyricsfreak.com/b/bryan+ferry/these+foolish+things_20025749.html>.

[263] See *"The Wizard of Oz* (1939)." *IMDb:* <http://www.imdb.com/title/tt0032138/>.

ingramcontent.com/pod-product-compliance
ning Source LLC
bersburg PA
W050851180526
59CB00007B/2646